ETHNIC AMERICAN LITERATURE

ETHNIC AMERICAN LITERATURE

Comparing Chicano, Jewish, and African American Writing

Dean J. Franco

University of Virginia Press · Charlottesville and London

University of Virginia Press

© 2006 by the Rector and Visitors of the University of Virginia

All rights reserved

Printed in the United States of America on acid-free paper

First published 2006

9 8 7 6 5 4 3 2 1

LIBRARY OF CONGRESS CATALOGING-IN-PUBLICATION DATA

Franco, Dean J., 1968–

    Ethnic American literature : comparing Chicano, Jewish, and African American writing / Dean J. Franco.

       p.   cm.

    Includes bibliographical references and index.

    ISBN-13: 978-0-8139-2559-2 (acid-free paper)

    ISBN-13: 978-0-8139-2560-8 (pbk. : acid-free paper)

    1. American literature—Minority authors—History and criticism. 2. American literature—Mexican American authors—History and criticism. 3. American literature—Jewish authors—History and criticism. 4. American literature—African American authors—History and criticism. 5. Ethnic groups in literature. 6. Identity (Psychology) in literature. 7. Bereavement in literature. 8. History in literature. I. Title.

    PS153.M56F73 2006

    810.9'920693—dc22
                                                     2006011469

For Adrienne

CONTENTS

Acknowledgments   ix

Introduction   1

PART ONE Traumatic History and Ethnic American Literature

1 ··· The Jew Who Got Away   29

2 ··· Working Through the Archive   55

3 ··· "She Has Claim": Material Justice and the Ends of History   73

PART TWO The Location of Cultures

4 ··· Borders, Diaspora, and Exile   99

5 ··· Outing Ethnicity, "Undoing" Nationalism   124

Conclusion: The Ethics of Ethnicity in Literature   153

Notes   183

Bibliography   201

Index   215

ACKNOWLEDGMENTS

When I began working on this book, I was renting a house with my wife in Long Beach, California. Our landlord, Dave—a spry, intelligent, and deeply religious seventy-year-old Baptist—asked me about my work, and when I told him that I planned on comparing Jewish, Chicano, and African American literature, he proceeded to explain to me why that made no sense at all. He delivered a long and compelling lecture, and though I am sure he was mostly concerned about my future financial welfare, he also made it clear that he had been around the block a bit and knew a thing or two about ethnicity—he knew a handful of Jews, Chicanos, and African Americans, in fact, as renters, and he wanted me to know that these cultures were quite different, hardly comparable. Since then I have been on the receiving end of many similar lectures from friends, colleagues, mentors, relatives, and sometimes complete strangers. At a minimum, these encounters sharpened my own thinking, and they often helped alert me to my own presumptions and blind spots. Besides the technical possibilities of comparison, I learned to account for the deep feelings associated with traditional concepts about ethnic boundaries. I learned that people have deep-set experiences and opinions behind their responses to multicultural America, thus leading to the book's focus, which is what we talk about when we talk about ethnicity in American literature and culture.

Tania Modleski, Teresa McKenna, and George Sánchez read portions of this book at a very early stage and patiently offered their advice. Vincent Cheng and Maeera Shreiber read and responded to versions of the manuscript from the very beginning, always believing in the project while helping me see its wider implications. I proceeded steadily thanks to their tremendous generosity and faith in me and my work. Thanks also to my friends in California who have always cheered me on: Chris Evans, Julie Frost, Timothy Caron, David Peck, Eileen Klink, and James Kincaid. My parents have been enduring champions long before I knew what this was about.

Wake Forest University provided a productive environment for writing. Thanks to my department for a semester-long research leave, and to the university for summer research support. Chris Margrave was my bright and efficient research assistant. Evie Shockley, Janis Caldwell, Jessica Richard, Anne Boyle, and Eric Wilson have been excellent role models and supportive colleagues. Gale Sigal, Phil Kuberski, Olga Valbuena, Michael Hill, and Gillian Overing all read drafts of chapters in progress and offered advice and support. Stéphane Robolin offered expertise and advice on chapter 3, though he is not to be held responsible if my claims seem outrageous. Neither is James Hans, who endured very rough versions of chapters 2 and 3, offering valuable commentary and direction.

My wife, Adrienne Pilon, is a constant source of intellectual stimulation and critical rigor. My best habits of thought—and some of the book's best ideas—come from her. Thanks also to my boys, Ari and Gabriel, who come to my office to raid the cinnamon candy in the dish on my desk. That is what it is there for, all for you.

A version of the first chapter appears in *PMLA* (March 2005) and is reprinted by permission of the copyright owner, The Modern Language Association of America. A version of chapter 4 originally appeared in *Cultural Critique* (Winter 2002) and appears courtesy of the University of Minnesota Press. Portions of the concluding chapter were previously published in *Post Identity* 2.1 (Winter 1999): 104–22. Lyrics from "An Undoing World," by Tony Kushner, Naomi Goldberg, and the Klezmatics, appear by permission (from *Possessed;* more information is available at klezmatics.com).

ETHNIC AMERICAN LITERATURE

INTRODUCTION

All National rootedness, for example, is rooted first of all in the memory
or the anxiety of a displaced—or displaceable—population. It is not only
time that is "out of joint," but space, space in time, spacing.
                    —JACQUES DERRIDA, *Specters of Marx*

eAnne Howe's 2001 American Book Award–winning novel, *Shell
Shaker*, contains one of the more bizarre scenes in recent fiction:
women who are kneading a bowl of dough suddenly find themselves
working through fistfuls of mud. The dough has been weirdly transformed, and it begins to rise, ooze, and creep out of the bowl onto the
counter, eventually forming a brown heap on the linoleum floor. What's
more, this is no ordinary mud, and these are no ordinary women. Although the scene takes place in Choctaw Country, Oklahoma, the mud
comes from Mississippi, specifically from the Choctaw *Nanih Wayia,* or
"mother mound," site of human origin in Choctaw creation stories. The
women are the aunts and friends of Auda, a Choctaw tribal administra-
tor who is being held for the murder of the corrupt tribal chief, Redford
Macalister. The older women have a long cultural memory of tribal customs and experience with the vast territory of North America, having
traveled across the continent working as actresses and performers. Furthermore, they are descendants of "shell shakers," or tribal peacemakers.
They are surprised neither by the transterritorial appearance of the mud
nor by the instruction, revealed in a dream-state, that Redford's body
should be taken to Mississippi and buried in the mother mound, lest his
malfeasant spirit reappear in future generations.

Redford, it turns out, is the re-embodied spirit of the eighteenth-century tribal chief Redshoes, a near-mythical figure who led the Choctaw
nation during their horrific civil war in 1748. Redshoes initially attempted
to broker a regional peace with warring Indian tribes, but his efforts
divided the Choctaw nation and the war began upon his murder later

that year. The motif of repeating history, where linear time comes "out of joint," is familiar enough to readers of ethnic American literature, but especially startling is the motif of place, the earth from the mother mound, quite literally displaced. Many readers of ethnic literature are familiar enough with the notion of recirculating or "oceanic" time in other Native American novels, and the compulsive repetition of past trauma is itself compulsively repeated in modern ethnic literature. Howe's allegory of "space-in-time" out of joint, however, is innovative and instructive, yoking together metaphors of home and history.

We should recall that the Choctaw nation, like many other Indian nations, has lived in diaspora for over 170 years following the signing of the treaty at Dancing Rabbit Creek in 1830. Prior to signing this treaty, the Choctaw had suffered the repeated violations of half a dozen previous treaties and had seen their land in the southeastern basin stolen by the federal government and migrating farmers. The treaty at Dancing Rabbit Creek arranged for the relocation and maintenance of tribal status for all willing Choctaw, while provisions for liberal citizenship were offered for those who wished to remain in Mississippi.[1] Choctaw were divided by their choice to remain or remove to Oklahoma. One group traded in geography for a continuity of historical identity; the other traded in historical identity for the permanence of place.

Shell Shaker, which narrates the aftermath of that divide, is a unique work, yet it presents many of the same themes and problems as other contemporary ethnic literature. For example, the novel stages a scene of working through history as a psychological and ethical process within the text, paralleling political and cultural processes for Choctaw beyond the pages. In *Shell Shaker,* politics is not an allegory for cultural trauma, nor does the psychological realism allegorize the political implications of the novel's plot. Instead, politics and historical trauma and its aftermath are homologous realities, and are the result of upheavals produced by war and relocation. The warrior-leader Redshoes represents and reconciles the political divisions within the Choctaw, while his re-embodiment as the contemporary tribal leader Redford Macalister eventuates a symbolic reunion of Choctaw otherwise dispersed across two states.[2]

In Howe's novel, Redshoes succumbs to the corruption and demagoguery potential in all politics, where the expedient logic of conflict trumps the imaginatively difficult logic of peace. Indeed, as Howe tells the story, the Choctaw civil war is the moment when the "shell shakers," or tribal peacemakers, lose their cultural and political efficacy. Redshoes's reincarnation as Redford Macalister presents an opportunity for the Choctaw to recognize that in the historical repetition is an opportunity to end the cycle of conflict. His exhumation and reburial amount to a ritual of reunion, joining disarticulated spaces-in-time.

Sections of *Shell Shaker* are narrated in the colonial eighteenth century, well before the United States was established, and at a time when the French and the British competed for hegemony in the southeast delta region. The novel depicts complex political alliances among the region's different Indian tribes, and demonstrates how the French and the British negotiated with Indian nations largely on the Indians' own terms and according to local custom. This period in U.S. prehistory obviously contrasts prevailing American myths about the nation's future space as a blank or empty frontier. While most late eighteenth- and early nineteenth-century U.S. maps of the southeast show the space as unexplored, European maps of the region, stippled with villages and accurate indications of different Indian nation's territories, were widely available (White 17–19). *Shell Shaker* makes clear that not only was a socially complex indigenous culture present in the region, but that a realist political agenda prevailed, thereby producing a renarration of the origins of the U.S. nation that is simultaneous but by no means the same as our well-known American mythology. In this way, *Shell Shaker* is part of a pluralist American literature.

Also in common with other recent works of ethnic American literature, *Shell Shaker* is a "multicultural" novel, deeply implicated in the cultural customs, legal practices, history, and beliefs held by Choctaw Indians which either contrast or have no comparable correlative in Western Anglo culture. Simply put, while *Shell Shaker* is entirely readable for someone without a deep knowledge of Choctaw culture, it produces a kind of knowledge that can only be considered Choctaw. In this sense *Shell Shaker* is what Howe calls a "tribalography . . . , a story that links Indians and non-Indians" ("Story" 46), but that linkage is not the same as an assimilation, or merging of stories. Instead, Howe suggests that the history of "America" and the history of Indian nations are, or must be, mutually implicating. *Shell Shaker* demonstrates both the malleability of cultures, as Choctaw and other tribes strategically incorporated French and then American cultural customs and values, and the enduring particularity, even incommensurability, of cultural epistemologies, religion, and ethics. Opening the discussion with *Shell Shaker*, then, introduces this book's three guiding critical themes: history, geography, and cultural specificity. The latter term is an effect of the prior two, and, in fact, cultural uniqueness creates problems for comparative work which may perhaps only be solved through careful retheorizations of history and geography.

LeAnne Howe's roots in Cherokee and Choctaw cultures illustrate the critical difficulties and opportunities of attending to cultural specificity. It is a scholarly truism that non-Western cultures may indeed operate according to different cultural values and epistemologies, and with radically different perspectives on history and time. Besides the common Indian concept of time as oceanic, many Native American writers innovate on Western literary forms in order to translate indigenous oral culture. Writers of the Native American "Renaissance" (1965–75) were especially conscious of the difficult but important task of communicating Indian ideas, values, and customs by hybridizing the novel. The availability of many volumes of supplementary scholarly material, including critical guides, MLA "approaches to teaching" series, "cultural casebooks," and video interviews attest to the ability of writers like N. Scott Momaday and Leslie Marmon Silko to break open the Western canon, and to their success in maintaining sufficient cultural specificity as to require all the supplements in the first place.

What is more, the Native American literary renaissance occurred during the formation of multicultural pedagogy in elementary and high schools, and in concert with the institutional recognition of multiculturalism in universities across the country. Though weakly misappropriated and under attack on many fronts, multiculturalism and the general shift toward self-identification and self-description by Americans of color is an attempt to recognize the unique historical and national origins of different social groups in the United States, thereby valuing multiple cultures' ways of knowing and being in the world. Black and Black Atlantic studies, Chicano studies, Native American studies, Asian and Asian American studies, and certainly the new Jewish cultural studies movement (more virtual than institutional) represent the attempt to locate the cultural specificity of these groups while granting that distinct peoples and their cultures can be studied, shared, and compared with one another or with the Western tradition.

The institutionalization of multiculturalism occurred simultaneously with and remains dialectically engaged with the philosophical and theoretical projects of poststructuralism and feminist theory and epistemology, especially the critique of universalism presumed in Enlightenment philosophy and political thought. In truth, poststructuralism and postmodernism are at once the ally and the bane of ethnic studies programs. The multicultural decentering of Western values and history opens up a conceptual space for the study of non-Western peoples and cultures, on the one hand. On the other hand, with strategies of knowing, identifying, and representing cultures themselves deconstructed, and with academia itself subject to skeptical scrutiny, the institutional study of multiple American cultures is forced to constantly question and retheorize not only its methods but also its existence.[3]

In some ways, the institutional anxiety attending ethnic studies is comparable to the challenges feminist theory continually faces, namely the problems of essentialism versus aggressive skepticism, coalition-building versus respect, and pragmatic versus radical political activism. In feminist theory, the conundrum is to imagine an identity or point of view stable enough to be politically effective, but aggressively skeptical so as to avoid replicating social regimes of gender, a productive tension in Robyn Wiegman's exemplary work of feminist criticism *American Anatomies,* for example.

Within ethnic studies, the conundrum is yet more complicated (the subject of chapter 5). The quote from Jacques Derrida at the beginning of this introduction suggests the contours of the problem. Multiculturalists and ethnic studies specialists would indeed deconstruct a Western teleology of space and time which prioritizes west over east, light over dark, and so on. But with "space-in-time" out of joint, on what grounds do ethnic studies scholars construct knowledge of their respective cultural traditions? The same question has many versions: how can we presume to know the other? If we grant the existence of the other as a separate culture, do we not also reify the logic of centers and margins? Hasn't the "cultural logic of late capitalism" turned culture into kitsch and authenticity into a commodity? If so, wouldn't the contingency of cultures result in a contingency of values, a scenario where no single culture can be studied on its own, but must be understood as emerging precisely in the moment of its differentiation from "other" cultures, with difference giving way to *différance*?

As spurs for scholarly study, these questions are productive, but they limit or even undermine the practical and political goals of ethnic studies, namely, advocating for cultural rights and recognition. The problems generated by these sorts of questions are finally problems of knowing and doing: how to know the content, the history, and the location of a given culture, and, more specifically, how to link texts with their contexts—that is, how to know what ethnic literature is, and then how to proceed pedagogically, institutionally, and politically to teach, represent, and organize on behalf of any given culture in the United States.

Without wishing to further complicate or overly vex these questions of knowing and doing, I should add that they are all limned by a set of ethical imperatives: Representations of a culture's past ought not amount to arrogant misappropriations that merely serve the interests of the present. Historicism ought not give way to commodifiable sentimentalism. Encounters with the other (the racial other, the other of history, the human other) which presume the privilege of self-presence are arrogant; instead, encounters ought to be mutually and dialectically interrogative, where literature and criticism, say, are mutually responsible. And last, ethnic literary criticism ought to be comparative.

This list of ethical imperatives is derived from a generation of criticism in print already, save for the last item about comparisons.[4] That is my own suggestion. And it is an ethic posing as a method. Or perhaps the reverse, a method that can be a strategy for addressing the postmodern problems of knowing and the pragmatic problems of doing, while maintaining respect for multiple cultures and literatures. My ethic of comparison is not transcendent, but is dialectically derived from the literature and culture itself, and from the two fundamental thematic concerns of ethnic literature, history and geography. Culture is what we do in the present, of course, but cultural difference in the United States is produced by history, including the histories of slavery, colonialism, and genocide, as well as physical displacements of people through immigration and exile. These historical phenomena are cataclysms for groups of people and constitute ruptures in cultural history, and are often ruptures of the relationship between people and place.

Moreover, for contemporary ethnic Americans, the very fact of their social difference and often marginalization is traceable to these historical events. As Timothy Powell puts it, explaining his term *historical multiculturalism,* "cultures do not exist in isolation but are inextricably intertwined in infinitely complicated ways. To study African American or Asian American or Chicano literature in isolation risks unwittingly reifying an essentialist conception of cultural identity" (10).

For most of a century, the efflorescence of ethnicity in the United States has been historically matched by a deafening scholarly silence. As Homi Bhabha explains, the plurality of cultures, histories, and places in the space of the nation threatens the very coherence of the nation itself:

> Counter-narratives of the nation that continually evoke and erase its totalizing boundaries—both actual and conceptual—disturb those ideological manoeuvres through which "imagined communities" are given essentialist identities. For the political unity of the nation consists in a continual displacement of the anxiety of its irredeemably plural modern space—representing the nation's modern territoriality is turned into the archaic, atavistic temporality of Traditionalism. The difference of space returns as the Sameness of time, turning Territory into Tradition, turning the People into One. The liminal point of this ideological displacement is the turning of the differentiated spatial boundary, the "outside," into the authenticating "inward" time of Tradition. (149)

Drawing on Benedict Anderson's popular thesis on the nation as an "imagined community," Bhabha explains the nation's need for the suppression of difference, and how difference "writes back." Bhabha aims not for "reconstruction" following deconstruction, nor is his work "actively" deconstructive—the quixotic sentiment of embattlement that inhabits the work of some activist criticism. Instead, following Derrida, he points to the way texts and cultures in general manifest their own incoherence. The consequences of such an observation, then, include the recalibration of the political space of the nation, inhabited by newly empowered participants previously excluded from spheres of agency. Instead of a reconstruction, such as simply writing new history books, Bhabha suggests that narratives constantly reform the nation insofar as the nation is the starting point for all contemporary cultural identities. This puts *reading* at the center of politics (the topic of chapter 6). And to the extent that politics stems from ethics, or following Levinas,[5] because the ethical encounter is the precondition of the political encounter, reading the other into history, and folding the margins of the nation into the center through reading, locates literature at the nexus of a critical re-evaluation of the history and geography of the nation. Simply put, studying ethnic American literature and allowing its narratives to emerge alongside others pluralizes and thereby expands the cultural space of the nation.

Another, perhaps more pressing, reason for comparative ethnic literature study is to critique and retheorize the field of study itself. It seems true that in all fields of literary study buzzwords and jargon become placeholders for actual thinking, but the earnest study of ethnic literature seems especially susceptible to this maneuver, because the critical language is so politically satisfying. Geographical descriptors like *the nation, empire, borderland, migration, colonization, exile, diaspora, the middle passage, the conquest,* or historical terms like *mourning, memory, trauma, repression, slavery, postcolonial, postmodern,* and *postethnic* have taken on a critical life of their own, independent of the particular situations they would describe. They are often used for their expediency and for their formulaic efficacy; as nouns or proper nouns, they seem to need neither contexts nor even actual people. While theorizations of language and culture regularly dwell on terms and ideas detached from contexts, theorizations of the experience of social difference are so dialectically wedded to the groups in question, as they draw from, respond to, and often aim to change our conception of a particular social group, that the ethics of specificity and respect mentioned above require commensurate attention to context of the group under study.

As a problematic example of jargon-slide we might consider Paul Gilroy's well-known suggestion that Black Atlantic culture ought to alter its paradigmatic self-perception from the organizing idea of "race" to the concept of "diaspora." In the closing pages of *The Black Atlantic,* and throughout his later, *Against Race,* Gilroy argues that the idea of "race" depends on a fixed relation between people and their place of origin, while the study of the Black Atlantic culture is precisely the study of the severing of that connection and its consequences. Diaspora, in contrast, is a more capacious and accommodating term that inverts a people's relationship to place and invokes a broad and ever-changing history of migration and resettlement. "The idea of Diaspora," Gilroy explains, "offers a ready alternative to the stern discipline of primordial kinship and rooted belonging. It rejects the popular image of natural nations spontaneously endowed with self-consciousness, tidily composed of uniform families" (*Against* 123). And, "more than a voguish synonym for the peregrination or nomadism . . . [diaspora] connotes flight following the threat of violence rather than freely chosen experiences of displacement" (123). Acknowledging that diaspora may be thought of as nothing more than "race in motion," Gilroy suggests we attend to the performative aspects of diaspora, as it is a cultural descriptor finally dependent on iteration over and against reification.

Gilroy's recourse to the performativity of the term matches my own general sense that culture is performative. But if culture is uprooted from the logic of place, can it also be divorced from history—the history of past dispersal and the future anticipation of regathering and return? And return to where? We are back at the poetics of place. (Incidentally, in his latest book, *Postcolonial Melancholia,* Gilroy fesses up to his own diasporic blues, as a British citizen pining for proper fish and chips in Connecticut.)

Gilroy's consideration of and attempt at rejecting the race-and-place denotations of diaspora point finally to methodology, the search for a critical analytic that is at once accurate for the object of study and ethically progressive as a thesis about culture in its own right. The difficulty of a term like *diaspora,* however, is that it is at once a noun indicating a group of people, a historical state of being, and a geographical locale (as the dialectical antithesis of Homeland, the diaspora is everywhere except home). Furthermore, *diaspora* connotes a distinct sort of now. For Jews living out of Israel, Gilroy's paradigm, diaspora is a present-time lasting over two thousand years. Jews in the diaspora are not now "fleeing from violence" as Gilroy would have it, or they are not but might be in the future. Or, even better, Jews simultaneously are and are not fleeing violence depending on where Jews happen to be in the world at any given time. From the point of view of Jewish culture, the term *diaspora* is accommodating and protean, and especially since 1948, the term fuses a racialist sensibility of Jewish self-perception—along with a stern disavowal of the logic of race—with an ambiguous sense of free choice for Jews who could at last "return" to the Homeland, but in all likelihood will not. Jews in America have literally chosen to regard themselves as in diaspora, as Arnold Eisen observes, and for American Jews the term has a borderlands connotation meaning not at home, but also not in exile (this is chapter 4's concern).[6]

If Gilroy counterposes diaspora against race, for twentieth-century American Jews "diaspora" contrasts the more felicitous and synthesizing term *immigrant*—as in "we are a nation of immigrants," and "everyone is an immigrant from somewhere." This term carries with it, like a snail with its home on its back, a built-in narrative of homecoming. According to the typical paradigm, migrants to the United States come looking for a better life, eventually shedding their old-world customs, or at least their American-born children do (the melting pot may simmer benignly or scald, but eventually all immigrants melt). The immigrant and his or her descendants become "ethnic"—properly American, with a cultural heritage symbolized, codified, and tamed. Closing the door on one country, or home, immigrants, according to this paradigm, also close the door on another time.[7] The immigrant paradigm implies one sort of logic: one person, one place, one time. The diasporic individual, however, is in more than one place in more than one time. The difference between Gilroy's use of the term and the American Jewish use of the terms is that his usage brings cohesion to an unwieldy group of people, while for Jews *diaspora* describes variety over similarity. I do not intend to take back "diaspora" for the Jews, but to return our attention to the specificity of histories signaled in our terminology.

To illustrate another instance of the need to retheorize within the field, consider the critical itinerary of trauma theory. Presently, trauma theory is widely used to explore literary representations of cultural cataclysm brought on by slavery, genocide, forced exile, or war and imperialism. In its origins, trauma theory was a Yale-born cousin of poststructuralism, combining Lacanian and Demanian theories of language, memory, and presence to analyze cultural representations of historical trauma, initially and chiefly the Holocaust. Trauma theory reacted to the problem of aesthetics after Auschwitz when Auschwitz itself was based on the manipulation of figurative language for the purpose of dehumanizing the Nazis' victims. Trauma theory also attends to the fundamental problem of the erasure of the witness: Auschwitz torqued reality in such a way as to make it impossible for its survivors to bear witness in the ordinary language of the real world.

Since its advance in the early 1990s through the work of Santner, Felman and Laub, Caruth, and LaCapra, the insights of trauma theory have calcified into a collection of buzzwords describing "unclaimed experience," the "presence of the past," "haunting," and "mute witnessing" as belated responses to trauma, all sorts of trauma, from slavery, to colonialism, to war and exile. The terminology of trauma theory is efficacious and compelling because it grants the aporia of history and the impossibility of self-presence described in poststructuralist theory while bridging those aporias with affective and nonrational encounters with history, through experience. At once sophisticated and expedient, the discourse of trauma theory, like the terms *diaspora* and *the borderlands,* has been eagerly and widely appropriated, and in the process has lost its specificity and efficacy (the subject of chapter 3). More to the point, theorizations of cultural trauma have become "trauma theory," distancing the theory from its object of study. To cite but one example, in an essay on the ethics of encounter Judith Butler draws on the rhetoric of trauma to describe how our lack of self-presence is made evident when being addressed by an other: "To be addressed carries with it a trauma, resonates with the traumatic, and yet this trauma can only be experienced retrospectively through a *later* occurrence. Another word comes our way, a blow, an address or naming that slaughters, even as one lives on, strangely, as this slaughtered being, speaking away" ("Giving" 38). I can find no theoretical fault with Butler's statements here, and I am, in general, moved by her effort to integrate Levinasian ethics with poststructuralist philosophy. But *trauma? Slaughter?* A dozen years ago we used to speak of "the split subject," but that phrase is more buzz than word by now, and the term *slaughtered being* seems like the equivalent of turning up the volume. What began as a theorization of cultural responses and representations of the traumatic past has turned into "trauma theory," a free-floating mode of inquiry independent of any particular history or phenomenon.

My goal in part 1, on traumatic history, is not to put a stop to trauma theory but to knit the theory into specific contexts in order to see how it applies and is implied by them. If the general triptych of trauma theory is "catastrophe, cultural mourning, recovery," different catastrophes will necessarily require different cultural work. More to the point, different cultures will do different sorts of cultural work and deploy different symbols and representative or reparative devices depending on the culture's understanding of, say, history, religion, and the afterlife. Furthermore, the very historicity of the cultural group in question implies different strategies of cultural mourning. For Jews after the Holocaust, theorizing trauma requires the theological work of integrating the Holocaust into the history of biblical exile and persecution, and the narrative work of reading the postwar waning of anti-Semitism in the United States or the successful establishment of the Jewish state as the redemptive ending to a horrific story. An entirely different historicity prevails for Chicanos who look back at the sixteenth and seventeenth centuries' history of European colonialism and nineteenth-century American expansion as founding tragedies. Chicano culture, with its radical politics and Marxist roots, is distinct from Mexican American culture, emerging at the point when Mexican Americans recognize their social oppression as the latest moment in a centuries-long history of oppression. For Chicanos, representing the cultural devastation wrought by colonialism and then American imperial expansion is as much a strategy for producing the present as for working through the past.

Though many Jewish academics are flattered by Paul Gilroy's appropriation of "diaspora," American Jews are wary, to say the least, about the appropriation of the Holocaust for comparison with other cultures' history. The problem is not only the draining of cultural specificity from the terminology, but also the turf battles within the field, and different conceptions about the values and goals of ethnic literary study. Within the broad field of literature study, constructivist accounts of culture rule the day and the authority of postmodernist and postethnic theory establishes one controlling paradigm. Within ethnic literature study, however, especially among cultural groups in the process of defining themselves within and against recently contrived bureaucratic and institutional discourse— think of the 1970s-era strategic coinage of "Native American," the Chicano rejection of the Nixonian term "Hispanic," or the amalgamating and eliding term "Asian American"—historicism, cultural materialism, and archivalism comprise the important work of stabilizing the culture in question. Within this breakdown, Jewish American writers have traditionally been suspicious of group identities, often rejecting the label "Jewish writer" and pioneering postmodern aesthetics that undermine concrete determinations of group boundaries.

Meanwhile, prominent Jewish critics hold notions about cultural difference quite at odds with critics from other minority groups. Thus, when the Jewish critic Sander Gilman edited a special issue of the literary establishment periodical *PMLA* on ethnicity in 1998, three of the six essays were on Jews or Jewish literature, and most were invited essays by senior scholars. In contrast, when the Asian American critic David Palumbo-Liu gathered essays for his 1995 collection, *The Ethnic Canon,* not a single entry was on Jewish literature or culture. Indeed, no derivation of the word *Jew* shows up in the index. In a subsequent issue of *PMLA,* Vincent Cheng complained that "the moment that the marginal seems finally to be gaining access too the center, it is . . . well-known senior scholars . . . who get to speak for the margins" (450). Gilman's unconvincing reply was to say that "like gender in the eye of Judith Butler, ethnicity is inherently ambiguous" (451). A senior Jewish postmodern critic pointing to the theory of a senior postmodernist Jewish theorist for justification hardly suggests critical self-reflection!

Cheng may find more satisfaction consulting Palumbo-Liu's introduction to *The Ethnic Canon,* where the author states that the goal is not for the marginal to gain access to the center after all: "In the instance of *The Ethnic Canon,* the goal is to resist the essentializing and stratifying mode of reading ethnic literature that make it ripe for canonization and co-option" (17). That is, the critical practice of ethnic literature study has to anticipate gestures such as Gilman's and, by developing an antiauthoritarian and counterhegemonic discourse and practice, resist the bland norming of ethnicity. To hasten to the point of this overview, and to anticipate my own discourse and practice in this book, can the margincenter paradigm and resistance-based reading practices truly accommodate the diversity of the field "ethnic American literature"? If Jews and Jewish literature are too much a part of the establishment for *The Ethnic Canon,* what about the status of a wildly popular teaching text like Toni Morrison's *Beloved*? Or the ascension of border theory in the 1990s? In the case of Jewish criticism, ethnic scholars fear the eclipse of the truly marginal by the center, but in the latter two examples there is the problem of the potential draining of cultural specificity and political agency as the literature and criticism becomes canonized.

If there are different ways of conceiving of "ethnic" encounters, it is because we have very different stories of "being ethnic" told in the United States over the last century. First of the two dominant types is the immigrant American as the paradigmatic ethnic prior to World War II, and second is the ethnic American of color, actively resistant to assimilation following the civil rights consciousness-raising of the late 1960s and the 1970s. The former group produced a substantial body of literature matched by critical attention up to and following the rise of multicultural consciousness. The latter group effectively contested the prominent representation of the former and successfully established a new critical ethos in ethnic literary study.

I would link these two paradigms to my broad axes of analysis here, geography and history respectively, though again, the categories bleed into one another. Early ethnic American identities in the late nineteenth and early twentieth centuries were defined by geography, though geography is something of a double-edged sword. Jewish, German, Slavic, Irish, Italian, and Scandinavian immigrants defined their relation to the United States in terms of the distance traveled. Great journeys were floated on myths of the American dream and the promise of settlement opportunities. First sightings of the Statue of Liberty, arrival at Ellis Island, and the movement west into the American frontier are all staple conceits of early immigrant literature. Furthermore, for these groups, becoming American—even ethnic American—meant assimilating into U.S. culture in order to bridge the cultural gaps determined by geographical distance.

Ethnic literature written since the 1960s forces us to rethink history, especially the history of cultural geography. Black, Chicano, and Native American cultural nationalist movements drew attention to the histories and legacies of their oppression in the United States, helped produce new cultural knowledge for their respective groups, and rejected assimilation or hyphenation. Through the establishment of Black studies, Chicano and Latino studies, and Native American studies departments and programs on the West and East Coasts, and in concert with the broadening of multicultural curriculums and affirmative action policies, a generation of scholars and literary writers came of age at the apex of transformative ethnic consciousness-raising. Scholars, editors, and critics—or sometimes one individual wearing all three hats—began to archive the literary histories of their cultural group while gathering together new literature that was specifically ethnically self-conscious. Doing so was not only an artistic enterprise but a political one: Since the Phillis Wheatley court, producing a culture has always been part of the process of claiming rights in the United States.[8]

The literature that comes out of this multicultural moment, particularly by Chicano, Native American, African American, and Asian American writers, bears the politicized aspirations of these ethnic movements, drawing on newly formed cultural histories attesting to the experiences of slavery, colonialism, and imperialism. As a case in point, we might look to the Chicano literary project, *Recovering the U.S. Hispanic Literary Heritage Project* (4 vols.). The publisher, Arté Público Press, was founded as an offshoot of the Chicano cultural rights movement in the early 1970s, and in carrying out its mission to publish and foster Chicano and Latino literature and culture, the press fuses critical, political, and artistic projects as one. The press gathers and publishes emerging writers *and* critics, while "recovering" the roots of Chicano culture from historical elision.

Chicano literature is particularly noteworthy for its cultural self-consciousness. For example, in her acknowledgments page of her short story collection *Woman Hollering Creek,* Sandra Cisneros thanks not only her editors, readers, and family, but the Chicana feminist theorists Sonía Saldívar Hull and Norma Alarcón. Cisneros includes art, politics, and transformative theory in a single gesture, and instances of similar gestures can be found in African American literature in the work and career of Toni Morrison, Ishmael Reed, or Charles Johnson, and in Native American literature in the work of Paula Gun Allen and LeAnne Howe. In all these examples, the literature participates in an oppositional and historically tuned project of cultural materialist revisionism.

The divide between old and new conceptions of ethnic American identities is formed in part by a color line, but also in part by a theory line. Politically charged theory, especially Marxist and postcolonial theory developed in the late 1970s, changed the terms of analysis from cultural comparisons and the dynamics of assimilation to an analytic about power, resistance, and the strategic manipulation of race for the persistence of white supremacy. At the same time that peoples of color were advocating for rights and recognition, groups of white ethnics advocated for the "new pluralism," a reconsideration of the centrality of WASP culture. Several studies were published in the early seventies advocating for white ethnicity, significantly changing the public as well as academic discourse on ethnicity and assimilation. Consequently, white ethnic literary criticism, based on liberal conceptions of the self and employing a semiotics of ethnicity, sits uneasily alongside multicultural literary criticism focused on collective cultural expressions. Michael Novak's *The Rise of the Unmeltable Ethnics* (1971), Joseph Ryan's *White Ethnics: Their Life in Working Class America* (1973), and especially Nathan Glazer and Daniel Patrick Moynihan's *Beyond the Melting Pot* (1963, 1970) carefully and persuasively argued that white ethnic identification was not only on the rise, but an obdurate characteristic of twentieth-century American self-definition. In a later book, Glazer and Moynihan summed up their study this way:

> In *Beyond the Melting Pot,* we suggested that ethnic groups, owing to their distinctive historical experiences, their cultures and skills, the times of their arrival and the economic situation they met, developed distinctive economic, political and cultural patterns. As the old culture fell away— and it did rapidly enough—a new one, shaped by the distinctive experiences of life in America, was formed and a new identity was created. (273)

The insights here are of major importance to ethnic studies, for the suggestion is that different ethnic groups share vast common ground simply by being ethnic. If ethnicity is a culture formed through experience with American mainstream life, it follows that all ethnic groups share a common consciousness of disenfranchisement, alienation, and discrimination. But what of resistance? A book like Robert Lecky and H. Elliot Wright's 1970 anthology, *The Black Manifesto: Religion, Racism, and Reparations,* imagines an American entirely different from the one described by Moynihan and Glazer, and, needless to say, responds to the nation in dramatically different ways. Thus we have the divide in twentieth-century conceptions of the ethnic American: While pockets of pre–World War II new immigrants resisted the hegemony (in the classical sense) of white America, others negotiated a position of (mostly) give and (considerable) take. In contrast, minorities of color, including African Americans, Asian Americans, and Chicanos, have actively resisted a paradigm of assimilation, and in doing so they have overtly (re)linked ethnic identity with left-wing politics. The alliance of African American, Chicano, Native American, and Asian American studies with postcolonial studies, materialist, and nationalist-oriented theory points to the vast gap between how white ethnics and ethnics of color figure the place of ethnicity and cultural difference in American writing.

The clear difference between an early generation of ethnic Americans of European heritage and a more recent generation from colonized or third-world countries creates a significant gap in scholarship on ethnicity in America. The easiest thing to do, perhaps, would be to say the old (white) ethnic folks are no longer ethnic, and ethnicity means something else entirely now. But has the population of people we now call ethnic changed? Or have we changed the way we look at ethnicity? Why did these things change? And what has changed about America? Perhaps most critically, we might ask in what ways have earlier European ethnic Americans changed America itself or our notions of what and where America is, and how has this impacted the culture of contemporary ethnic Americans?

Ultimately, as Michael Omi and Howard Winant persistently argue, the ethnicity paradigm is easily appropriated by the mainstream and offers no basis for activist criticism. The writers proffer a paradigm based on a legally and politically configured concept of "race" instead. In fact, this presumption sways many who now write on ethnic literature. It would be hard to overstate the influence of Omi and Winant's critique of ethnicity and championing of a race-based paradigm for literature study. Besides being a standard citation in studies of race and ethnicity in literature, their seminal *Racial Formation in the United States* presents an alternative way of writing about race which rejects biological essentialism and maps out how legal and political racial configurations form and conform social racial being, giving rise, in part, to the ethos behind Critical Race studies.

One negative consequence to this development is the extent to which literature by white, European ethnics has been cut off from advanced theoretical literary study. Though Omi and Winant and those who write in their wake rightfully observe that white ethnic groups assimilated into American culture and gained access to its privileges by buying into hegemonic whiteness, the structure of such an analysis relies on and reproduces stable concepts within the terms *white* and *American*.

A key question, then, is how to approach these schisms within the field. For multiculturalists who assume that distinct cultures in the United States have distinct histories, historically oriented ethnic literature creates an imaginative provocation for readers to see separate and distinct histories where before there was only one. This latter point especially is what Bhabha means when he appropriates Derrida's idea of dissemination, recast as "DissemiNation," for postcolonial critique. Reviewing the nation through multiple and at times contradictory stories of counternationalism, or resistance to the nation, results in a plurality of irreconcilably politicized identities and a deconstruction of nationalist logic. A committed multicultural approach necessarily drops the deconstructive method here, for multiculturalism as a political and pedagogical practice is committed to holistic and coherently self-present cultural systems, distinct from one another. For a number of reasons advanced below, I am skeptical of a strictly multicultural approach to ethnic literature, though I am sympathetic to the aims of multiculturalism as an intellectual and pedagogical strategy. Multiculturalism finally implies static and homogenous cultures. More problematically, because multiculturalism presumes that individual selves are dialectically attached to their culture of origin, cosmopolitan individuals who may consider themselves also part of a local culture have no terms for encounter with that culture.[9]

My favored term, *ethnicity*, is not without its own messy history, of course. *Ethnicity*, as Werner Sollors reminds us, is relatively new, coined early in the twentieth century, and only widely used in the late 1960s and early 1970s (*Beyond* 23). The term *ethnic*, on the other hand, has a long and nasty history, and the gap between the origin of one and then the other points to a sea change in the way social difference is conceived in America. *Ethnic* derives from the Greek *ethnikos*, a word that pejoratively denotes "otherness" akin to the Hebrew term *goy*. The latter word refers to non-Israelite nations, and so connotes a fundamental theological otherness, a valence *ethnic* shares in its historical usage. Indeed, the word *ethnic* is a root source for the latter-day term *heathen*, and in their historical usage both terms suggest an other who is different not only in the eyes of humanity, but of God as well. As Sollors usefully notes, Puritan settlers in New England alternately used the terms *ethnic* and *heathen* to describe the Natives they encountered (*Beyond* 26). In the latter half of the twentieth century, however, *ethnic* and *ethnicity* have come to mean cultural (and, especially in recent decades, nonhierarchical) difference, located squarely in cultural customs rather than any essential racial makeup. Sollors observes that ethnicity connotes differential social relations and concludes that ethnicity is finally defined by the boundaries of any given cultural group rather than by the group's cultural content: "Ethnic groups in the United States have relatively little cultural differentiation, . . . the cultural *content* of ethnicity . . . is largely interchangeable and rarely historically authenticated. From such a perspective, contrastive strategies—naming and name calling among them—become the most important thing about ethnicity" (28). Sollors concludes that ethnicity pertains primarily through symbolic representation and differentiation. Of course, we might wonder about the use of the term *symbol* at this point. Is the border a symbol? To the U.S. government, which puts up fences and mans the border with a military police force, especially since 9/11, the border is highly symbolic, matched by the flag in its anxious definition of the nation. But it is by no means "just" a symbol, or if it is a symbol, its connotations for Chicanos are not only different but in conflict with mainstream connotations. Indeed, we would be grossly in error if we believe, first of all, that the border, the Middle Passage crossing, and Ellis Island were mere symbols with little constitutive efficacy in the lives of respective ethnic Americans. To conflate one with the other, to say that the content of ethnicity is less important than the symbolic boundaries, where all symbolic crossings would be the same, tautologically separates literature from its material and affective contexts.

The symbolic or semiotic analysis of ethnicity and race is inherently politically tuned toward laying bare our country's devastating fictions of racial difference. In general, deconstructive criticism exposes the (false) assumptions and (flawed) structures of knowledge that give rise to our cultural constructions. The deconstruction of the logic of race in particular aims to combat the menacing legacy of those constructions. Useful a process as this is, there is something glib about the conclusions that we move "beyond" ethnicity as Sollors suggest, or that we are now, finally, "post-ethnic" as David Hollinger would have it. These gestures too easily write off a history of racism, facilely moving "beyond" a legacy that persists still.

In contrast, critical race and postcolonial theorists and critics argue that the term *race* provides a more apt logic for analyzing how cultural communities are constructed and operate in America. Critics favoring this strategy recognize that biological race is a misleading concept that has in fact been a tool of racist domination for at least four centuries, but this is precisely the point. Biology, cultural anthropology, political legislation, and a broad network of cultural texts have construed people of color in America as racial others. To turn race into ethnicity, or more starkly, to view America as "post-" ethnic, does not alter the fact that the otherness of color, articulated over centuries, is manifest in significant inequalities of justice, or economics, for "race resides not in nature but in politics and culture" (Jacobsen 9). Advocates of symbolic multiethnic or multicultural study, race critics argue, miss just this fact. For this present work, I would say that ethnic cultures are contingent, protean formations, and produce serviceable identities for all sorts of critical practices. *Ethnicity* is a catch-all term that points to the deconstructive potential in cultural pluralism, but the term is ultimately breached itself by the specificity of individual ethnic groups.

It would be problematic to assume a critical practice that speaks to and for all ethnicities. As Lisa Lowe puts it, such a practice

> levels the important differences and contradictions within and among racial and ethnic minority groups according to the discourse of pluralism, which asserts that American culture is a democratic terrain to which every variety of constituency has equal access and in which all are represented, while simultaneously masking the existence of exclusions by recuperating dissent, conflict, and otherness through the promise of inclusion. Multiculturalism is central to the maintenance of a consensus that permits the present hegemony, a hegemony that relies on a premature reconciliation of contradiction and persistent distractions away from the historically established incommensurability of the economic, political, and cultural spheres. (86)

Lowe's claims is sweeping and does not distinguish between the several types of multiculturalism and pluralism that exist,[10] but it nonetheless poses a strong challenge to a project like this one, which frequently compares the literature of a group widely regarded as white and ethnic— Jewish Americans—and the literature of Chicanos, people of color for sure, historically regarded as racially distinct from whites in America. Lowe points to the sociohistoric differences among ethnic groups and cautions us that though it would be tempting to compare these histories and even seek out similarities, this may indeed lead to a premature reconciliation of the contradictions ethnic groups pose for each other, and for America at large. On the other hand, and from my point of view, not to compare is to miss the opportunity to critique the postethnic school of thought, and to examine the historical and literary development of different social identities in relation to one another.

Precisely in order to avoid the premature reconciliations described by Lowe, I choose to defer a straightforward theorization of ethnicity or race in favor of a developing hypothesis that through comparative analysis of different ethnicities' literatures we can observe the external pressures and internal maneuvers of group identity which produce overlaps and divergences in the mechanisms of group identity formation. For this reason, my analysis reflects back on the critical scene and not only on literature. Despite the recent scholarship that indicates that white European immigrants to America in the late nineteenth and early twentieth centuries were indeed typed as racially distinct, even "colored," it is also quite clear that these same immigrants or their children gained their white status in differential relation to African Americans, Native Americans, Asians immigrants, and Mexican Americans. Thus, though we may say that Jews, Italians, or Irish were considered racially different upon arrival in America, America itself fundamentally altered its concepts of race through federal legislation, liberal social reform, land-grant policies, union construction, and (crucially) literary imagination in order to reinscribe the white/colored racial dichotomy.

According to Matthew Frye Jacobson, "white privilege in various forms has been a constant in American political culture since colonial times, but whiteness itself has been subject to all kinds of contests and has gone through a series of historical vicissitudes" (4).[11] Clearly, a study that compares ethnicities in America must attend to these vicissitudes, and a treatment of differing histories for ethnic groups is in order, but here too we have a compelling topic: America is a site of internal contradiction, constructing and constructed by ethnic difference. Again, Jacobson makes the point: "By looking at racial categories and their fluidity over time, we glimpse the competing theories of history which inform the society and define its internal struggles" (6). Though this is not a book about race, I cite Jacobson because what he has to say about being white can be broadly appropriated for thinking about the normative idea of "America" at large. Too much ethnic scholarship (or mainstream for that matter) posits a stable America in relation to ethnicity, but this distinction becomes increasingly difficult to maintain.

Keeping in mind Sollors's insights on the symbolic construction of ethnicity, but also maintaining the point of view of Lowe, Jacobson, and others, I would argue that a theory of the symbolic construction of eth-

nic literature would also be a deconstruction of American narrative coherence. Deconstruction is not the same as dismantling—the dismantling of racism, say, or the undoing of racist narratives—and such a project would certainly not aim for the kinds of premature reconciliations
Lowe warns against. Rather, deconstructing American narrative coherence means investigating the contradictory symbolic designations of identity that a mainstream American identity necessarily suppresses.

Furthermore, such a project includes an honest reckoning with the
mutual implication of mainstream and minority cultures. Not only is
America a site of internal incoherence, but so too are minority cultures
constructed by the contradictory claims that ethnic and national histories and symbols make on them. In fact, many Chicano scholars and
artists have drawn on this contradictory logic to ironize and therefore
make present an ethnic culture otherwise suppressed. I am thinking about
the logic of the border, an official barrier against the other, which also
enfolds the other into America, but I would argue that the material history of ethnic groups, when symbolized in culture performance, may be
coded to deconstruct the mono-logic of mainstream versions of national
citizenry.

If this sounds too much like a "celebration" of ethnic difference, I
should quickly note that histories of ethnic Americans may be devastat-
ingly painful, standing outside the economy of symbols that would
attempt to represent them. These include histories of slavery, genocide,
and colonization—American history—but also to contemporary mani-
festations of ongoing racism: English-only laws, sweatshops, armed border guards throughout the Southwest, and the now fully embraced practice of ethnic profiling. There are no easy symbols or narratives, ironic or
otherwise, to deflect the danger of persistent racism, nor will an analysis
of ethnic literature open up a safe space for victims of state-sponsored or
publicly sanctioned racism. Instead, what I hope to achieve with the critical comparisons of multiple ethnic groups in this project is a clearer picture of the process of cultural construction—mainstream and ethnic—
which at once attends to the separate histories of each group while
symbolically implicating each into the center of a discourse on American
culture at large. My interest in "ethnicity," then, springs from the insight
that cultural contingency and geohistorical contiguity end up so muddying the waters of identity that any account of where cultural identities

come from and how they function must necessarily be one that favors impurity over purity, dissonance and a bit of chaos over harmony and order.

In order to explain these competing analytical tendencies and theoretical strategies, most chapters here focus on Jewish and Chicano writers and critics, with glances toward African American and Native American literature and criticism as well, thereby provoking the problems occasioned by the different paradigms and histories of ethnicity. I am using those convergences and clashes to explore the limits of some critical concepts in ethnic literature study. Of course, the differences between the groupings "Jewish writers" and "Chicano writers" is obvious. While many Jewish writers are recipients of major national and international literary prizes, and have access to elite publication venues, Chicano writers are nowhere near as popularly or critically disseminated. Chicano authors write from the margins of the literary establishment and many rebel against prevailing aesthetic and ideological norms, while Jewish writers all but comprise the establishment and have been on the vanguard of literary trends throughout the century, from Henry Roth's modernism to Philip Roth's postmodernism. Perhaps not surprisingly, in an academic multiculture that has adopted the ethics of resistance to American hegemony, Chicano writers have helped form the very language of counterhegemonic cultural criticism, while Jewish writers and critics have been comparatively absent from multicultural critical dialogues. I take it as a sign of cultural self-confidence and stability that so many Jewish writers continually reject the label "Jewish American writer," and even the value of the category itself. African American, Chicano, and Native American writers are much more willing to embrace their respective ethnic categories and to recognize the value of cultural archiving.

Yet there is more in common between Jewish American and Chicano cultures than we initially think. Both Jewish and Chicano writers meditate on alternative homelands, histories of migration and displacement, and the discursive space between inherited race and chosen cultural identity. Furthermore, both cultures' contemporary self-articulations resist black/white binaries, and both are in the midst of a set of challenges to the shape of identity which are demographic, cultural, and class-based. Though both Jews and Chicanos fold historical legacies into contemporary self-constructions, neither is solely comprised of nostalgic longings for the motherland, nor is either reducible merely to a set of materially empty symbols. I should pause to recognize the same and more can be said about African American, Asian American, and Native American writers. Recent studies in Italian American and Irish American cultural identificatory practices indicate that this heterodoxy extends at least somewhat across the colored/white divide.[12] This, then, is the primary purpose for examining two very different bodies of literature and criticism in comparison: to suspend the prevailing academic assumptions about both race and ethnicity which persist when examining literature only under one heading or the other; and to see how certain critical methods help us account for a wide array of literatures, while at the same time observing how the diversity among those literatures would cause us to rethink the objectivity of our critical tools.

The first three chapters consider the large question, how do American ethnic writers represent and respond to cultural histories of trauma and loss? Our popular culture is saturated with books, films, photos, museums, and memorials that attempt to symbolize (and thereby make present) past instances of war, slavery, genocide, or colonialism. Both academic and popular writing about these sorts of memorials presume that different American cultures can work through and mourn the horrific past, thereby healing it. Likewise, a trend in recent literary criticism is to say that contemporary ethnic literature effectively mourns the past. I respond by asking what mourning means in different cultural contexts, and whether in fact mourning is an adequate critical description of how different cultures' literature responds to the past. Chapter 1 asks, how can Jewish literature authentically respond to the Holocaust when that historical event is already sentimentally embedded in American popular culture? Reversing the question in chapter 2, how do Chicano writers represent the cultural cataclysm wrought by colonialism and racism when there is a near-total absence of popular historical awareness of their side of history? And for African Americans who would write about slavery, in what ways does the project of cultural healing become a program for recognition, rights, and social justice? This is the subject of chapter 3. With Jewish literature, two examples of "acting out," or the narrative repetition of loss, rewrite a broader American cultural appropriation of the Holocaust. For Chicano writers, mourning is secondary to producing a cultural history, or archive, which links the past and present, and allows for a progressive vision of the future. Archives are not static authoritarian libraries of cultural knowledge, but ever-growing and changing bodies of literature that require contemporary writers and critics to draw from and add to them constantly.

Turning to African American literature and criticism, I consider whether the psychological apparatus of "mourning" is in fact relevant to historically engaged literature. Focusing on Toni Morrison's celebrated novel *Beloved*, I propose an alternative goal, namely "reparations"—that is, monetary reparations for African Americans for slavery and Jim Crow segregation, but also national reconciliation between cultural communities and between the present and the past.

The three chapters of the second part may seem to broaden the book by considering critical concepts of space and place, but my methodology remains consistent: comparing literature and criticism across cultures to test and even reformulate those concepts. American ethnic writers and critics have long meditated on the ethics of diaspora, the porousness of borders, and the values and limits of nationalism. In the next two chapters I ask and answer the following questions: how are conceptions of diaspora similar to and different from the literary and critical metaphor of the borderlands? What sorts of political and ethical agendas does each concept suggest? Though some have held up one or the other concept as an exemplar of marginal critique, what does it mean to think of a borderlands Jewish culture, or a diasporic Chicano culture? Or a diasporic border? In chapter 4 I broach a thesis on the border that is less a metaphor for cultural geography and more a critique of American conceptions of national boundaries. Next, in order to expand thinking about the limits of ethnic nationalism, I turn to a very different sort of nationalism, namely the activism of Queer Nation, and the subsidiary gay-ethnic nationalist activism in radical ethnic literature. From the very start I concede the many obvious problems with a politics of nationalism, but I show how writers and critics have explored boundary breaking gay social activism in order to locate and even transcend those limits.

The book closes with a full-length concluding chapter that makes explicit the ethics of criticism implicit in the preceding chapters. All along I demonstrate that a comparative approach to ethnic literature must begin by accounting for the intrinsic historical, political, and ethical contingencies of different ethnic American cultures. In the conclusion I show how those contingencies dictate the very critical perspectives which produce discussions of ethnic literature in the first place.

PART ONE··· Traumatic History and Ethnic American Literature

1··· THE JEW WHO GOT AWAY

The title of this chapter comes from Nathan Zuckerman's description of his idol, E. I. Lonoff, in Philip Roth's *The Ghost Writer* (1979): "I think of you as the Jew who got away" (50). "Got away" from what is clear enough: Burning Europe, the raucous dynamism of Jewish New York, and the pull of the traditional Jewish family. But what does he escape to? When you get away from tradition, history, religion, culture, and emotional family ties, what can you possibly be? The question is doubly pressing applied to Lonoff since he writes about nothing but Jews with apparent "Jewish irony" and obviously extends to the broader question of how to think about the meaning and content of the category "Jewish American writer."[1] For writers and critics thematically interested in this sort of escape, or who are interested in escaping themselves, typically figured as *assimilation*—a term so open to interpretation as to be empty of all meaning—does literature disassociate or integrate the past from the present, the living from the dead; does literature break or produce a trajectory of culture? For those who want to get away, is literature the escape mechanism itself, or is literature the sentimental dwelling place where exiles go to reconnect with culture? James Young, citing David Roskies, points to the problem underwriting such questions:

> That an individual can be "cut off from the sustaining archetypes, from the exalted messianic schemes . . . , from the communal saga, from the past, from his own set of inherited symbols," implies that one can cut oneself off from one's tradition, or leave it behind somehow. But in fact, the individual "cut off . . ." might only exist hypothetically as the emblematic modernist or freethinker, or in fiction as *"der Mann ohne Eigenschaften."*

For only the desire to cut oneself off from the tradition and all of its cumbersome, informing, and constraining myths might be represented and speculated upon in writing; inasmuch as language and narrative are essential parts of any tradition, however, this desire to be "cut off" can never actually be enacted in writing. (*Texture* 97)

In *The Ghost Writer* Nathan and his literary patriarch Lonoff perform the paradox Young describes: both long to be totally removed from anything like Jewish culture and community, yet both write about Jews consistently. Compounding the paradox, for readers of the fictional Zuckerman, Lonoff, and (more important) real writers like Roth, Ozick, Malamud, and Singer—Jewish writers who write recognizably Jewish literature—does literature draw one back to the past? Sentimentally, falsely? Or intellectually and critically? Or might literature be precisely that which blocks out the past, either because writing objectifies or because it makes the transcendental radically subjective? This is a chapter about literary encounters with an alienated and alienating past. My principal subject is Holocaust narratives that perform multiple problems of identifying with the past. If individuality competes with cultural memory for Jews in general, the conflict is all the more substantial with Jewish thinking about the Holocaust. An enormous amount of scholarship exists on the efficacy, ethics, and politics of literary representations of the Holocaust, but what I consider here is slightly different from what has been studied and stated thus far.[2]

I begin by establishing how popular American culture reifies and universalizes the Holocaust through ideological appropriation. Then I trace how Cynthia Ozick and Philip Roth resist the totalizing gravity of Holocaust history in America.[3] In Roth's *The Ghost Writer,* the freedom required to write truthfully requires a total escape, including the escape from some form of Holocaust identification that is mandated not only by Jewish culture, but by American ideologies. Ozick, in *The Messiah of Stockholm,* narrates the reverse, arriving at a similar conclusion: her protagonist is so totally absorbed by a suspect identification with the Holocaust as to lose all sense of himself as a living contemporary person who might relate to the Holocaust historically rather than immediately. Partly because Roth and Ozick are working against an already developed memorial project, this chapter ends without broad theoretical conclusions, but my intent is also to set up the two chapters that follow, which examine the construction of alternate sorts of cultural memorializing in literature.

National historiography is ideological insofar as it draws narrative threads from disparate cultural strands and knots them together to produce a self-strengthening, tight reality, and a vision of what the nation should look and act like. Specifically, popular U.S. history assimilates the histories of ethnic groups into a single history, often divesting plural histories of their particularity.[4] Similarly, Ethnic American writers, from Mary Antin to Gish Jen, use stories of ethnic encounters with American culture to establish a felicitous place for their group in a conservative national imaginary, to weave into or tighten the knot. As Lisa Lowe has suggested with Asian Americans, popular and political historiography and narrative not only exclude the presence of ethnic and differently gendered "others" from the mainstream culture, they work precisely in opposition to the otherness of the "foreigner," the queer, or the historically exploited and oppressed.[5] Benedict Anderson may be correct that nations are "imagined," but as Lowe (following Bhabha) indicates, the imagined homogeneity of a nation is a dynamic *repression* of a nation's difference. Fracture perceived as a placid whole—so goes the psychoanalytic critique of subjectivity, and so too might we clarify Anderson's theory of imagining the nation. Those renditions of the nation's history in literature, criticism, and historiography that are inassimilable (or "un-meltable," as Novak memorably puts it) would present to a national narrative the uncanny challenge of other histories and other stories.

Such a pluralism suggests not only a multiculture, but multiple versions of the same nation. In instances where histories and cultural experience are co-opted, literary writers resisting that co-optation perform a dialectic of appropriation and resistance, but this raises the recurring question: can literature offer a counternarrative to the prevailing hegemonic narratives that result from cultural appropriation without performing a ritual of authentic discovery? The catch in this question is that while writing the past always requires a skillful rethinking of the present, the traumatic past, including histories of genocide and colonialism, may be psychically as well as narratologically inaccessible.

Attempting to represent the traumatic past has become something of an ethnic, and perhaps national, pastime. From the sublime to the banal, memorials, libraries, shopping malls, street names, rap music, comic books, children's books, cartoons, holidays (folded into pregame festivities at baseball stadiums throughout the summer) respond to and aim to memorialize—that is, remember through some version of representation—the traumatic history of just about any and all ethnic groups in the United States. Add to that the ever-growing list of critical titles that extract a scene of mourning or memorial from literary texts.[6] Without claiming that historical trauma is in fact *essential* to ethnic identity in America, it seems clear that when ethnic Americans critically and creatively think about their identities, communities, or cultures, they look back into a history of war, colonialism, genocide, forced relocation, enslavement, or perilous migration. Meanwhile, the uncanny gaze of American culture is looking along, over the shoulder of ethnic America.

Precisely because contemporary ethnic Americans are generally not faced with such perils—and a whole generation of ethnic Americans has never personally known them—history itself is profoundly otherworldly. Holocaust survivors and their descendants live oddly bifurcated lives in America, like "two side-by-side refrigerators/(one in the kitchen, one in the basement)," as Jacqueline Osherow puts it in her poem "Conversations with Survivors" (23). The hyperbole of life that results from escape, whether it is through assimilation, exile, or reclusive withdrawal, is itself a failed trope and a exorbitant doubling back onto the past. How does literature represent and respond to the hyperbole, the exorbitance, the duality implied in such an image—two lives, one subterranean, one above ground, which combined imply an evasion of the real? A superficial multiculturalism that celebrates diversity and fits days of remembrance on the calendar is the above-ground, placid surface of ethnicity in America. But rumbling just below that surface is a subterrain of unincorporated experience. Representing the subterranean experience may well turn into appropriation, but we look for the rupture of the one into the other to see where the line is drawn.

Though the Holocaust seems to have passed fully into American culture, much has been lost in the transfer.[7] Transference might be just the term here, since what follows is a sketch of how American nationalist culture has transferred its own cultural problems onto the story of the Holocaust in a kind of wish-fulfilling narrative act. The Holocaust has become woven into the narrative fabric of America, a part of the ideology of the nation as we will see below, but as is the case with official narratives, the specificities of survivor experience have been repressed. A catastrophic event without redemption which poses a challenge to the very conventions by which we understand history has become overwritten in American culture with the narrative of hope and renewal.

A somewhat poignant but startling article in *Fortune* magazine published in 1998 suggests the point and offers some insight into the "trade value" of survivor narratives in America's economy of exchange, the immigrants' rags/*shmattes* for the nation's riches. The article is not unique by itself, but is characteristic of a type of celebratory thinking about Jews in America, and of the larger discursive interpolation of ethnic narratives into the dominant ideological narratives that construct the U.S. nation. I don't mean to say that Jews have always been or are only celebrated. In fact, in 1936, as the Nazis were coming to power in Germany, *Fortune* undertook an in-depth survey of American public attitudes toward Jews, their fate abroad, and the supposed power they wielded at home, concluding, "for centuries Jews had refused to accept the cultures of their host countries and were unable to accept American culture, despite their will to do so because the 'habit of pride and stubbornness or their ancestors is too strong in them'" (in Eisen, *Chosen* 33). *Fortune*'s reversal suggests the Jewish reversal of fortune, as America has become a remarkably comfortable place for Jews, many of whom have earned fortunes of their own.[8]

The cover story for the April 13, 1998, issue, written by Carol Loomis, is titled "Out of the Holocaust," suggesting the Holocaust is a place, a site of emigration from which Jews originated and arrived in America. Jews have been coming to the United States since its founding, out of Germany, Russia, or Poland, Cuba, Mexico, or Turkey, but apparently it is not until they came out of the Holocaust that Jews became properly American: "What did it take to survive the Holocaust's death camps and start over with little or nothing in a strange land—and then build enough wealth to give away millions?" (65). The question rings strangely for those who have read Primo Levi or Elie Wiesel, both of whom tell of the lack of logic and sense to survival or death during the Holocaust. *Fortune*'s question implies its answer: the survivors profiled had "the right stuff," some characteristic which, when retroactively applied, is uniquely American.

The article is didactic, less concerned with the psychology of the survivor than with asserting the survivor as proof of a process the author calls "the American dream in action" (65). Each profile has two parts; the first, in italics, is a brief synopsis of the individual's Holocaust experience—"Part One." "Part Two" is the journey to America, and the individual's rise to success: "most of these young men had little English and less money. They lacked friends and mentors and the familiarities of family and home. They reached, nonetheless, into unfathomably deep pools of resilience and found the drive to succeed." Not content to marvel, however, the author interpolates the survivors' tales into the mythic experience of immigration to assimilation, rags to riches. The point turns here, from awe at survivors to a didactic chastisement: "but many millions who were unencumbered by the heavy, exhausting baggage of the Holocaust had the same opportunities and never reached out to seize them as these men did" (65). The point, then, is not only to marvel at the stories, or even to "warm the pages of this magazine" (64), but also to promulgate an ideology that at once interpolates survivor-Jews into the American immigrant myth, while chiding readers into an identification with Jewish loss and industrious return: "Hey, you! You think you got it bad? Look at these guys—*they're* not complaining!"

The breakdown of profiles into a "Part One" and a "Part Two" forms each profile into a mini-epic of dispossession and return; America becomes the putative "home" to each protagonist's destiny. With each of the five profiles there is no looking back to the past, and few regrets, not to mention trauma-induced crises. For example, Fred Kort narrowly escaped an execution-style slaughter of all the men in his camp barracks and lost his father, brother, and sixty other relatives (68). Of his life in America, we are told, "Kort is in no way locked into the memories of the past. Deeply aware that America has been good to him, he is instead propelled by the thought that he'd just better bounce out there and 'do more'" (70). The profile of Bill Konar, survivor of Auschwitz, ends with his reflection, "What a country!" (76). And Nathan Shapell's story ends with his triumphant reprivatization of a company which, to his dissatisfaction, he had previously taken public: "It hardly ranks with the first, of course [!], but he calls [the reprivatization] his 'second liberation'" (72). Finally, there is Sigi Ziering, who wonders "whether the 'training' of the Holocaust—'unless you work you are destined for the gas chamber'—

may not have permanently bent him and many other survivors to work" (84). The musing merges posttraumatic stress disorder with the Protestant work ethic, prompting the authors of the article to conclude that the five profiled "picked themselves up from the worst and darkest of beginnings and triumphed in the best tradition of the American dream" (84).

In each case, Jews not only escaped, but transformed or transposed themselves into typical Americans. And not by assimilating—at least not in the story told—but by inserting "Jewish survivor" into the very typology of the American Dream. The individuals profiled are complicit with *Fortune*'s point of view, each having recast himself as an American (with all ideology and outlook intact), and now re-presenting their Holocaust experience as the binary contrast to freedom in America. But "freedom" in the *Fortune* essay is specifically the freedom of free enterprise, as capitalism is synonymous with liberation. According to an editor's note at the beginning of the article, the subjects interviewed were sought out because they were listed on a donors wall at the U.S. Holocaust Memorial Museum in Washington, D.C., all in the million-dollar-plus section. As Vivian Patraka has observed, the D.C. Holocaust Museum is a site "where a cultural performance of Holocaust history is being staged for public consumption," and the fundraising itself may perform the ideologies inherent in the museum project (62). Patraka concludes that the museum is as much a monument to America as the antithesis of Germany as it is to Germany's victims: "If what is critical for the museum's project is to extend our fictions of nationhood by the premise that a democratic state comes to the aid of those peoples outside its borders subjected to genocide, then the conferring of liberation becomes the story of American democracy" (62–63). The very idea of the nation requires an ideology, and consequently Jewish stories are appropriated and drawn into American fabulations and felicitous dreams.

On the co-optation of memory and personal history for the construction of national narrative Homi Bhabha explains, "to be obliged to forget—in the construction of the national present—is not a question of historical memory; it is the construction of a discourse on society that *performs* the problem of totalizing the people and unifying the national will" (160). Bhabha recognizes that although popular discourse tends to totalize and usurp unique ethnic narratives, this point of co-optation is also a potential point of intervention. It is precisely because of the deep implication of the people as the object of a national narrative that representations of social difference and cultural complexity can lay bare the homogenizing capacity of nationalist discourse (161).

Bhabha begins his essay on postcolonial identity and literature with a question that may help us see how to place popular myth-making like that of the *Fortune* article alongside novels that explore and trouble received notions of ethnic-group trauma: "How does one write the nation's modernity as the event of the everyday and the advent of the epochal?" (141). In the term *everyday* we may consider the constant struggles the profiled survivors faced to enter into and merge with America as well as the quotidian lives of American Jews whose families were established in the United States long before the outbreak of war, and who did not relate directly to the Shoah's victims. The "epochal," of course, resonates with the solidification of America's exceptionalist mission in world history. We should also keep in mind, as we will see below, the history of America as the darkly epochal event in the lives of many of its citizens, including Native Americans, Asian Americans, African Americans, and Chicanos and Latinos. The history of U.S. conquest across the continent fuses the epochal with the everyday for those whose histories originate here.

Bhabha's theory turns on a concept of the "meanwhile," or "simultaneity" (also figured as Freud's' "uncanny"), outside of a narrative scope that otherwise constructs the "time" of the modern nation (161, 159, 145). Anderson's famous theory of "Imagined Communities" is predicated on the imagination of a synchronous time-space of the nation, and Bhabha's intervention suggests that simultaneity does not mean sameness. Bhabha points out that the signifier, vehicle of synchronic representation of the people in Anderson's theory, "is condemned to slide ceaselessly" between a discourse of the pedagogical (the people ideologically totalized) and the performative (everyday lived heterogeneity) (149). Bhabha explains that this disjunction "introduces a signifying space of iteration rather than a progressive or linear seriality. The 'meanwhile' turns into quite another time, or ambivalent sign, of the national people" (159). "Explains" might be going too far: What Bhabha apparently means is not only can we read a national literature's ambivalence against itself, but minority discourse can also emerge from this ambivalent time by proffering a version of the nation's subjects that is simultaneous but not the same, thus challenging the dominance of prevailing narratives (149). This is the "menace" of postcolonial literature, and the implicit critique of the national imaginary in American ethnic postmodernism. With Roth's and Ozick's novels, we find multiplications of stories-within-stories that critique the wish-fulfilling tendencies of America and American Jews and the archive-ism of Holocaust melancholy, respectively. Characters in both novels are also writers and they allegorize the writers' dilemma: rejecting the ideological types of identity means escape and isolation, which is not the same as freedom from identity. Instead, the Jew who gets away is still Jewish, but only, borrowing from Ozick, as an auto-iconoclast, negating the position of standing in for something, constantly crushing the idols of identity one necessarily creates for oneself. What emerges productively from this dilemma? For Roth, there is at least criticism and satire comprising an ethos of Jewish culture, if not an identity. But Ozick herself is self-negating, self-flagellating, scouring all aesthetics of Jewish identity, including Jewish identification with history, with a swipe of ruthless ethics, the ethics of ultimate respect for the alterity of the Holocaust and its victims.

Roth's version of Anne Frank, imagined into being by Nathan Zuckerman in *The Ghost Writer*, is a nearly assimilated American Jew, a lover of letters—she goes by the name Amy Bellete—an adoring fan of the patriarchal American literary tradition, similar to Nathan himself. Roth's appropriation of Anne is certainly scandalous, but no more so than her appropriation by dominant American ideologies of liberal identity and the ethics of freedom and liberation. In *The Ghost Writer*, Nathan Zuckerman is struggling for artistic freedom from the provincialism of his slightly hysterical Jewish family, acknowledging all the while that he is emotionally and morally bound to that family regardless of his duties to Art. Amy Bellete appears as a mysterious student and paramour of Nathan's literary hero E. I. Lonoff, with just enough physical resemblance and historical baggage to provoke Zuckerman's speculation that she could be Anne Frank, or if not Frank, then someone analogously but anonymously tragic. She is Amy in the first and third sections of the novel, Anne in the second, but I call her Amy-Anne here because the hyphen signifies the tension of unresolved possibilities in history (as hyphens often do), the simultaneity of the "meanwhile," and the mutual canceling effects of each persona against the other. Were Anne to have lived, she would only be Amy, largely unknown and unread, while the historical Anne's tragedy and fame cancel out the banal survivor identity of Amy. Furthermore, the ambiguity in the novel over Amy-Anne's identity, her function in the story as the potential hyphen for Nathan's American-Jewish identity, and the humorously easy conflation between her literary interests—sex, family politics, and her literary heritage—and Roth's own would bridge the otherness that separates the Holocaust and Jewish American cultural life in a radically different way than so far seen. The split from and the attraction to the Holocaust, or at least its aura, is best displayed in a scene late in the novel, as Nathan Zuckerman looks lustily at Amy-Anne, while longing to redeem his own Jewish life. Asked by Amy-Anne what occupied him during the war, while she was presumably awaiting the gas chambers, Zuckerman replies flatly, "my childhood" (168). The vast gap between the American Jew and the European Holocaust victim/survivor produces *The Ghost Writer*'s paradoxical problem. In Zuckerman's fantasy, Anne's escape into Amy's life would result in Zuckerman's return to a Holocaust-identified Jewish family. Only one Jew can get away, in the fantasy anyway. The ideological traps of identifying with the past are clear enough in the *Fortune* article. But the broader question, even beyond Holocaust identification, persists: is there a way to be a liberal Jew, free of attachment and responsibility? *The Ghost Writer*'s paradox is that we are all inevitably interpellated into the normalizing logic of communities and cultures, just as we inevitably yearn to resist, even escape that normalization.

Complicating Nathan's struggle for independence is fear of American anti-Semitism, which fuels Holocaust identification. As Nathan's father puts it: "there is very little love . . . in this world for Jewish people. I don't mean in Germany either, under the Nazis. I mean . . . run-of-the-mill Americans, Mr. and Mrs. Nice Guy who otherwise you and I consider perfectly harmless. Nathan, it is there. I guarantee you it is there. I *know* it is there. I have seen it, I have felt it, even when they do not express it in so many words" (93). Such a perspective comes with its own aesthetic theory, which rules out ambivalent depictions of ethnic groups in America. Under siege, the argument goes, Jews cannot afford to acknowledge any kind of factionalism, while sectarianism must give way to clear demonstrations of patriotic national affiliation. Because of Mr. and Mrs. Nice Guy, literature by Jews is always-already ethnic insofar as Jews in America are hedged in by the total alterity of the Holocaust and concomitant strains of philo- and anti-Semitism, whether real or imagined. Nathan's duty to his Jewish community is to occlude that ethnicity, deracinate the narrative, and represent an ideal of liberal familial conformity at the core of his stories—in short, to be a good Jewish "ambassador" to the wider gentile community.[9]

The conflation of texts with cultures or personal identities is simplistic and reductive, and readers no doubt sympathize with Nathan's rejection of his father's limiting and defensive advice. However, if we grant that Nathan is not responsible for Jewish culture when writing his stories (and by extension neither is Roth), we also loosen the synecdochal bind of Frank to the Holocaust. Amy Hungerford insightfully names the problem, "the personification of texts," a phenomenon wherein literature, sacralized as the liturgy of culture, takes on the status of the human. This way, Holocaust literature, exalted by the critical urge to rescue, archive, and publish, stands in for what is otherwise inaccessible because it was lost, murdered, or otherwise irretrievable. Hungerford rightfully rejects the elevation of the text to the status of the human, as well as the conflation of cultural loss with the deaths of people, but she misses the extent to which this phenomenon is produced by a very human longing for identification with the other, lost to history or otherwise. Longing for connections within cultures and across cultures *produces* culture.

The power of *The Ghost Writer*'s critique of American Jewry is not—or is not only—its rejection of the conflation of writer and text, but the degree to which it takes it seriously, represents it as a psychical and ultimately cultural given. For Roth, the bedrock epistemology is always Freudian—the unconscious needs what it needs, and consciousness can resist those needs or reroute them through socially acceptable symbolism. As clearly as we see what is wrong with conflating people with texts, we also see across Roth's entire Zuckerman series at least a very familiar longing for such a conflation. Narrative is the only way we know the other, even if it is a partial or even failed way of knowing.[10] As much as Roth satirizes the facile associations among author, text, and culture, he also accurately represents a psychical hunger for such an association.

The problem of identification and overidentification with the Holocaust for American Jews, and ethnic identification overall, is further vexed by the double-edged sword of genealogical configurations of group identity. The term *genocide,* coined in the 1950s as the Nuremberg trials progressed and the magnitude of the Nazi final solution was crystallizing in the public mind, presented for American Jews a conundrum: how to reject the racist logic inherent in genocidal ideology, yet claim kinship with the dead across national lines.[11] Turning to religious commonality makes sense, but notably, in *The Ghost Writer,* as with Holocaust-themed works by Bellow, Malamud, or Ozick, religion is not the issue.[12] Bloodlines are the tie between people across nations, simply put. The genealogical interchangeability of Jews in Newark and Jews interred at Bergen-Belsen suggested in a heated exchange between Nathan and his mother typifies the need for and limits of such identification:

> "We are not the wretched of Belsen! We were not the victims of that crime!"
>
> "But we *could* be—in their place we *would* be. Nathan, violence is nothing new to Jews, you *know* that." (106)

What Ashkenazi Jew is not somehow victimized (by the loss of distant relatives, or ancestral villages) by the Shoah? What Jew of Eastern European descent has not thought, "That could have been me"? Yet the identification produces a black hole whose pull overwhelms the centrifugal inventiveness of art. The long flashback memory of Nathan's battle with his parents is book-ended by an oft-repeated Henry James line, "we do what we can—we give what we have. Our doubt is our passion and our passion is our task. The rest is the madness of art" (77). The solipsism of the quote and the assignment of madness to art—instead of to life— matches Nathan's and Lonoff's yearning toward a priestly freedom from worldly concerns. The insertion of Anne's story and its conflation with Amy's, and the simultaneous evasion and confrontation with the Holocaust it bears, suggests the hyperbolic extent to which art's madness confronts and competes with that other madness, the irrationality of history.

Rather than shy away from this gross confrontation, Roth emblematizes it, imagining a scene where Amy-Anne sits half-naked on Lonoff's lap, imploring for his affection:

> "Oh, tell me a story. Sing me a song. Oh, imitate the great Durante, I really need it tonight. . . . Sing 'I Can Do Without Broadway.'"
>
> "Oh, I know don well I can do widout Broadway—*but* . . . can Broadway do widout meeeee?" (119)

This is a rich moment for Roth. Durante is famous for his performances with the icon of American innocence, Shirley Temple, while the Broadway version of *The Diary of Anne Frank* rendered Frank as a Temple-like universal innocent. Transposing Shirley Temple over Frank is both seductive and obscene, an emotionally transgressive combination literalized in the positions of Amy-Anne and Lonoff. The scene is a tight allegory of how Frank seduces American Jewry, but to embrace her amounts to a betrayal of American affiliation on the one hand, and a betrayal (by reduction) of the rest of the six million dead on the other. The solution, typical of adulterous rationalization, is for American Jewry to become complicit with the Americanization of Frank. To become the Jew that got away is necessarily to get away from being Jewish, a self-negating, self-annihilating act.

Capitulating to a celebratory identifications between Jews and Americans is far more obscene and violent to Nathan's way of looking at things than any representation of gritty reality: "Ma, you want to see physical violence done to the Jews of Newark, go to the office of the plastic surgeon where the girls get their noses fixed. That's where the Jewish blood flows in Essex County, that's where the blow is delivered—with a mallet! To their bones—and to their pride!" (106). Nathan reveals a brutal relationship between aesthetics and reality here. "The madness of art" is mad indeed when it takes the form of a hammer blow to the face, willingly received for the sake of negating an identity inscribed in physiognomy. But we are in an endless loop: While it seems earlier in the conversation that Nathan refuses to conflate Jewish life in the United States with Jewish extinction in Europe, we read here just the opposite: To obsessively look overseas for object-lessons of Jew-hatred is to miss the distinctly American form of hegemonic anti-Semitism. Where Jews in Europe were forced into camps and subjected to obscene "medical" experiments, including freezing, burning, amputations, and yes, bone crushing, Jews in America walk freely into the plastic surgeon's office to have their noses "fixed."

Obviously vastly different in source and outcome, nonetheless there is a common (il)logical overlap in Nazism and self-hating corrective surgery. With either there is the weird-science of genealogical purification: "Fixing" the nose corrects the mistake of genetic race, thereby confirming the fact of racial inferiority.[13] The efficacy of the nose job is also consequential to the makeup of the American national character: the nose is straightened, the Jew can "pass," and deracination—the first step to the full emptying out of a heretofore racialized multiculture in America—can proceed. The Jewish hegemonic celebration of Anne Frank's diary is not a hyper-identification with Jewishness but a similar conflation of a Jewish icon with American values.

Mediating Jewish self-perception in *The Ghost Writer* is the popularized legendry of Anne Frank, whose diary is in first-run on Broadway during the novel's setting. Characters in the novel attempt to claim Anne as a signifier for their own sense of Jewish nationhood. The struggle for control of Anne Frank's "message" prompts the novel's overarching question: what does Anne Frank signify? Universal goodness, or man's capacity for evil? More focused, what does she signify about America? The diary's American Jewish champion, Meyer Levin, battled with Otto Frank over who would produce the play. Levin insisted the diary presented a Jewish story, but Otto finally chose a Hollywood screenwriting team well versed in homogenous American culture to produce a universal "Anne Frank."[14] What does it mean to have "her" play produced in America? The play as performed became, in Irena Klepfisz's words, "the Holocaust of glamour . . . , of American Big Business [which] is awarded Emmys, Oscars, Tonys" (64). Klepfisz identifies this "phenomenon of co-opting" as "very very American. It is the process of mainstreaming whatever seems real and genuine, whatever seems threatening" (64). With the *Fortune* article and with the Broadway version of Anne Frank's story, the desire of the audience for stories that fit the prevailing ideology—whether capitalist, Christian-redemptive, or American-universalist—clears the narrative landscape of any such threats, any available plotline through which to convey such a threat. Frank's story, according to its playwrights, is a universal testament, not necessarily a Jewish story, but one which little girls all over the country could relate to. The play and the diary would seem to function similarly to the *Fortune* profiles, fixing the Holocaust in the past, burying the victims, if not outright transmogrifying them into always-already Americans. The signifier/survivor in America belongs to America, signifies American values, and even functions to help construct postwar America in heroic terms.

In this way, to answer Lonoff's Durante riff, Broadway cannot do without Anne Frank. Her martyrdom sanctions and enables a perfor-

mance of grief necessary for writing the past into history. Amy-Anne
realizes this when she goes to see the play in person: "Carloads of women
kept pulling up to the theater, women wearing fur coats, with expensive
shoes and handbags. I thought, This isn't for me . . . and of course it happened. It had to happen. It's what happens there. The women cried.
Everyone around me was in tears. Then at the end, in the row behind me,
a woman screamed, 'Oh, no'" (123). Ritual displays of material wealth
and the shared desire for catharsis consolidate the audience into a gener-
alized American norm, and the play reflects the American bourgeois
response to the Holocaust. The woman's scream, "Oh, no," is a soliloquy,
a performance of American naiveté and sympathy for the victim. It is
unlikely that anyone in the audience would not know how the play ends,
nor how so many millions of diverse lives ended in the Holocaust, but
the "Oh, no" performs a realization, as if innocence was shattered for the
first time. The cry puts the drama in the audience and punctuates the
play as *the* experience of Holocaust narrative, the satisfaction of a cultural
desire for some kind of boiled-down meaning.

The play was written and received as a populist, even celebratory account of Anne's courage. According to early reviews from the play's initial run, "it is not grim"; rather, it is "glowing, moving, frequently humor-
ous," with "just about everything one would wish for" (quoted in Ozick,
"Who Owns Anne Frank" 86). One wonders, just what does one "wish
for" from a play about the lead-up to the murder of a handful of people,
and we are reminded again of the *Fortune* article, which performs what
Dominick LaCapra calls the "projective or wish-fulfilling tendencies"
attendant with "an attempt to engage critically the problem of one's relation to the past" (*Representing* 71). In Roth's account a lone woman's response to the play's end signals the wish for sympathy and belated horror and performs the fulfillment of the wish all at once. But here sympathy
implies an understanding of, even an identification with, the victim insofar as the audience itself is afflicted—a closed circuit that ends with the
audience's response. Roth's Amy-Anne hears this and realizes that she cannot contact Otto: "if he knew, if I told him, then they would have to come
out on stage after each performance and Announce 'But she is really alive.
You needn't worry, she survived, she is twenty-six now, and doing very
well.' . . . I couldn't when I heard that woman scream 'Oh, no.' I knew
then what's been true all along: I'll never see him again. I have to be dead

to everyone" (124). The lessons of the play are contingent on the death of its principal subject, which allows for a neat mourning experience without the difficulties of encountering the survivor, rendered radically other by the experience of trauma.

By the end of *The Ghost Writer* Roth splits the appropriated object in two—the unsignifiable (because still living) Amy and the dead, martyred Anne, and it is here that Bhabha's thoughts on the "ghostly" or uncanny quality of the *time* of nationalist discourse becomes clear. Roth's novel offers two versions of the tragic Holocaust victim, the "official" version, and the imagined "meanwhile" of Nathan's fantasy narrative. To an American mainstream, including writers and dramaturges, theater reviewers, and Broadway ticketholders, Anne is the victim of not having lived in America, a country where girls with her "vitality" are tolerated and grow up unmolested. However, in Roth's representation, American Jews read the play as a warning about the world, America included, further consolidating the community amid fear.

The two perspectives are equally real and posit contrasting images of the United States. The living Amy haunts the Anne Frank of the play, not because she lives, but because of the ghostly presence of her possibility which haunts the reified Anne of popular culture. Anne's vitality (in the diary and play) is never in question, and in fact it is her urge for life experience which is such a draw on audiences. As Walter Kerr put it, reviewing the play's first run, "Anne is not going to her death; she is going to leave a dent on life, and let death take what's left" (quoted in Ozick, 86). Kerr's conceit of the dent is apt, and makes the point: a dent is the *impression* of an impact that has already happened. The object that had made the dent is gone; the damage to that object is irrelevant; if the dent is the point, the impact, or crisis, is beside the point, is history. Nathan's fantasy woman is not history, nor does she signify survival; instead, she portrays the ongoing impact of traumatic events; not dead, she leaves no "dent" on life, lives without presence. Roth neither celebrates the real Anne Frank nor (merely) critiques the universalized Anne of Broadway. More than that and less, his representation of Amy-Anne illustrates the way the racialized Jewish past disappears in postwar "Jewish American" ethnicity. The ghostly quality of ethnic difference described by Homi Bhabha is effectively illustrated by Roth, especially if we consider his novel's overall structure. Anne is always present, but never there, first a fiction, then a fantasy, an ever-receding but ineluctable "real" for Jewish Americans.

By the novel's close, there are a number of candidates for the title, "the Jew who got away." Lonoff's escape from Jewish cultural identification provides the model, but it is hardly viable, and the novel's close has him running after the kinds of entanglements that he was supposed to have escaped. Amy, finally a real person and not Anne as Nathan dreams, is apparently a survivor of some sort from the war, but the very fact that she is the tailor's dummy for the drapery of Frank's life in Nathan's fantasy suggests she is nearly as enmeshed in history as Frank herself. The novel ends with Nathan standing all alone in Lonoff's house. He is the Jew who gets away, at least for the moment, though his is an escape from the very thing he longs for, family, culture, and history.

Roth's meditation on Anne Frank ultimately takes the problem of her present absence and loops it into a discussion of American Jewish escape from the historical bind of ethnic identification. Typically, Cynthia Ozick, in her own analysis of the Americanization of Anne Frank, does Roth one better. Writing ruefully about the 1997 restaging of *The Diary*, Ozick suggests an alternative to the omnipresent social performance of the diary: "One can imagine a still more salvational outcome: Anne Frank's diary burned, vanished, lost—saved from a world that made of it all things, some of them true, while floating lightly over the heavier truth of named and inhabited evil" ("Who Owns Anne Frank," 87). This is Ozick's great theme, in her essays and fiction: how to escape the hypostatization of culture that reifies—idolizes, Ozick would say—the past and thereby paralyzes the present? If Philip Roth illustrates a metaphysics of Anne—the present absence of the Holocaust in Jewish American life—Cynthia Ozick describes an ethics of Frank, and the identificatory impulse behind Holocaust representation at large: "any projection of Anne Frank as a contemporary figure is an unholy speculation: it tampers with history, with reality, with deadly truth" (76). In this essay and elsewhere, Ozick is committed to a representation of the real, a de-aestheticized, unsentimental reminder of the "facts" of Anne Frank's story: Where Roth has Nathan praise Frank's lack of "poisonous" pretension, Ozick is quick to remind us that Frank died a poisonous death (76). The title question of Ozick's essay, "Who Owns Anne Frank?," is not just about the reading reception of her diary; Ozick concludes that we cannot access her story because it is incomplete, because it does not tell the end, her death. Thus all productions, all editions, all popular considerations of what Anne Frank's story means, and where it fits in the litany of testimony—all are distortions of the real, her horrible murder. The diary distracts us with its brightness, deflects our attention from the actual context of its writing, the dark and nearly incomprehensible Shoah; it is a dangerous text.

For Ozick, the idea of the lost or burned text signifies the otherwise unfathomable loss of the Shoah more than any published story could. In *The Ghost Writer,* Amy-Anne repudiates her own text, confirming the present crisis of Holocaust representation. The spectacularly ironic scene of Amy-Anne reading her diary and commenting in the margins on her own style and imagery in Roth's novel illustrates a fundamentally deconstructive critique of the presence of the author in his or her own work which is also a critique of the personification of the text and of the appropriability of history. Ozick's own novel about a lost text and dead author, *The Messiah of Stockholm,* takes up the problem of the presence of the dead at precisely the moment that presence is transferred into the present as a narcissistic and melancholic identification between reader and writer. *The Messiah of Stockholm* is dedicated to Roth, and it revels in his themes, seeming at times to be a revision of *The Ghost Writer.*

The protagonist of *Messiah,* Lars Andemning, is an underread book reviewer whose interest in obscure Eastern European fiction is so absorbing that he finds in the fiction a mirror of his own identity. Lars is an orphan, and though he knows almost nothing about his parents, he comes to believe that he is the refugee son of the Polish Jewish Modernist writer Bruno Schulz, who was killed at the beginning of the Holocaust. Lars has no evidence that he is Schulz's son other than his consuming identification with Schulz's fiction, including stories about fathers and sons, estranged but reaching toward each other. Lars is enabled in his identification by his book-dealer ally Heidi, who provides him with a steady stream of Schulziana, old letters, obscure translations, and book reviews, which she claims her husband, an unofficial diplomat to European Jewry, finds for her. The novel pivots on the authenticity of Lars's identification, paralleling the dubious authenticity of the Schulziana Lars collects. The only thing that is real and sure in Ozick's novel, replayed relentlessly, is Schulz's murder in 1942. For Ozick, the traumatic death disrupts sentimental appropriations of history, but like Roth, she grants the compelling power of desire for cultural community and history that produces such identifications. European literature, retrospectively folded into a Holocaust archive, becomes a contact zone between the past and the present, one that necessarily grants agency to the living reader, producing but simultaneously resisting the desire for sentimental identification. Ozick reproduces this paradox in *The Messiah,* only to rupture it with an ethics of iconoclasm, where the responsibility of the living to the dead mandates a respectful alterity between the two.

Very little is affirmed in *The Messiah of Stockholm;* the taint of forgery attaches to characters and texts alike. Heidi and her husband manage to produce what is likely an entire forged manuscript, and a forged daughter of Schulz—who mirrors Lars's usurpation of identity—to go along with it. The manuscript is supposedly Schulz's lost masterpiece, "The Messiah," and the cabal presents it to Lars for his authenticating and likely profitable approval. Lars's great conflict is between his desire to believe in this forged text, and his recognition of the lie of the book's and his own identity. Lars's heroic act at the end—he burns the book—is an immolation of all that he desires and, characteristically for Ozick, the story is finally about ashes.

With its immediate past plundered of family and culture, the generation following the Holocaust has both the responsibility and the burden of redacting the past into a kind of metatext, first by articulating a patchwork of textuality—letters, diaries, testimony—and then by entering into relation with it in institutions like the Yale Holocaust Video Archive, the National Holocaust Museum in D.C., or archival projects like David Roskies' *Jewish Search for a Usable Past* (1999). This is not a draw on the poststructuralist impulse to imagine all the world a text; rather, the impulse is archival, to produce cultural memory and bridge the gulf between past and present. Ozick's *The Messiah of Stockholm* is an investigation into the origins and the limits of this urge. Lars and his comrade Heidi compulsively collect Schulziana in order to track down Schulz's lost manuscript, "The Messiah," so Lars can erect a textual patrimony in absence of a real history and fulfill a favorite Schulz maxim which Lars frequently repeats: "reality is as thin as a sheet of paper." For Lars, the fabric of reality—the names of his family, towns associated with his heritage, and, more esoterically, his own psychic formation—is a patchwork of yellowed paper he pieces together with Heidi late at night in her bookstore. Lars increasingly locates himself and his origins in Schulz's gnostic stories, which are themselves often plotted around a son's approach to an estranged father. The paper-thin reality is sieve-like for Lars as he eerily moves between past and present. All around him, in Stockholm's winter nights, he senses "a smell of something roasting, what was that? Chimneys" (17, 49). The incessant smell of smoke, the roasting, evokes the crematoria of the Shoah, returning Lars "again and again . . . back to the shooting . . . [t]he corpse thrown into the oven; smoke up the chimney" (38).

Lars is living in a metatextual space in which Schulz's stories and Lars's life mingle, both pointing obsessively toward one common moment, Schulz's murder. Lars slips between the bizarre gnosticism of Schulz's writing and the reality of his own orphanhood, and this slippage is both an elevation and a questioning of the status of textuality as a mode of reality. Lars attempts to live in his father's texts, and thereby claim a past that is otherwise unavailable, but the efficacy of the revisionist history, pejoratively marked as fiction-making by Ozick, is ever in doubt.

Ozick enacts the yearning for social solidarity, though there is no bridge to the past, and Lars's attempts to live in his father's past are psychical symptoms of history's aporia, not effective means for breaching it. As Ozick presents it, the surviving generation's obsession with the past amounts to "extreme 'acting-out' wherein one is possessed by the past and tends to repeat it compulsively as if it were fully present" (LaCapra, *Representing* 12). The work of mourning is foreclosed by melancholic attachment; a "victim" of history, the individual in this situation is unable to mediate the past through socially constructive narrative, nor can he perceive the past as a distanced story. Lawrence Langer has observed that this is indeed the struggle for many Holocaust survivors, who are caught between immediate, or "deep," memory, and the socially collective "common" memory (Langer, *Holocaust Testimonies* 6). The former is the survivor's painful recall of events that transport him to the past, replaying the trauma on his mind and body; the latter form of memory allows the individual to occupy the anonymous and historicizing point of view of society at large. This latter type of memory is dependent on the historicity of narrative, art, and philosophy to offer a socially distanced point of view from which to recall without reliving the past. But as we see with Roth's novel, direct lines to the past, and cultural representations, can be hegemonic stand-ins for the inaccessible, unsignifiable real. In *The Messiah of Stockholm* the function of "common memory" is further complicated because of the very odd motives of the novel's two main characters. Lars is not, after all, a "survivor" of the Holocaust as the term is commonly understood. He does not know what he is, and neither do we, all the way up to the end of the novel. He has appropriated common memory in order to fabricate a highly subjective deep memory, the memory of direct experience that he can never really have. On the other hand, his partner in Schulziana research, Heidi, may indeed have been in the camps, though this remains unclear, too. She reminds Lars that "death is reliable," and continually tethers his flights of imaginative association with Schulz by bringing him back to the author's murder. In either case, because too distant or too close, Lars and Heidi are fixed into an obsessive, melancholic relationship to the Holocaust that is at once possessive and absorbing.

Lars's plot problem—encountering the past, being seduced by history, killing it off—is also the metatextual problem Ozick produces. The narrative encounter with the found manuscript poses the fundamental question of ghostly literature: what is the relationship between text and trauma? The novel suggests that the found manuscript is actually a forgery, but hints that it might have been real. The ambiguity pushes the question toward a broader theoretical and critical purview beyond Lars's own condition, also likely forged. What would be gained—for Jews, for the world, for history—by the resurrection-like discovery of a missing manuscript? Does it produce more historiographic context? Or does it collapse past and present, allowing access to the aura, if not the life of the Holocaust victim? Does the psychical paralysis occasioned by the absence of the real give way to yet another kind of disruption of living, the results of co-optation, universalization, or forged sentimentality? In either case, the enduring problem that Ozick critiques is the facile identification between self and other, including the other of and within the text.

Ozick telegraphs her ethics of alterity fairly clearly. During the moments preceding Lars's destruction of the manuscript, Lars is discomfited by the surprising familiarity among the cabal of seeming strangers in the room, suggesting a conspiracy, the conspiracy of the "we" against his own individuality. Recognizing a latent "we" where individuals once stood, he is also able to recognize inversely that his own "we," his commune with his supposed father, is a self-deception and an arrogation of the being of the other, one that also eradicates his own being.

Identification does not give way to individuality but to iconoclasm—an intimate relation through negation with the idols of the past. Lars's burning the manuscript means fully losing his identification. What remains after the idols are smashed is a respectful distance between past and present, living and dead, a relation achieved in psychical as well as ethical terms. A brief comparison of Lars's iconoclasm with a famous Freudian dream scenario helps establish how awaking from the illusion of identification amounts to an ethics of distance. This much-commented-upon scenario is of a father dreaming about his son, who has just died of a fever. The father, grieving for his son and pained by his inability to help him, lies down and falls asleep, only to see his son again in a dream: "After a few hours sleep, the father had a dream that *his child was standing beside his bed, caught him by the arm and whispered to him reproachfully: 'father, don't you see I'm burning?'*" (547–48; italics in the original). The father awakes from his dream to the smell of smoke and finds his dead son's clothing has been ignited by a nearby candle, thereby doubling his death by fever.

The dream scenario is typical of the fantastic desire for repression of the traumatic moment of loss, a repression that transmutes painful experience into a phantasmagoria of revivification. Roth and Ozick, and Morales and Morrison (as we will see in the next chapters), all present protagonists who encounter their dead on some continuum of working through loss and grief, and Freud's dream scenario helps us see that such an encounter always leads back to the same place, the repetition of the original loss. "Working through" in general is theorized by Freud and neo-Freudian literary theorists as a process of repetition with difference, the restaging of trauma for the sake of its mastery. Though the father/son roles are reversed, *The Messiah of Stockholm*'s plot is structured like Freud's anecdote, as Lars oscillates between the moment of loss—the death of Schulz in Poland's "wild action"—and the dreamy communion with Schulz's writing.

The manuscript of "The Messiah" is the material form of Lars's fantasy of Schulz, though initially he does not see it as such. With the manuscript, the hallucinatory threatens to become material reality, fixing Lars ineluctably in melancholic identification with Schulz. However, Lars's fantastic dreams of Schulz—either that a celebrated Schulzian oeuvre will take its rightful place in the canon, or that Schulz's genius will transmute to Lars—are ever threatened by the lingering signifiers of the real, Schulz's death. The pervasive smell of smoke, roasting, burning flesh, and chimneys that pursue Lars all over the city signify the death of Schulz in the Shoah, and this in turn parallels the correlative burning—the real burning of the child's corpse—which in Freud's anecdote pervades the father's sleep and shapes his dream.

When the forged text, the supposed masterpiece, is presented for his authenticating approval, Lars is confronted with a choice: to authenticate the text would be to raise Schulz's work from the ashes, play Elijah to Schulz's "Messiah." But to reject the manuscript as a forgery would repeat the traumatic moment of original loss. The awakening to loss is indeed a repetition of the trauma—"a rite, an endlessly repeated act" Lacan calls it in his interpretation of the dream scenario—though "not a simple repetition of the *same* failure and loss . . . but a new act that repeats precisely a departure and a difference" (Lacan, in Caruth, "Traumatic Awakenings" 101).

For Lacan, the father's awakening merely replays the moment of trauma. It is "an act of homage to the missed reality—the reality that can no longer produce itself except by repeating itself endlessly in some never attained awakening" (Lacan, in Caruth 101). Indeed, Lars's decision to burn the manuscript is an homage to the reality of his loss, but it is repetition from the point of its mastery, or a mastery of the claims the trauma has on him. In a flash of clarity, Lars breaks from his melancholic dream, recognizes the manuscript is a "false messiah," and sets it ablaze before the forgers can stop him. The moment is dramatic and marks a profound turning point for Lars. Burning the text allows him to claim his orphanhood; though he loses a longed-for family, he gains a history, the history of the loss of Eastern European Jewry.[15]

Regarding Freud's dream scenario, Cathy Caruth suggests that "to awaken is thus to bear the imperative to survive: to survive no longer simply as the father of a child, but as the one who must tell *what it means not to see*" (101). In *The Messiah of Stockholm,* traumatic loss is similarly figured as a loss of sight. Lars's specular communion with Schulz is figured as the sharing of Schulz's eye, an image itself suggesting a gaze fixed on the past, fixed *by* the past. By the end of the novel, Lars learns that survival occurs in the present, and the present is sustained by hope for the future. Mourning, then, is not a movement from the traumatic imaginary into the symbolic order, but a relegation of the past into the Real, that psychic lacuna which is the location of that which is not there. Lars lives committed to the real world and all its possibilities. No longer withholding himself, he begins writing engaging, witty, popular book reviews that elicit written response in return.

Traumatic histories have made groups of people—ethnic communities—"other" to "host" communities; alterity is integrally a part of the ethnic community's identity, not due to internal or cultural essence, but as the excess of traumatic history, whether it be colonization, genocide, or enslavement. At the same time, traumatic histories interrupt generational continuity, dividing ethnic communities across political or moral axes. In the two examples we have seen so far, the text—real or imagined, sustained or erased—transforms difference (even while maintaining alterity) into community. The text is not a bridge of difference; it does not create some ideal unity, nor does it offer an ideal portrait in which each member of an ethnic community can find her- or himself. On the contrary, the harrowing history within *The Diary* or around "The Messiah" alienates future readers from the text. But the voice of the author persists into the present lives of the characters within each novel. The author-figures—Frank and Schulz—do not recede into the past as "voices of history," but speak in the present, interpolating their interlocutors into their story, subsequently locating them in ethnic community.

Bhabha describes the longing for mourning in Morrison's *Beloved,* perhaps the most prominent example of a ghost story that mourns the past: "to live in the uhomely world, to find its ambivalencies and ambiguities enacted in the house of fiction . . . is also to affirm a profound desire for social solidarity" (18). This seems to me an enormously significant point— perhaps Bhabha's strongest contribution to ethnic studies—and a compelling rebuke to ideological or deconstructive accounts of identity which do not take affect into account. Drawing on Lacan, Bhabha points out that we are not free agent "humans" but subjects born into a symbolic order that is always already marked by the trauma of race oppression and classification. What we call history—a narrative story of things that happen to different people at different times—is as much produced by as it produces a multicultural symbolic order. In virtually any history, any work of literature, any utterance, we may find racial and ethnic difference marked by the aporias of trauma, shame, guilt, and grief. The turn to cultural identities is not a choice bespeaking individual agency (free agency, the choice not to choose) but a social response to a pre-existing symbolic order. Thought of this way, the desire for a noncultural social order is not an ethical pathway out of our social schisms but an imaginary-order return to a fictive state of being. For Lars, born an orphan, the desire for belonging is sensible and validated, though his appropriation of Holocaust history is finally akin to a forgery.

The Messiah of Stockholm ends with a kind of communal identification that transcends the particular and narcissistic melancholic identification Lars suffered previously. By the end of the novel Lars, in fact, achieves a more powerful position, able to see Schulz as both a nameless victim of the Nazi war machine and a lost, individual artistic voice: "When, less and less often, the smell [of smoke] flushed up out of the morning's crevices, Lars inside the narrow hallway of his skull caught sight of the man in the long black coat, hurrying with a metal garter box squeezed under his arm, hurrying and hurrying toward the chimneys. And then, in the blue light of Stockholm, among zebra fumes, he grieved" (144). The image is a palimpsest of the general and the specific. "The Messiah" is there in the metal box, unnamed; the long black coat is a metonymy of shtetl Jewry (lost) in general, the "zebra fumes" condense prisoner uniforms and the Holocaust itself, the burning of European Jewry.

Finally, however, this is Lars's interior vision of a world he can never be a part of, but only grieve. He is not publicly a Jew, or even an ethnic minority in a cosmopolitan city of refugees and exiles. His identification with the past is more a recognition of his place in relation to it, and less a fully realized identity which would inform his present. For Ozick, as with Roth, there is no means of recuperating the human and cultural losses of the past through representation. Ozick critiques the extreme choice of identification and appropriation of Holocaust history by non-survivors; Roth critiques the extreme distancing of the Holocaust in American life through banal and universalizing performance. For all his high-flying fantasy, Nathan Zuckerman's most compelling statement comes in response to the question posed by Amy Bellete, what did you have instead of the war?: "My childhood" (168). "My childhood" instead of the war rings with Nathan's mother's claim that we could have been them, in their place we *would* have been them. Between us and them exists the tension between same and different, appropriation and respect. Lars finally gets on with the business of living in the present, while retaining a circuit of memory for the past. *The Ghost Writer* and *The Messiah of Stockholm* do not resolve this tension between survivor and belated witness; rather, both novels reproduce it as a textual monument to an ethics of respect for histories not their own.

2··· WORKING THROUGH THE ARCHIVE

A merican Jews writing about the Holocaust do so in an environment where Holocaust facts are iconic, where Holocaust memorials occupy sacred national space, and where memorial events regularly find American statesman donning the kippah to speak at synagogues.[1] Within this environment, Jewish writers can and perhaps must write against the institutional awe toward the Holocaust, and so besides Roth and Ozick's novels, we have the peculiar ironization of survival in Nathan Englander's stories, the kitsch-inspired return of the avenging golem in Michael Chabon's and Thane Rosenbaum's novels, and the justly famous comixnarrative by Art Spiegelman, *Maus.* However, a simultaneous but very different environment prevails for other Ethnic American writers who write about their cultural group's traumatic past. For Native Americans, African Americans, Chicanos, and Asian Americans, the traumatic past is eclipsed, or overwritten by American history itself, and narratives about historical trauma have to counter ignorance about not only colonialism, Indian removal, or slavery, say, but also prevailing histories and narratives that stand in for, speak over, and thereby mute voices from and of those histories. Both theoretical investigations into the problems of representing the past and narratological theories of trauma draw substantially on the phenomenon of historicizing the Holocaust, but clearly we should be cautious about assuming that theorizing about the Holocaust is fully portable for reading other American ethnic literary responses to historical trauma.

With this chapter and the next, I examine historiographical narratives that are more or less knowing of the historicist problems associated with the Holocaust, and that perform cultural work very different from Jewish American writing on the Holocaust. In this chapter, I examine how Alejandro Morales's trope of the archive allegorizes the role of literature for constructing usable narratives of both the past and the future. Morales is canny about his novel's intersection with Holocaust-oriented tropes of history and draws on the Holocaust as a signifier of trauma. In the next chapter, we will see how Toni Morrison's *Beloved* is also knowing of the prevailing problems of representing the traumatic past, but Morrison offers a materialist-oriented response very much at odds with the deconstructive or allegorical writings of Roth, Ozick, and Morales.

Critical writing on *cultural mourning, historical working-through,* and the persistence of *cultural memory* in ethnic literature participates in a larger conversation about the passage of ethnic histories into the present, the need for access to those histories—difficult, to be sure, when the history is in fact a history of erasure—and the constructive deployment of those histories for culture.[2] Broad-scale cultural mourning and working-through involve a negotiation between the traumatized past, repressing present, and (hoped-for) progressive future, with narrative providing an ethical dimension to this struggle. In this chapter, I turn to the Chicano author Alejandro Morales's novel *The Rag Doll Plagues* to propose and theorize the trope of the Archive as an apt figure for literature and criticism's reconstruction of ethnic histories, and as an allegory of the role of cultural critique in the development of ethnic cultural identity. In Morales's novel, the Archive is a catalyst for individual and collective working-through traumatic history and may serve as an allegorical model for critical approaches to ethnic literature which attempt to mourn history.

At this point, we might make a useful distinction between two concepts mentioned above, both of which are closely related in Freudian psychoanalysis: "mourning" and "working-through." In "Mourning and Melancholy" Freud defines mourning against melancholy as the normal work of the unconscious to detach the ego from a lost object of significant psychic value, a process that requires the ego to face the reality of the loss in the first place—"so and so is dead," or "such and such is gone." The pain of grief ensues from the conflict between the ego's attachment to the lost object (due to the libido's entanglements with that object) and the reality that the object no longer exists. Rituals of grief that assign symbolic value to loss facilitate the ego's perception of the reality of loss.

Melancholy, in contrast, is a relentless narcissism brought on by the ego's overidentification with the lost object, which, for the melancholic, results in the subject becoming lost to him/herself: "Melancholia thus emerges from a specific variety of mourning, one that has looped back around to engulf the mournful subject" (Avelar 232). Several scholars have theorized that Freud's theory of individual mourning may be translated into an analysis of *cultural* mourning, in order to chart the process a culture undergoes when it has experienced traumatic loss.[3] In this scenario, cultural groups enact rituals and stage symbolic repetitions of loss—with the erection of monuments, or staging of museum shows, and telling ghost stories—in order to master the reality of loss.

I find this speculation fruitful for thinking about ethnic American groups' relations to traumatic history, especially as played out in narrative. However, the speculation is finally inadequate, primarily because such a cultural mourning is dependent on a teleology of actual loss. Besides "loss" is the more troubling and difficult-to-work-through problem of *absence*—the absence of totality, wholeness, or cultural integration even prior to traumatic history. Ethnic Americans' status as cultural minorities in the United States in part derives from and is defined by an originary historical trauma rather than wholeness, and for some groups— African Americans, Chicanos, Asian Americans, and perhaps Jewish Americans—this history undercuts the possibility of redemptive psychocultural processes. For nonindigenous ethnic groups, the very experience of coming to the United States, or the preconditions of departure, make for fundamentally inchoate origins.

There is no utopian ethnic American culture that can be recaptured following historical loss, because original and whole culture is absent in the first place. Dominick LaCapra reminds us that the difference between absence and loss from the point of view of psychoanalysis creates a fundamental difference in the processes of mourning and working-through, both for individuals and for cultures:

> The affirmation of absence as absence rather than as loss or lack opens up different possibilities and requires different modes of coming to terms with problems. . . . Paradise absent is different from paradise lost: it may not be seen as Annihilated only to be regained in some hoped-for, apocalyptic future or sublimely blank utopia that, through a kind of creation *ex nihilo*, will bring total renewal, salvation, or redemption. It is not there, and one

must therefore turn to other, nonredemptive options in personal, social, and political life—options other than an evacuated past and a vacuous, or blank, yet somehow redemptive future. (*Writing History* 56–57)

These other, nonredemptive or nonrestorative options may be loosely gathered under the heading of *working through* trauma. Different from mourning (though at times, part of mourning's work), working-through is the effort to be conscious of one's own repetitive symptomatic behavior, especially on the road to recovery following traumatic experience. Obviously relevant for thinking about cultures that have experienced traumatic history, "working-through, as it relates both to the rebuilding of lives and to the elaboration of a critical historiography, requires the effort to achieve critical distance on experience through a comparison of experiences and through a reconstruction of larger contexts that help to inform and perhaps to transform experience" (LaCapra, *Representing* 200). Thought of this way, cultural working-through would be a cultural group's effort to recognize its implication in repetitive history, even to opt out of the repetition compulsion through cultural transformation, without necessarily transforming history or making it "come out right."

Emphasizing the experience, memory, and contexts of historical trauma, often called "the usable past,"[4] should prompt us to think about the role cultural *archives* play in attempts at ethnic redefinition and cultural working-through. Literally, archives are codices, letters, stories, myths, photos, and other like documents that are organized as collections of cultural knowledge. The noun *archive* indicates both the contents and the place where the archive is located, and the dialectical relation between the two is suggestive for thinking about how cultures produce self-knowledge. The contents of the archive, retroactively conceived as the root-source of a culture, creates the very need for the archiving activity, culminating in the physical archive itself. And archives, once established and named as such, give rise to cultures of response. By turning to archives, I do not mean to suggest an authentic blueprint of cultural origins, which could be consulted to restore or reconstruct present-day cultures, nor do I see cultural memory as unproblematically archival. Instead, a postmodern approach to the archive acknowledges the dialectics of reading and writing—a loop outside of time—where what is retroactively termed the archive in fact only comes to be called so when recognized as such from the standpoint of the present.

In this sense, the Archive is a necessary myth that acknowledges its own mythopoetical properties. (Forthwith, "Archive" is capitalized to indicate the critical trope I am describing; "archive" in the lowercase indicates literal archives, or libraries of information.) An Archive of cultural knowledge may indeed perform an "arch-ontic" function, as Derrida puts it, exerting a kind of restrictive cultural gravity, but the cultural turn to the Archive can be seen as a self-conscious performance of cultural working-through.[5] The Archive in this sense is a symptom of and a catalyst for working through historical trauma. Literal archives, or libraries of cultural knowledge, are always belatedly constructed if only for that fact that they are retroactively discovered, named, or redacted as such. They are as much a product of present-day culture's ideologies and cultural longings as they are matrices of cultural origins.

A theory of the Archive is particularly apt for reading a Chicano novel because of its frequency as a trope of Latin American literature. Elaborating the function of the Archive in works by Borges, Fuentes, and García Márquez, Roberto González Echevarría explains, "the Archive keeps, culls, retains, accumulates, and classifies. . . . It mounts up, amounts to the law, the law of fiction" (18). Invoked and deployed self-consciously, the Archive may operate as a catalyst for cultural "self-discovery," a trope for cultural integration, and a site for holistic cultural memory. In a helpful gesture in her own theory of the Archive, Lois Parkinson Zamora adds that "the Ancestral [impulse is] the necessary complement to the Archival [impulse]" in any discussion of American literary history (125). In ethnic American literature, the erasure of the ancestral, through murder, genocide, enslavement, and the eradication of cultural memory, is precisely the trauma that must be worked through, and the Archive may facilitate this. With Morales's *The Rag Doll Plagues,* the complement between the Ancestral and the Archival is profound: it is the Ancestral—the ghosts/witnesses to historical trauma—that helps work through the Archival presence, a collection of literature, memoir, and medical journals.[6]

Alejandro Morales, the author of six novels (three originally written in Spanish), is a remarkably underread Chicano author, whose historicism and experimental style are challenging to those who would place him on syllabi or in tables of contents. Morales's early work was hailed by many as a breakthrough in Chicano aesthetics, and his depictions of barrio life and the tensions between Chicano and Anglo societies was initially thought to be the vanguard of the new Chicano novel. However, Chicano literary criticism has yet to sustain a substantial interest in his work. In the several major surveys of Chicano literature published since Morales began writing in 1975, there is almost no serious engagement with his work.[7]

Chicano autobiographers and novelists such as Ernesto Galarza, Arturo Islas, or Tomás Rivera successfully distill erudition in Mexican history into accessible symbolism and naturalistic prose, resulting in literature that reads as organic to its subject. Morales's fiction, in contrast, tends toward a baroque, even grotesque aesthetics, and his historical interests are considerably more opaque. In contrast to much-studied writers such as Rudolpho Anaya, Sandra Cisneros, and Ana Castillo, whose literary voices are effortlessly engaging, Morales's voice, especially in his early novels, consistently draws readers away from the subject at hand and into a linguistic house of mirrors, where characters, themes, and ideas anarchically reflect and absorb each other. And though he writes about the history and people of the American Southwest, his literature, especially recently, draws from theory and criticism usually associated with European history and culture.[8]

In *Retrospace* (1990), Juan Bruce-Nova explains that Morales, with his use of fantasy, his gritty depiction of the barrio, and his interest in Mexican literature writes fiction "challenging the concepts of Chicano literature" (85).[9] Still, Chicano critic Ramón Saldívar has argued that Chicano literature opts for "open over closed forms, for conflict over resolution and synthesis" (7), and in this sense, Morales's deployment of the Archive in *The Rag Doll Plagues* is a typically Chicano literary gesture. Book 1 is set at the end of the eighteenth century in Mexico and observes spiritual and physical catastrophes of colonialism while anticipating the coming Mexican war for independence. Book 2, set in Orange County, California, during the early Reagan era, draws parallels between the previous book's colonial devastation and the violence of gang warfare in a Mexican American barrio, simultaneous with the early spread of AIDS in the United States. Book 3 is set in a not-too-distant dystopic future, and describes a new hemispheric order where, post-NAFTA (and with allusions to international trade wars), national borders are broken down but class division has solidified into a caste system, regulating cultural strata from Canada south into Mexico.

The plot of each book centers around the rise of a devastating plague—termed *La Mona,* or the "Rag Doll plague" in the first book because it reduces the victim's body to a loose pulp—and the recurring protagonist is a doctor with an ambivalent relation to Mexican or Mexican American culture. This recurring cycle of devastation matches the Aztec cosmology of recirculating apocalypse, and in the novel's final section the new NAFTA-inspired government is titled "The Triple Alliance," the term used to describe the Aztec political alliance with other Indian nations prior to Spanish conquest.

It is appropriate, then, that the recurring protagonist in all three books is named Gregorio or Gregory Revueltas, which might be translated as Gregory revolving or returning.[10] Gregory is never entirely either history's agent or history's victim. As a doctor in each epoch, he is chiefly a witness to historical trauma, though always serendipitously at the center of historical transformation. Nor does he have a transcendental consciousness that would allow him to make sense of the repetitive traumas of history. What he does have, however, putting him in good company with other protagonists in ethnic literature, is a pair of ghosts, one who is the apparition of the other Gregories, and the other the grandfather of book 2's Gregory, Papa Damian.[11] Though the ghosts never speak in any of the novel's three books, they stand on the edges of the text as witnesses to historical trauma. The ghosts and the protagonists all read and write, both while living and dead, documenting history (including the future), and constructing an Archive that ultimately collapses the distinctions between the three epochs/characters. These are not the unmourned dead who return for unfinished business. Rather, Morales's ghosts have lived fully and return to help the living work through their own lives. Each knows the wisdom of his respective era and exists to help the living locate it.

The novel's structure, themes, tropes, events, and characters loop back into one another and effect a kind of simultaneity of events, people, and, crucially, traumas. Melancholic as it seems, history itself is caught up in a repetition compulsion. Poverty, disease, cultural dominance, and racism recur and rend the fabric of linear history in the novel. This raises two questions whose answers the novel works toward: Are cultures whose pasts are marked by trauma capable of finding an apt set of signifiers for this trauma, allowing for constructive working-through and the articulation of a usable past? And how can individuals participate in a history that seems locked into a fated repetition compulsion, a history where the culturally oppressed are not masters of their fates or agents in their destinies?

The recurring plague prompts these questions more than anything else. Writing about another literary plague, Shoshana Felman remarks, "[The Plague] occurs . . . as what is not provided for by the conceptual framework we call 'History,' as what, in general, has no place in, and therefore cannot be assimilated by or integrated into, any existing cultural frame of reference" (104).[12] The novel begins with the Spaniards' point of view: progressive forces of history, namely colonialism, Western culture and medicine, technology, and religion, should triumph over the unenlightened, primitive New World. The plague sweeping New Spain, however, is antimodern, and fittingly, kills Indian and Spanish alike, reversing the status of deity-through-immunity established for the Spaniards at the beginning of Colonization. Upon close inspection of the "new world," Spanish physician Don Gregorio faces an epistemological crisis, as he tries to fathom that the poverty, disease, and oppression he sees are "not a nightmare, but His Majesty's Empire" (26). Sent to cure the disease, Gregorio must first confront the fact that his modern science, modern medicine, and rational inquiry—the distillation of European culture—are not only powerless against the plague, but in part the cause of it.

The plague allegorizes not so much oppression, or colonialism, but history itself, and the startling lack of agency for individuals caught up in history. La Mona strips victims of their subjectivity, rendering them objects in its march through history. One scene in particular presents the point with deadpan irony and Morales's characteristic graphic horror. Gregorio's first encounter with the disease in a makeshift hospital stages this dissolution of subjectivity. Pausing to note a man whose leg is swollen and liquid with infection, Gregorio observes as the man picks up a knife and "slit[s] his leg from the knee down to his foot. The leg tissue offered no resistance. We watched a substance slowly pour out from his body" (32). The visual image, like so many others in the book, is written to make the reader squirm, but the highlight here and elsewhere is the dual role of witness and sufferer that the plague victim plays. Consistently throughout the novel, victims of plague and political and racial oppression struggle to actually be present in the moment of their suffering, to resist being made invisible or silent both to the world at large and to themselves. The peculiar instance at the beginning of book 1 emblematizes the challenge, however: as the diseased man pierces his leg with a knife, then passively observes the results, we wonder at the extent to which the man's flesh any longer belongs to him.

There is no cure for the plague's ravages, though amputation slows its progress. However, the human costs of amputation mock the very concept of palliative medicine and paradoxically oppose modernity against human agency. Late in book 1, Gregorio is summoned by the Viceroy of New Spain to attend to his mistress, Marisela, an Indian woman who is pregnant and suffering from La Mona. Gregorio's task is not to cure, which he knows is impossible, but to keep her alive long enough to deliver her baby. Gruesome amputations ensue, first of the forearms, then the arms up to the shoulder, and later the legs. The body, reduced to its barest functions, is more object than subject, a receptacle of life while barely holding onto life itself. The woman delivers her baby via C-section, and unable to hold her newborn daughter, nonetheless begs to have it placed on her chest, after which she dies. The dramatic death of Marisela and the birth of her daughter, whom Gregorio names Monica Marisela, mark a turning point in the novel. Don Gregorio adopts the baby, a true *mestizo* (the father, the Viceroy, goes mad), and commits to living in Mexico permanently. La Mona, meanwhile, begins to loosen its grip on the colony, simultaneous with the rise of revolutionary, anticolonial sentiment among the intellectuals and Spanish-born sympathizers like Don Gregorio. Part of a trend of Chicano and Mexican revisionist writing that would reinscribe Mexican *mestizaje* with constructive connotations, Morales uses Monica Marisela's birth to symbolize the roots of Mexican and, subsequently, Chicano culture—anticolonial, revolutionary, mixed, and born out of fragments and the desire for human agency.[13]

Book 1's close, especially the unsettling, fragmentary birth of Monica Marisela, poses a question that the other two books will have to deal with: how to integrate the many fragments of a nation, a culture, and even an individual? The question presupposes that the three are linked somehow and, moreover, bound up in the same historical and psycho-historical processes. This is Morales's own presumption, but it becomes the reader's as well, for the novel asks the reader to make connections between the protagonists, their relationships, and then, in turn, the historical patterns each is woven into. Each connection is the product of the recurring metatextual quality of the novel. Though we never see Don Gregorio writing in book 1, his descendent, also Gregory, finds his medical journals in book 2, and this second Dr. Gregory Revueltas's writing—fantastic novels, including one called "The Rag Doll Plagues"—are discovered by book 3's Gregory, also a doctor/decoder of repetitive plague and trauma.

All three protagonists are to some extent alienated from their putative culture, in part because of their relatively high economic class and Western identification, but also because in each epoch there is no solid ethnic culture that Gregorio/Gregory can identify with. Instead, cultures are in flux, redefining themselves in light of colonialism, gang affiliations (which divides Mexican Americans in southern California in the 1980s), or class alignments. The recurring plague is at once the cause and the allegorical symptom of cultural destabilization. Seen this way, history is allegorized as a clash between those who have power and those who do not, or cultures of agency working to destabilize indigenous or oppositional cultures. Though this view of history seems simplistic and overly dichotomous, the narrative solution Morales presents seems on the mark. The successive Gregories who write and read one another's writing are constructing an Archive of cultural knowledge that is simultaneously cultural history and an exorbitant critique of historiography.

The Archive in *The Rag Doll Plagues* is actually composed of several physical archives, or libraries. Book 2's archive, for example, is the *Biblioteca religiosa* in Tepotzotlan, Mexico, ruled by the librarian/healer figure, Señora Jane. A powerful figure, Señora Jane commands the knowledge contained in the *biblioteca,* and she guides Gregory who has come to Mexico in search of a cure for his wife's fight with AIDS. This time, Gregory experiences the plague not as a cultural or national crisis, but as a personal tragedy, as his wife is among the disease's earliest victims, and he has not yet come to understand the broader cultural implications of the disease. Nonetheless, the search for a cure for his wife, Sandra, will prompt his encounter with his ancestor (the first Gregorio) and an ancestral culture. After Sandra and Gregory visit the ancient medical archives at the *protomedico,* they see a local *curandera* with an archival memory of history, culture, and healing. The library and the curandera are both transformative for Gregory and Sandra, linking both to a broader cultural history. The curandera recognizes that Sandra's disease is a variant of La

Mona, and though she cannot cure the disease, Sandra's alienation is ended as she is linked to a historical continuum and finds comfort from her isolation.

Gregory's visit to this medical library prompts the uncanny encounter with his *tocayo* or namesake ancestor, resulting in Gregory's reflection that the physical archive may integrate him into a larger historically developing culture. Indeed, these continual incursions into the Archive—the space of the library-archive, the immersions in various texts and creations of new ones—provoke in Gregory the psychical repetition and comprehension of traumatic events. The remove he feels toward his Chicano brethren in California by virtue of his education and class standing is echoed in the first Gregorio's initial relationship with the indigenous he treated. The growth of empathy and the process of assimilation the first Gregorio undergoes charts a path toward cultural cohesion for the second Gregory. Immediately and locally, the archives may offer a medical clue for Gregory and Sandra as they deal with her plague. But more broadly speaking, the Archive assists Gregory as he works through his relation to a fragmented history and culture. After Sandra's death, Gregory returns to California and begins writing fantastical novels, inscribing himself and Sandra into the Archive.

In each book, as history's cycles recur, the physical and psychical efficacy of the Archive grows to match the melancholic scenarios of the present. Increasingly, Gregory needs to approach the Archive proactively, seeking its mental and physical security from an outside world hostile to cultural continuity. In the dystopic book 3, "Lamex," the Archive is represented by an immense library of hundreds of thousands of volumes, and again, its contents interpolate Gregory into a historical cultural identity. Formidable, and referred to as a "prison" by Gregory and a "fortress" by its keeper, this archive stands as an atavistic challenge to Lamex skepticism toward what is considered sentimental book culture. Gregory is confined to this library as a punishment for insubordination in his role as medical director for the greater Lamex region, Mexico City north to Los Angeles. Later, when relieved of his duties, Gregory will retreat to his family home in the California desert, the house that Gregory of book 2 built, and which houses his own immense library. Faced with terrifying and dehumanizing choices about his life and career, he returns to the Archival home, which provides a place "where continuity and discontinuity are held together in uneasy allegiance" (González Echevarría 24). Roaming through his grandfather's library, Gregory comes across the uncanny novel written by his grandfather, titled "The Rag Doll Plagues." This dystopic novel, like book 3 itself, forecasts a horrific future of disease, racial oppression, and the cold hand of technology against the will of humans, effectively emplotting history with a narrative thread. This uncanny encounter helps Gregory cut through the ahistorical cultural skepticism toward reading and prompts his growing awareness of a larger historical context to his present circumstance.

The writing and reading woven through the novel, especially the uncanny moments of recognition, allow for Gregory's working through history—not so much history's mastery as the recognition that he is embedded in repetitive historical tragedy. At the same time, the reader is prompted to see the allegorical implications of working-through as a version of critique. The amputation of diseased limbs in book 1 is echoed by the appearance of concentration-camp tattoos on the arm of Gregory's Holocaust surviving physician-partner in book 2, another form of bodily objectification. Book 3 amplifies the trope of the body-as-object, as Gregory's partner Gabi has had her arm voluntarily cut off and replaced by a computerized prosthetic. Gregory is being pressured to make the same decision, and the choice is really one of two archives. The computerized arm will link him to the information databases of Lamex, unleashing a flood of decontextualized statistical and medical information, lacking narrative structure or plot. But to choose against the arm means a demotion in his position, and possible relegation either to the fortress of old books or to his home library. The choice would seem clear and stark, but the hegemonic force of Lamex ideology presses Gregory to believe that he can perhaps do more for the poor as a doctor than as an outcast.

Gregory's choice is made less stark by his growing fondness of books, and Gabi's simultaneous wasting away due to infections in her arm. Both Gregory and Gabi witness the ravages of the plague, but Gregory is able to "unplug" by retreating to his library, while Gabi must literally plug in, or recharge her arm, remaining ever connected to a force that eradicates her identity. For Gregory, the retreat to the library becomes homeopathic. There he can read and absorb (and so come to recognize) the arc of Western history and colonialism. Encountering his tocayos in his grandfather's library, Gregory traces history's ruptures and finds continuity. This slow process of coming into conscious awareness and integration is contrasted with Gabi's hypercharged life patched into a constant stream of information and energy. The continual recharging of the arm, a repetitive anti-ritual born of technological necessity, leaves her drained over time. Contrasted with Gabi's arm is the "cool, almost living skin-like paper" of Gregory's books (142). As her bones and flesh begin to singe with each charging, she literally becomes split between subject and object.

Her auto-destruction becomes an object lesson for Gregory: "Gabi moved closer. While she stared down at me, a wall of my grandfather's books framed her body. I returned to my reading" (141–42). In such moments, the Archive stands as an affront to the forces of medicine, technology, and official historiography. Framed by the wall of books, Gregory and the reader see the increasingly objectified Gabi as most human within a larger historical context, linked with the amputee Marisela and the bleeding Sandra of books 1 and 2. But Gabi's computerized arm and her attachment to objectifying mechanisms of Lamex society obviate her understanding of how she participates in her own subjugation. Ironically, then, every time Gabi reconnects her arm, ostensibly an act of linking, she effectively restages her severing and resituates herself as an unwitting victim of history. Ultimately, Gabi resists her objectification, but her response is melancholic rather than healing: Aware that her life has been co-opted by Lamex authorities, and slowly dying from the effects of the arm, she jams the prosthetic into a charging outlet, dials up an overdose of electrical voltage, and explodes.

Gregory's rejection of technology and his refusal to have his arm amputated coincides with the recognition of his self in the humanity of another, the Mexicans he encounters as he searches for a cure for the disease among in the poorest sections of Lamex. But the debate over the prosthetic arm is matched by a broader allegory of racial objectification and cultural amputation. Book 3's plague "Blue Buster," like the first, leaves its victims hollow, limp vessels, and its unusual spread—among both lower and upper classes—threatens the social order. Miraculously, Gregory discovers the cure in the blood of Mexicans hailing from Mexico City, dubbed technically as "MCMs" or Mexico-City-Mexicans. This miracle blood is a wry gesture by Morales. The blood is curative because it has evolved to be resistant to centuries of toxic pollution, malnutrition, and disease. The blood itself is an Archive of Mexican history, anti-essentialist because constantly mutating, and triumphantly historical. The "superiority" of the MCMs, of course, threatens the caste-like social order. Ironies are heightened, however, when wealthy white families hire MCMs to live in their homes as continual live-in blood donors, thus effecting a restaging of colonization and enslavement of the putative "master race" of MCMs. Staring into the eyes of a Mexican soldier, soon to be conscripted as a blood donor, Gregory whispers to himself, *"mi raza"* (144) and later thinks,

> In the past, it was Mexican blood that was spilled during the conquest; it was Mexican blood that ran during the genocidal campaign of the Spanish Colonial period . . . it was Mexican blood that provided the cheap labor to California during the first half of the nineteenth century and that now provided the massive labor force in the *maquiladora* factory belt. . . . In a matter of time, Mexican blood would run in all the population of the LAMEX corridor. Mexican blood would gain control of the land it lost almost two hundred and fifty years ago. This thought originated in Grandfather Gregory's long forgotten histories. (195–96)

This historical reflection marks the peculiar efficacy of working though the Archive. The recitation of historical trauma creates a mournful history indeed, but the Archival sweep—and the Archival trope of blood—establishes a counterhistory that challenges not only the dominant narrative, but the dominant structures of historiography as well. Cyclical rather than linear, the history of trauma for Mexicans and their descendants, which would putatively chart the decimation of a culture, in fact becomes the Archive of that culture. In turn, the Archive facilitates cultural working-through, which ultimately allows for the radical revision of the Archive itself. Here, the trope of blood is most sneakily ironic. Each time the narrator mentions "blood" in the passages cited above, he gathers a different racial group under the category "Mexican," including precolonial indigenous Aztec, Mexican *Mestizos,* and, presumably, Chicanos. Blood, then, is a gesture, or a trope, which gives Archival coherence to the history described.

The novel ends on a hopeful note. Gregory is removed from his position as medical director, but joins up with a revolutionary political and spiritual movement growing in the rising poverty classes, comprised mainly of Mexicans and Asian immigrants. As the "Blue Buster" plague recedes, Mexicans remain nonetheless in the homes of their patrons, part of a potential revolutionary force. Gregory is no longer forced to merge his individual self with a hegemonic political force, but he is now in a position to choose to identify with his "people"—a group and a concept ever in flux—a move facilitated by the Archive, itself ever in a state of revision.

Though the novel ends optimistically, there is nothing to suggest that the tragedies of history will be redeemed, or somehow undone, or even fully overcome. It is not even clear what that would mean, given the transformation of culture—and so the bounds of identification—by the vicissitudes of history over the centuries. Pointedly, there is no mention of "Chicano" in book 3. Whatever transformations take place in the revolution to come, they will not involve the restoration of a Chicano community in, say, a putative homeland like *Aztlán*. Furthermore, at the center of the revolutionary movement are Ted and Amalia Chen, a Mexican and Chinese couple whose mixed-race child is prophesied to be the new spiritual leader of the revolution. In short, the comeuppance of the impoverished minority community of Lamex draws from class and religious inspiration outside of the novel's purview.

What, then, of the efficacy of the Archive? Throughout, the Archive has been the source and catalyst for Gregory's own personal revolution and integration with his family and family history. But the Archive obviously has no power to stop the plagues that routinely come, and certainly Gregory cannot wield his books against the various colonial armies. The Archive is not meant to be the antidote to cultural oppression in this novel, but the response to it. The Archive effects a kind of paradox. On the one hand, it narrates and embodies the condition of absence of totality or wholeness at the root of Mexican and Mexican American culture; on the other hand, it allows for the development of cultural consciousness, even becomes culture itself, a source for Gregory to understand and respond to his bewildering, dehistoricized present. The Archive is at once the result of and the means for working through traumatic history.

Though the Archive's agency is limited to only one individual's working through within the novel, its reach beyond the book's pages may be considerable. I want to conclude by suggesting that Morales's trope of the Archive is an allegorical offering to those who read and write about trauma in U.S. ethnic literature. I began this chapter with what might have seemed like theoretical hair-splitting, distinguishing between loss and absence, mourning and working-through. I want to return to those distinctions and place them in a much broader discourse about ethnic American literature. Where loss and mourning would imply a teleology of (potential) cultural wholeness and redemption, absence and working-through more accurately capture ethnic Americans' cultural processes, including the kinds of self-conscious cultural constructions ethnic scholars themselves acknowledge.[14] A psychoanalysis of culture that grants the legacy of historical trauma without using that history to reify the cultural group—by "restoring" culture, or locating "authentic" culture, or some other essentialist gesture—and which accounts for the cultural legacies of trauma without facilely positing redemption may indeed be suggestive for a whole host of issues having to do with multiculturalism, canon and curricular debates, and even the identification of who or what is ethnic (as opposed to racialized, or mainstream). Working-through suggests an approach to ethnic history which privileges reading and critique, and ever-expanding archives over closed canons.

Consider, for example, how the figure of the Archive participates in an ongoing discourse in Chicano literary and cultural criticism about the very meaning and character of Chicano identity. In fact, Chicano criticism's strongest contribution to ethnic studies is its self-conscious and deeply political meditation on appropriate figurations of the group, from the image of *la Virgen,* to the semimythical national space of *Aztlán,* to the hugely influential trope of the border and the border-dwelling people— the "new mestiza" as Gloria Anzaldúa puts it. For Chicano cultural criticism, the Archive is a kind of meta-trope, descriptive not only of the *rasquache*-style literature and culture, but also of the criticism that responds to this culture. When the Chicana poet Lorna Dee Cervantes writes, "I come from a long line of eloquent illiterates," she refers not only to her own recent contribution to the Archive of Chicano culture, but to the retroactive process of organizing a history of cultural change and response to change, not necessarily written down, but passed on in folklore, mural art, or through ancient and modern codices.[15]

The relationship between the Archive and its readers is especially instructive for responding to contemporary ethnic literary criticism. In *The Rag Doll Plagues,* the knowledge the Archive presents is always, and cannily, exactly the knowledge its readers require. In this way, the novel matches Ramón Saldívar's conception of the dialectics of Chicano literature: For Chicanos, "to write is preeminently a political act seeking to fulfill the potentialities of contemporary life. It is also, ultimately, an attempt to recall the originary myths of life on the borders of power in order to fashion a new, heterogeneous American consciousness" (218). This dialectical model of reading and response (leading to cultural reconstruction) has parallels in other cultures' history, too. In *The Jewish Search for a Usable Past,* David Roskies explores the rise of documentary writing among religious, secular, and intellectual Jews in nineteenth-century post-Enlightenment Europe, and explains that at the very moment Jews were faced with a various ways of being Jewish, Jewish memory shifted from a liturgical field to a political act. Jewish memory-making for this milieu was less a process of recalling a receding old-world culture and more one of charting a retrospective trajectory from past to present—the contested present in need of validation. In a chapter titled "The Library of Jewish Catastrophe" Roskies explains that the impulse to archive the past fed into an urgent quest to document the mounting disasters for Jews in the early to mid-twentieth century. "Thus, the modern Library of Jewish Catastrophe both grew out of Jewish collective memory and fed back into it" (19). Prior to and following World War II, the writing that comprised the Library of Jewish Catastrophe took on sacred, talismanic status for those producing it and those who would subsequently research it. Roskies explains, "[T]he most lasting legacy . . . was the archive itself—as model and metaphor. For the archive was never safe from the hands of those who wished to see all evidence of this crime destroyed" (20). Consequently, the value of the archive rendered "every scrap of paper . . . sacred" (20); demand for such writing resulted in the new genre of Jewish autobiography, as well as Jewish archival anthropology and Jewish testimonial projects.

Though Roskies superbly charts the open-ended, recirculating nature of the Jewish testimonial library and effectively demonstrates a process of Jewish cultural reflection that is similar to working-through, he nonetheless concludes by succumbing to the seduction of a master-narrative that would finally collate all others, once and for all. Writing about Zionism, Roskies begins with the iconoclastic observation that "exile is a literary construct. And so is Zion" (169). That said, "Zionism is protean, inclusive, and heteroglossic," containing the multitudes of contradictions within contemporary Jewish life, and finally, Zion itself is a "covenantal community" and "home" for Jewish culture (171). Such a statement in this context grossly understates the depth of Jewish theological and ideological difference regarding Israel and other matters, and swerves away from a sophisticated exploration of the open-ended archive of Jewish culture. Not only are there fracturing debates among Jews about both Israel and memorializations of the Holocaust, Jewish critiques of contemporary Zionism are also often in part responses to the nationalist narrative emerging from one wing of the "Library of Jewish Catastrophe."[16] Roskies' turn to Zionism as a sort of denouement to post-Enlightenment Jewish history is belied by Derrida's observation that "all national rootedness" is in fact "rooted first of all in the memory or the anxiety of a displaced—or displaceable—population," and that such an anxiety requires ever-fresh additions to and consultations of the Jewish library, prior to and following catastrophe (83).

If favoring open-ended archives and cultural working-through means resisting the gravitational pull of large-scale memorials, museums, and final rituals, we might in closing look to Betonie, the humble and marginalized archival-healer in Leslie Marmon Silko's novel *Ceremony.* Like Gregorio, Betonie is a medicinal healer of mixed racial background, straddling two cultural worlds. His task in the novel is no less than to heal the wounds of historical trauma as they appear in the protagonist, Tayo. Asked about his collection of traditional Indian medicine kept in store with old calendars, municipal phonebooks, newspapers, and other American cultural detritus, Betonie explains he's just "keeping track of things" (121). Betonie's Archive is the "medicine" that initiates Tayo's cure, and Tayo's eventual working through trauma confirms the efficacy of ethnic cultural Archives. Keeping track of things, an endless process, means keeping track of cultural change, always adding to the Archive of cultural knowledge, at once granting its authority while asserting its malleability, a self-conscious gesture that allows for a culture's recognition of its own process of construction, its own embeddedness in history.

3··· "SHE HAS CLAIM": MATERIAL JUSTICE AND THE ENDS OF HISTORY

What are we personally willing to sacrifice, give up for the "public good"?
What gestures of reparation are we personally willing to make? What risky,
unfashionable research are we willing to undertake?

—Toni Morrison, "How Can Values Be Taught in the
University?" Princeton University, April 27, 2000

Alejandro Morales stands out among Chicano writers because although
his aesthetics are underwritten by a materialist critique of capitalism
and imperialism, his vision of a better future does not rely on or produce
a more stalwart cultural identity. Instead, along with Roth and Ozick,
and in contrast to contemporaries like Ana Castillo, Arturo Islas, or even
Sandra Cisneros, Morales's protagonist transcends the material precisely
at the moment when he arrives at a broad historical consciousness. His
allegory of the role of criticism for producing a dialectical and ultimately
revolutionary consciousness certainly draws on the anticolonial critique
of Chicano and postcolonial criticism, but as we have seen, his work also
suggests an ultimately discursive model of identity formation, based on
the production of historical consciousness through an intellectual engagement with the past.[1] Though Roth's and Ozick's novels are more about
the business of negating reified or co-opted histories, the three are finally
more alike than different, since all three recognize that cultures with traumatic pasts require historical memory and mourning, and that literature
can further this process. It is also the case that for Chicanos, as for Jews,
skin color or physiognomy is not finally the ultimate determiner of social
identity in America. Rather, the identities "Jew" and "Chicano" imply
some historical interpellation for its subjects, and also depend on, even as
they produce, some anticipated revolutionary or quasi-messianic future.

The same certainly cannot be said for African Americans, nor does
African American literature operate in such a psychical space of historical memory. Instead, African American literature has been categorically
involved in producing the terms by which a community battles for recog-

nition and rights in a social and public sphere in the nineteenth century, while presenting devastating social critiques of both white and black social orders in the twentieth century. This is not to suggest that Jewish literature has not been involved in social critique. Instead, in landmark works of social criticism by Abraham Cahan, Michael Gold, Anzia Yezierska, or Henry Roth, for example, social criticism does not secure the viability of Jewish identity, but radically critiques the very concept of the "Jewish American." African American literature may critique the black cultural imaginary, but as the genre of the "passing" novel makes clear, there is no escaping the ultimately material consequences of being black in America. I offer this sketch of a comparison in order to raise a question about the way we read and respond to ethnic American literature. Allegories of mourning, melancholy, and working-through make sense for reading a culture that is necessarily anxious about producing a group-consciousness, ever under attack or the threat of co-optation, but to the extent that working-through is primarily a psychical process, it does not adequately describe other kinds of cultural work—material work, including the struggles for civil rights and ending racism in the social and legal system. Sticking with the basic premise of this book, I think literary criticism can and should adopt its strongest critical tools for dealing with kinds of cultural difference I am describing.

Simply put, trauma theory and theories of mourning in literature might be adapted to account for the material critiques and consequences in African American literature. This chapter models one way to structure this adaptation, by borrowing the structure of trauma theory and investing it with the ethic of material social criticism in relation to Toni Morrison's celebrated novel, *Beloved*. Already a substantial amount of critical writing about *Beloved* is invested in the ethically problematic and politically limited discourse of co-memory and co-mourning. This kind of criticism is what I would call "critical wish fulfillment,"[2] a critical projection of real-world ethical and political goals onto the reading scene, allowing readers to identify facilely with the novel's characters and their experiences. However, by passing the prevailing discourse of trauma studies through a more overtly politicized analysis, we can arrive at a critical approach that both advances the ethical and political claims a literary text such as *Beloved* has on its readers—the claims of the past on the present—and acknowledges the limits of reader-text identification, or the otherness of text and reader. I begin with an analysis of psychoanalytic approaches to Morrison's novel but I end in a very different place, suggesting we read the novel as a contribution to the contemporary national discussion of reparations for slavery and Jim Crow segregation.

The critics surveyed in this chapter already presume some sort of ethical project at the center of their own writing, at least insofar as they presume that a study of mourning and healing in literature is on the side of what is good. The analysis here aims to examine what critical, theoretical, and ethical presumptions prevail in the criticism, and to show how psychoanalytic discussions of agency in *Beloved* can be translated into an activist public sphere. Making this explicit will not undermine the value of such trauma-studies readings. On the contrary, under the adage that where there is quantity there must be quality—or something that is deeply valued—the prevalence of the ethical impulse underwriting so much of *Beloved* criticism tells me that it is a good thing, worthy of clarification and praxis.

That *Beloved* is a ghost story is well known, and it is not hard to imagine how a contemporary novel about a historically distant but nonetheless always present time—the period of American slavery and Reconstruction—participates in something like mourning for the past. The story is overwhelming, as is its genesis in the real-life incidents of runaway slave Margaret Garner, who in 1856 killed her own child to keep it out of the hands of her pursuing owner. In *Beloved* the murder of the child by her mother, Sethe, is in the past, but Sethe remains literally haunted by her dead daughter, right up till her ghost materializes as a young woman named Beloved, come to live with Sethe and her other daughter Denver. Sethe's haunting, dispelled at the end of the novel by a stirring exorcism, resonates so awfully because, as the highly applicable formula puts it, the reader is made to experience the presence of the past. Appropriately, therefore, scores of critical articles and book chapters have been devoted to describing the machinations of the novel's mourning, its role in cultural healing, its quest to rebury the dead, or its program of redeeming black female subjectivity from the damning criticism of analyses like the Moynihan report and its bastard children, the Reagan-era bashing of "welfare queens," and Dan Quayle's pathologization of single-motherhood.

The tenor of this criticism is well matched to the novel's achievements. But the claims that the criticism makes are far from transparently self-evident, and the performative power ascribed to literature in such claims bears some scrutiny, if not from the point of view of narratology, then from the perspective of cultural criticism, or even metacriticism. The criticism cited in this chapter claims that novels *do* things, presumably in the world at large. What do novels do and how do we know they do them? If I were to claim that a novel builds a bridge, I could then empirically say, "and look, there it is, right there—the bridge." But we do not claim that novels do things in three-dimensional space, and no such empirical knowledge is available to us. Novels build bridges across time or among cultures, but these are metaphors only and express what we wish on their behalf. However, if novels build metaphorical bridges, this implicates a wider reading culture in the process. I suggest that mourning, like bridge-building, may likewise be a metaphor that points us not only to what happens in the novel, but also to what responsibilities and actions the novel establishes for readers. A theory of how literature participates in cultural transformation needs to tap into the transformative potential in literature in both psychical and material ways. Psychoanalysis or materialism: this suggests a divide in approaches to African American and other ethnic literatures, and to *Beloved* in particular. Activist, Marxist-materialist criticism in African American and ethnic literary critical practice is one way of putting literature into conversation with the social reality of the world "out there"; with postmodern novels like *Beloved,* formal, linguistic-oriented, or psychoanalytic studies suggest a still deeper if less popularly accessible way of relating literature to lived social experience. I would like to examine how criticism on *Beloved,* informed by the insights of trauma studies, can participate in a wider political activism.

A current of literary criticism exists that advocates for and finds in literature a process that is variously called mourning, healing, working-through, or redemption. Characters, history, and cultures are on the receiving end. Texts—usually novels—do the cultural work, while critics serve as attendants, making the literary and cultural work transparent. Nancy Peterson, the editor of *Toni Morrison: Critical and Theoretical Approaches,* offers a reading of *Beloved* in *Against Amnesia* (2001), an analysis of "women writers of color,"[3] linking *Beloved* to what she considers a wider project of writing counterhistories in contemporary American literature. Concluding her book, Peterson sums up,

[T]he preceding chapters have emphasized history as wound, history as trauma, in order to call attention to an important dimension of contemporary women's writing: the need for these texts to bear a double burden—and to function as both history and literature. . . . These literary texts, however, are not only about history; they are also about healing the wounds of history. (169)

The goal of ethnic literature, according to Peterson, is not only descriptive, but constructive. Her writers "use literature to tell the other side of history and to refashion the narrative so that history comes out right this time" (183). Peterson's analysis is substantially derived from an optimistic reading of Cathy Caruth's theorizing of literary trauma in her justly celebrated book, *Unclaimed Experience.* Quoting Caruth approvingly, Peterson writes,

[T]he link between trauma and the initial missed experience leads to a model of reference that is not direct and immediate, but belated, displaced, and oblique. For Caruth, such a theory of trauma and its indirect referentiality suggests "the possibility of a history that is no longer straightforwardly referential." Where better to find an obliquely referential history than in literature, which by virtue of its figurative language constantly exceeds straightforward understanding? (13)

For Peterson then, literature offers a "counter-history" (13).

Besides the disciplinary slide from history to literature, Peterson has subtly translated Caruth's language. A history "no longer straightforwardly referential" is Caruth's beginning description of narrated traumatic experience (*Unclaimed Experience* 11); but Caruth concludes, trenchantly and with demanian overtones, that surviving to tell the story of trauma means telling *"what it means not to see"* (105; italics in the original).[4] The deconstructive loop in bearing witness to blindness suggests that the experience of historical trauma is rescued from melancholy only insofar as the suffering subject can narrate his or her own melancholic experience. To the extent that history is a "wound," a reimagining of history along the lines Caruth suggests is always in danger of succumbing to a "repetition compulsion . . . [manifest in] allegories of excess, incomprehensibility, and empty utopian hope" (LaCapra, *History and Memory* 208). Simply put, the wound either throbs and festers, or the text heals it: repetition or closure. This obviously endows the literary author with an impressive capacity for power over the past, especially in Peterson's analysis of *Beloved* where the status and meaning of the concepts *history,* *memory,* and *imagination* are interwoven and ceaselessly give way to one another. But can we so facilely collapse linear time in order to recast history? Can we claim that *Beloved* does things with and for culture and history without also claiming that it somehow is involved in and with the past? And in what way: repetition or closure?

Sharing Peterson's critical agenda and conclusions, many critics have credited Morrison's novel with "working through history and memory . . . [and] building new social configurations of family and kin" (Jesser 325). Others go further, arguing that "Morrison constructs history" and that such "history-making becomes a healing process for the characters, the reader, and the author" (Krumholz 395). All are healed because "Beloved is both the pain and the cure" (Krumholz 400). According to Wardi, "By participating in acts of homage and commemoration, [Morrison] resurrect[s] the spirit of those that came before and raise[s] monuments for the dead" (51). In this way, *Beloved* is a "visible marker that provide[s] a resting place for the ancestors" (51).

In her analysis of the "call-and-response" quality of *Beloved,* Maggie Sale argues that "*Beloved* presents a new way of conceiving of history, one that refuses and refutes master versions of history" (43). Sale explains that the novel's "call for communal response is part of the contemporary healing process that this text is involved in" (44). Sale insists on the corrective and therapeutic value of the novel—the novel *does* things—but she credits the reader with participating in the novel's action. Paying more attention to the function of the reader strengthens an overall analysis of how the novel operates in the world at large.[5]

Sale's discussion of the importance of the reader for realizing *Beloved*'s healing hints at how the novel's achievements—healing, mourning, countering history—may be accomplished in the world outside the pages of the book. I want to trace this insight in another author's analysis of *Beloved* to show both the limits of trauma-theory approaches to *Beloved* and what lies beyond those limits.

Kathleen Brogan's analysis of *Beloved* in her *Cultural Haunting* (1998) echoes Peterson's, but goes further in theorizing the effects of *Beloved* on its readers. Citing sociologist Robert Hertz's description of a "second burial," Brogan explains that "the movement Hertz describes from preliminary to final burials, in which a dangerous, spiteful ghost is translated into a benevolent ancestral spirit, closely corresponds to the masterplot of possession and exorcism that structures so many stories of cultural haunting," including *Beloved* (66). Suggesting that "final burial shifts power from the dead to the living" and "integrates the dead (as newly accessible spirits) into the ongoing life of the community," Brogan nevertheless stops short of claiming that such a ritual has been fulfilled by the end of Morrison's novel (67). The exorcism of the ghost by the community of women re-establishes the claims of the living over the claims of the dead, but the women, Sethe, and Paul D cannot or will not pass the event on into a symbolic narrative. In this way, "*Beloved* performs the final burial, but leaves the grave open," calling on readers to "join the author in forming a community of mourners who commemorate the dead" (91).

Brogan ephemerally concludes that the novel's haunting becomes the reader's "historical consciousness," but she precedes this with a hint of a more material call for justice: white readers are invited to make "an unpalatable identification with the novel's [hateful] Schoolteacher or well-meaning but condescending Bodwins," and thereby "take responsibility for both the past and the present" (92). Now we're getting somewhere! Taking responsibility takes historical consciousness seriously. We not only remember, or even "re-member." Instead, we are asked to bear some sort of ethical responsibility for the story we read, the story we live. Brogan's assertion that Morrison's novel is an "invitation" to ethics, however, implies an ethics that undermines its own purpose (92). What we are invited to do, we may also refuse. Historical consciousness of this sort separates knowing from doing, inclination from imperative.

Avery Gordon offers a more amplified discussion of the compulsion for (and limits of) ethical identification for readers of *Beloved*. As Gordon puts it, readers are not so much invited into relation with the text as *haunted* by it:

> To be in the seemingly old story now scared and not wishing to be there but not having anywhere else you can go that feels like a place you can belong is to be haunted. And haunting is exactly what causes declarative repudiations and voluntary identifications eventually to fail, although it must be said that they can be sustained for quite some time. Reckoning with ghosts is not like deciding to read a book: you cannot simply choose

the ghosts with which you are willing to engage. To be haunted is to make choices within those spiraling determinations that make the present waver. To be haunted is to be tied to historical and social effects. To be haunted is to experience the glue of the "If you were me and I were you logic" come undone. Though you can repeat over and over again, as if the incantation were a magic that really worked, I am not Schoolteacher/He is not me, the ghostly matter will not go away. (190)

The tone of Gordon's passage suggests the anxiety of being haunted by the novel, and the compulsion to take its claims seriously. As Thomas Keenan puts it, "It is when we do not know exactly what we should do, when the effects and conditions of our actions can no longer be calculated, and when we have nowhere else to turn, not even back onto our 'self,' that we encounter something like responsibility" (2). Like Coleridge's "Wedding Guest" we can neither turn away nor fail to "pass on" the story of *Beloved*. Or, as Adam Zachary Newton writes, "one faces a text as one might face a person, having to confront the claims raised by that very immediacy, an immediacy of contact, not of meaning" (*Narrative* 11).

Rather than choosing to identify (or not), we "face" the novel and submit to its claims. For what? What do we owe it, its characters, its historical antecedent? The "we" of such questions is a polyglot "we" of the present, a catch-all pronoun that only makes sense in the language of politics—"we Americans." Of course there are a plurality of "we's" to consider: black folks, white folks, and others dissimilarly but simultaneously dispossessed of life and property during the eighteenth and nineteenth centuries, not to mention African readers who would reflect on their continent's losses and culpability in the slave trade. How exactly this responsibility translates is not clear, but this is not beyond the scope of a critical reading of *Beloved*. Brogan does not follow up with a materialist analysis of the status of property and the physical claims the dead might have on the living, but precisely by not doing so, Brogan points to the breach between a criticism that offers a psychoanalysis of literature and a criticism that drives towards material and political response to literary claims. Brogan's and Peterson's commitment to psychoanalysis ultimately positions the text as consciousness itself, acting out, working through, and mourning its own narrative, but we can follow Gordon's hint to see how the novel participates in the world at large—the world of the reader.

The word *claim* has shown up in this chapter frequently already, and it is prominent in many analyses of *Beloved,* for good reason: the novel's plot, its discursive texture, and its characters' development all pivot on the word *claim*. The shifting, multivalent meaning of the word produces a lexicon that compliments, if not outright challenges, the discourse of trauma. For example, as all the black characters in the novel come to realize, "freeing yourself was one thing; claiming ownership of that freed self was another" (95). Running away north is freeing, but is owning yourself similarly material, or purely psychological? Or is the psychology of self-ownership necessarily dependent on the material? Perhaps the difference between freeing and claiming is the same as the difference between doing and claiming: "Sethe had done what she had claimed" (165). What Sethe had done is kill her baby; in what way is this claiming ownership? After he sees what Sethe has done, "right off it was clear, to schoolteacher especially, that there was nothing there to claim" (149). Nonetheless, schoolteacher "filed a claim and rode off" (183). In the first instance, schoolteacher sees that among all the blood, terror, and outright refusal, he has lost what he came for, his property. The second instance is more subtly suggestive of Morrison's awareness of the pervasive and ambiguous business of slavery.[6] Apparently, schoolteacher files an insurance claim on his property, cashing in on a policy such as the ones that modern insurance giants like New York Life sold for slaves in Kentucky during the mid-nineteenth century.[7] Nothing to claim/file a claim; doing/claiming; freeing/claiming ownership: in each instance, "claim" is the simultaneously complimentary and contradictory term in the pairing, the term that negates the other, even itself. As the narrator says of Beloved, "Although she has claim, she is not claimed" (274). Not claimed because forgotten, repressed, not sought after . . . but what sort of claim does she have, and on whom?

Claim is one of those brilliant words that refracts when read through the lens of the *Oxford English Dictionary:* A demand for something due; an application for compensation, especially for damage to property; right or title; (redundantly) that which is claimed; (obscurely) a call, shout; (verbally) to assert and demand recognition of (an alleged right, title, possession, attribute, acquirement, or the like). . . . *To call for, demand, or require; to be entitled to, deserve, have a right to.* . . . "Beloved, she my daughter. She mine" (201; italics added). Possessive intonations run throughout the final third of the novel as characters claim each other as mother, daughter, and sister. Sorting re-enslaving possession from nurturance and loving is the tricky task before us. Can Sethe use the syntax of the slave owner, while speaking as a mother? "*When I tell you you mine, I also mean I'm yours*" (203; italics added).

Most readers of *Beloved* skeptically conclude that a property-based epistemology is the root of all the novel's evil. For example, Trudier Harris observes that the characters in *Beloved* consistently think of themselves in monetary terms that are ultimately inadequate or self-negating (333). Building on that observation, Erik Dussere argues that "if liberation is to be had at all for ex-slaves, it is not through the paying of debts or the balancing of books; Morrison deliberately denies the notion of justice implied by such acts" (343). Dussere is at least partially correct. *Beloved* is a novel that consistently pits the status of humanity against the status of property, and no amount of money can justly compensate the dehumanization involved in slavery.[8] However, precisely because the most daring acts of humanity are violations against the laws of property, the discourse of property in slavery is embedded with a dialectical and self-negating discourse of humanity. "Slave" aims to cancel "human," while freeing one's self is always freeing oneself from a state of property. There is no getting around what characters are freeing themselves into, as Houston Baker reminds us: "the creative individual (the *black subject*) must, therefore, whether he self-consciously wills it or not, come to terms with 'commercial deportation' and the 'economics of slavery'" (39).[9]

Beyond this dialectic, though, alternative conceptions of property among slaves not only did not cancel humanity, but in fact sustained, and even *produced* kinship ties. Because legal codes denied a slave's right to property, slaves who had acquired property displayed it publicly, in yards around slave quarters, or with special brands. And because money to buy property was so hard to come by, slaves depended on alliances with kin, or established quasi-kinship with others sharing quarters in order to attain group-owned property.[10]

What this means is that there is a way of reading Sethe's property-based discourse outside of the rhetoric of law. Property may ultimately be a material word, but it exceeds the rhetoric of legal codes and requires some form of human recognition to sustain. Rather than dismiss the discourse of property as "the master's language" to be overcome, we can read it as expressing the experience of slavery, including those recurring moments where humanity exceeds the legal codes that would bind it.

Of all the terms associated with property in the novel, *claim* best captures the slippery nature of ownership in the nineteenth century. Claiming is paradoxically performative and redundant: the declaration or act of claim establishes original possession. That is, you acquire the possession in the act of calling it yours. But claiming also means seeking compensation for something lost. As anyone who has filed an insurance claim knows, it is essential to prove your prior possession of what was lost before you can claim it. There's turning the screw of interpretation: how can you claim something you never had, how can you demand something be restored that was not there in the first place? Morrison sustains rather than elides the language of property, not to expose how susceptible her characters are to internalized self-perceptions as property, but to turn that discourse against itself, from the inside out. As Hortense Spillers has observed in other emancipatory texts, "the project of liberation for African-Americans has found urgency in two passionate motivations that are twinned—(1) to break apart, to rupture violently the laws of American behavior that make [dehumanizing] syntax possible; (2) to introduce a new *semantic* field to [one's] own historic moment" (226).

Making a new semantic field may take on a number of possible revisionary forms, but with *Beloved* the new field is necessarily written across the already existing one. Sethe's murder of her daughter is precisely her claim of ownership for her; breaking the law of slavery is an assertion of the "law of the mother" (Spillers 228). Trauma is experienced as the breaking and remaking of the law, and in this way Sethe's action is an injury to the law, and to the one who would claim her, at the same time that it is a trauma to her. Contrary to the way we typically think of injury, it is against the law she breaks that Sethe has claim and produces claim for others around her, because Sethe's humanity and her claim for her family precede the law. James Berger's superb analysis of *Beloved* as an "intervention" in contemporary debates about single black mothers and welfare is helpful for seeing the novel as writing a new field over the old. Berger focuses specifically on the 1965 Moynihan report that identified a "tangle of pathology" associated with the matriarchal black home as the source of black social problems in the 1960s. According to Berger, reading *Beloved* in the context of the Moynihan report establishes the novel as a response to the contemporary rhetoric of race and gender: "*Beloved* opposes neoconservative and Reaganist denials of race as a continuing, traumatic, and structural problem in contemporary America but also questions positions on the left that tend to deny the traumatic effect of violence within African American communities" (498).

I would extend Berger's analysis to say that several scenes in *Beloved* respond to Ronald Reagan's condemnation of black "welfare queens" by revising the terms by which we understand single parenthood. Reagan, we recall, erroneously and frequently cited the supposed example of one such "queen" who was using food stamps to buy steaks and champagne while driving around in a Cadillac. The image of conspicuous consumption by someone who, by virtue of her race and lifestyle choices would be regarded as undeserving of such privileges, garnered white resentment at her arrogance and presumption. Startlingly, we find a similar scenario in *Beloved* in Ella's resentment, first of Baby Suggs for living so well so soon after slavery, and then of Sethe, for demonstrating pride of ownership in herself and her children (187, 256). Later in the novel, the reader is confronted with another discomfiting example of Sethe's "lifestyle," when she and her daughters exile Paul D and spend every last cent on sweets and fine clothes. The portrait of their decadence is like a diorama of Reaganite rhetoric: "The thirty-eight dollars of life savings went to feed themselves with fancy food and decorate themselves with ribbon and dress goods. . . . Bright clothes—with blue and sassy prints. She walked the four miles to John Shilito's to buy yellow ribbon, shiny buttons and bits of black lace. By the end of March, the three of them looked like carnival women with nothing to do" (240). This final observation, with its outside-in point of view, suggests the double vision inhering in images of the black single parent, where the static looking in misses the story comprising the picture: "Sethe was trying to make up for the handsaw; Beloved was making her pay for it" (251). When the money runs out, Sethe, Beloved, and Denver survive off the anonymous "welfare" of neighbors, though this sustains rather than checks their "lunatic" behavior (251, 250). The novel's climax arrives when Bodwin comes to pick up his new employee, Denver—in a kind of welfare-to-work scenario—while the kind neighbors who had previously left food now organize to exorcise the ghost of Beloved. Bodwin's offer of employment is not unwelcome, but it first requires the intervention of the neighbors, who have come to reclaim Sethe as part of their community.

Just as "freeing" and "owning" are words loaded with political, ethical, and material meaning in the novel's setting of Reconstruction, so too

is *claim* a word under material and political legislation during the mid-
to late nineteenth century, as Dylan Penningroth explains in *The Claims
of Kinfolk* (2003). In 1871 Congress formed the Southern Claims Commission to investigate claims of property loss filed by Southern Unionists
who demanded compensation for property stolen by Union soldiers. According to Penningroth, in addition to the thousands of claims anticipated by white Southern landowners, the commission was also inundated
by hundreds of ex-slaves filing claims for similarly usurped property.
Despite the fact that slaves could not legally have been in possession of
property, the Claims Commission recognized alternative definitions of
property title and proof, for both black and white claimants. Ex-slaves
brought kin and neighbors to testify as eyewitnesses to property possession, and joint claims filed by several members of a family for property
were granted. Typically, we think only the state can grant property rights,
but in this case the state was forced to recognize or grant the right to property based not on pre-existing title but on claims that were harder to pin
down.

The Southern Claims Commission represents one aspect of a wider
renegotiation of property rights in the United States during the mid-
nineteenth century. Contemporaneous with the Southern Claims Commission, Congress also passed the General Mining Law of 1872, establishing federal procedures for staking and filing claims for mineral rights, in
concert with previous state-passed laws in 1866 and 1870. The new law,
which generally still holds, is remarkably simple: whoever so identifies a
precious mineral on previously unclaimed government property may file
a claim and thereby take possession of the minerals therein. Administra-
tive fees and proof of "improvement of the claim" are also required.[11] The
devil, however, is in the details, as Patricia Nelson Limerick observes:
"the events of Western history represent, not a simple process of territo-
rial expansion, but an array of efforts to wrap the concept of property
around unwieldy objects" (*Legacy* 71)—unwieldy because these objects
are minerals that are difficult to access, animals that move, or slaves that
run away. In this way, the Fugitive Slave Act of 1850 is one of a number
of mid-century attempts to codify property rights over resistant object/
agents in a heterogeneous nation. The General Mining Law, as well as the
Homestead Act of 1862, can be seen as revisions of the American theory
of property law that renegotiated the priority of individuals over things.

In "the wilderness," beyond the scope of the law, claiming required community.[12]

At the risk of running far afield from the subject here, it is worth mentioning that Denver—the city whose name is metonymically if not directly attached to Sethe's other daughter, born on the way to freedom in 1855—was founded in 1858, on the eve of the Civil War, by gold prospectors looking to establish a claim district, and during the 1870s—the novel's present time—the city was experiencing its first great population and financial boom due to goldmining.

I offer this information not as evidence so much as resonance in order to suggest how *Beloved*'s historical setting is underwritten by a set of complicated legal and extra-legal codes that at least begrudgingly privilege subjects over objects, people over things. *Beloved* is set during a period in history when claiming pillaged property, gold, or your own free self means establishing that there is something to be claimed in the first place, whether by securing the affirmation of family members or by digging down deep to uncover what is of value. And because "claim" is one of those redundantly performative practices—you establish ownership over what is rightfully yours through declaration—it suggests how claiming is less an act of liberation and more an act of restoration, returning yourself to you. Claiming rests on the veracity and verifiability of the "I," and to acknowledge the kinds of claims described so far means recognizing the life and work of the one who makes the claim. Are we back where we started, with another version of working-through? Is this not a material allegory of the Freudian formula, *wo Es war, soll Ich werden*—establishing the "I" in the territory of the material, the "it," thereby moving from repressed or absent experience to a worked-through and symbolically mourned trauma?[13] Perhaps so, if we grant what is also new, namely the material, financial implications of the discourse of property.

Property directs the plot of the novel, and it is where trauma and material possession meet. Drawing out the novel's multivalent utterances of "claim" does not change the subject from trauma to property rights; rather, it points out the novel's particular lexicon of trauma. The experience of the black characters is decidedly the experience of property—stealing or being stolen, freeing or being freed, repossessing, and hauntingly, claiming. Sethe tells Paul D this much near the novel's beginning, when he first observes the raised scars on Sethe's back:

"They used cowhide on you?"
"And they took my milk."
"They beat you and you was pregnant?"
"And they took my milk!" (17)

The repetitive exchange suggests that "they took my milk" is the clarifying corrective to Paul D's question. The trauma, Sethe tells him and us, is not the beating, but the taking, not the whipping but the stealing of her milk. The operative word in the exchange is "my" as in *mine*. Sethe lays claim to herself, and the product of her own body. Taking, later glossed as stealing (200), means taking what was rightfully hers. Her milk parallels and inverts the production of ink for schoolteacher. Though a formula not of her own design, Sethe mixes the ink just the way schoolteacher likes it (37). With this special-mixed ink schoolteacher records his observations of Sethe and the other slaves. The material rewrites the corporeal, the special ink, synecdoche of individuality, produces the logic by which schoolteacher can later come to claim his property, stolen away to 124 Bluestone, fatefully acting for all the world to see like human beings. Conversely, it is Sethe's own special mix, her breast milk, "enough for all," which impels her, with all the force of human love, to escape from Sweet Home, to claim her right to her own self, a right she has no right to claim. In this case the language of material possession is the best register for the expression of being human, the best way to claim humanity. Later, Sethe decides it is time to run when she realizes that her children, the product of her body's own labor, are increased property for schoolteacher.[14] In each case, assertions of self-ownership contradict Sethe's legal status as property and posit a different sort of claim, where kinship, family, and love produce and define humanity.

This meditation on the relationship between bodily trauma and the body as property, mediated by the language of "rights" and "claiming," points out the flexibility of concepts like injury and redress, which constitute the broader field within which trauma occurs. I am negotiating a reading of somatic or psychical trauma with an analysis of proto-legal injury by arguing that a discourse of ownership marks the experience of being a slave; it is through that discourse that Sethe and others are best able to affirm their being human. As Satya Mohanty puts it, "[E]xperiences are crucial indexes of our relationships with our world (including our relationships with ourselves), and to stress their cognitive nature is to argue that they can be susceptible to varying degrees of socially constructed truth or error and can serve as sources of objective knowledge or socially produced mystification" (211). Experiences index objective knowledge when they are indicative of our "objective social location," and they allow for self-knowledge when we are able to read our own experiences in light of our historical and theoretical moment (216, 229). This would mean that Sethe's and other characters' lexicon of property is the result of a conscious analysis of their own experiences—the experience of being raced, dehumanized, or made property.[15] It also suggests a realistic awareness of their social location as subjects and objects in the American capitalist economy.[16]

The discourse of Sethe's emotional and moral experience, performed in trauma-centered analyses of the novel, provides by far the richest possible description of her deep-textured humanity. However, in doing so this discourse invariably winds up in impossible ontological problems, especially given the extent to which trauma theory is wed to deconstructive accounts of being human. Passing the discourse of psychic trauma through the semantic field of injury and the adherents of materialism and property raises a new question. If the productive response to trauma is working-through and mourning, what is the right response to material loss? Or, to add another twist, is a psychoanalytically conceived effort of working-through adequate to the task when the experience of loss is mediated through the discourse of property?[17]

In a study of the intersection of narrative theory and critical race studies, Carl Gutierrez-Jones suggests ways of thinking about how the narrative depiction of trauma may participate in a materialist discourse oriented toward social justice. Gutierrez-Jones reminds us,

> Simply making power and injury visible in no way guarantees a more liberated society, although of course recognition of these injuries can be a crucial initial step. The key is appropriately mediating between such recognitions and the literacy that governs the interpretation of social and cultural problems generally. Without this mediation, the making visible of injury can easily be co-opted into a project in which conflicts are subdued, or worse yet, completely robbed of their ability to generate "alternative" political thought. (74–75)

Gutierrez-Jones's cautionary gesture points two ways: Mediation means speaking *for* those aggrieved and *to* a discursive system that sustains oppression; studies of injury need to provide methods of redress in order to be effective, and theories that do not account for material injury do not advance the claims of literature into the "literacy," or discourse, of the world at large. Among the limitations of trauma-studies readings of novels like *Beloved* is that they end up either serving as mute witnesses to a scene of destruction, like Benjamin's so frequently referenced "Angel of History," or they end up suggesting that something or someone has mourned and is now healed in or by the text, without adequately exploring just what and how this happens. Working within a psychoanalytic discourse, Gutierrez-Jones associates the first type of analysis with "acting-out" and the second with "working-through" (58). In the case of legacies of historical trauma such as slavery, political measures aimed at producing economic equality between black and white folks may result in reductive and narrow legal redress without addressing fundamental issues of ethics.[18] On the other hand, mourning through literature or other cathected cultural symbols produces a ritual of working-through and perhaps narrative closure, or even the possibility for ethical encounters between black and white as Brogan suggests, but without invoking the clearly central fields of law and property. The question I am driving toward the reader by now anticipates: is there a psychological formula, a form of justice, or a rhetoric, which comprehends and enables both mourning and material redress, and which is neither so wedded to the past nor so utopian as to supplant ethics with ideology, resentment, or facile fictions of narrative identification?

I suggest that a discourse of reparation is adequate to the task. To be more and less specific, by "reparation" I mean the idea of reparations for slavery and Jim Crow social oppression and marginalization, though I do not intend to debate the political and philosophical complications here, partly because such complications are so prohibitive, and partly because they are so compelling.[19] *Reparation* is another provocatively refractable word, meaning restoration, spiritual healing, mending, compensation, and reconciliation. Reparations claims brought forth against participants in the institution of slavery as well as Jim Crow segregation demand money, property retrieval, apology, and institutional redress. In short, the idea within "reparation" includes a combination of psychical and spiritual, as well as material and political, redress for wrong done to the injured party. Because the word's meaning toggles between spiritual and material repair it seems to symmetrically address trauma in *Beloved* as the experience of being property and the struggle to claim ownership of one's own self. Precisely because freeing the self is a process requiring, but not wholly facilitated by, the legal documentation of freedom, the up-front discussion of compensation for what Margaret/Sethe Garner and her descendants have claim for is part of the process of securing freedom. The materialism of the language associated with reparations may seem off-putting or reductive only when we fail to recognize that Morrison consistently twins the language of spiritual and psychic devastation with the language of material loss and legal injury, giving us a materially textured surface that conforms to the depths of the spirit.

Though there are substantial social and legal obstacles to even engaging a pragmatic conversation about reparations, this does not preclude thinking about the ethics and value of reparations. As J. Angelo Corlett reminds readers in *Race, Racism, and Reparation,* we should not confuse *ought* with *can* regarding reparations (192). In fact, the discourse of reparations is a helpful link between the discourse of trauma and a political and material discourse; furthermore, the ethics of reparation can be an appropriate compliment to the discourse of trauma studies when reading and responding to *Beloved.* Given the activist sentiment at work in trauma-studies readings of *Beloved,* and given the ethical perspective that accompanies so many of these readings, already embedded in this criticism is the urge for the novel to participate in something like political reconciliation. Considering too that the novel's own terminology for trauma includes property, legal redress, and injury compensation, a meditation on reparative justice is well within the scope of any account of the novel that aims to examine how it directly participates in an American context of political race.

A good deal of the intellectual energy for current reparations lawsuits originates in Boris Bittker's *The Case for Black Reparations,* brought to print in 1973 by Toni Morrison while she was an editor at Random House. It was at Random House that Morrison conceived of and researched the African American archival project *The Black Book,* published in 1974, which occasioned her discovery of Margaret Garner's story (Harris 1974); the overlap at least suggests that Garner's story and an interest in reparations were drawn from the same intellectual well. Commenting on the recent republication of *The Case for Black Reparations* by Beacon Press, Morrison writes, "publishing Boris Bittker's *The Case for Black Reparations* in 1973 seemed to me an important contribution to the fledgling reparations debate. Now with its focus on the legal hurdles of such compensation, his work is more than significant—it is vital" (jacket cover). Just as reparations paid to Jewish victims of the Holocaust testify to the present-ness of the past, so too should we see the present-day lawsuits for black reparations as part of a single trajectory of history that begins with the Middle Passage.

Critics of reparations, including the literary critic Walter Benn Michaels, are skeptical of the premise that present-day African Americans are uniquely tied to the experiences of slaves over one hundred years ago. Michaels, for example, attacks what he deems the logic of memory underpinning both Morrison's novel and the reparations movement. According to Michaels, both rely on a false kind of memory, for neither Morrison nor any present-day Black American who might receive reparation can claim to actually remember what in fact happened to his or her ancestors. According to Michaels, "To put the point in this way, however—to describe the goal of reparations as a racially proportionate redistribution of wealth—is immediately to invite the objection that it's hard to see how leaving the economic inequalities of American society intact while rearranging the skin color of those who suffer from and those who benefit from those inequalities counts as progress" (*Shape* 159, 164).

Michaels's understanding of reparations as taking money from one individual's pockets and putting it in another is a gross misunderstanding of the targets of reparations suits, namely corporations and federal and state governments. Be that as it may, for Michaels, the logic of cultural legacies and the logic of reparation are fundamentally opposed to one another, since the first depends on a notion of culture-as-property, while the second means disinheriting one group—whites, presumably—for the sake of another group. Michaels's analysis, and his mock-earnest commitment to the integrity of each separate notion, depends on a conceptualization of what it means to "remember" as strictly limited to the recall of events already lodged in the memory of the one who has experienced them. Of course, *remember* may also mean to honor, to study, to think about, or to commit something new to memory. This is the function of the Lincoln Memorial, for example, to mark and commemorate an event even well after those who experienced it have passed on. Memory has a public function and may be collective, not as a lazy false consciousness, but as an act of commitment to a narrative, an origin, and a set of values. As Randall Robinson, a leading proponent of reparations, puts it, "even the *making* of a well-reasoned case for restitution will do wonders for the spirit of African Americans" (232). Michaels accuses Robinson of just such a false memory, but Robinson's point is that the practicalities of filing for class-action lawsuits, including tracing family *and* corporate genealogies, and the genealogy of legal codes regulating slaves and ex-slaves furthers the recovery of our national memory (*Shape* 164).

Thought of this way, reparation is as much an imperative process following horrific and cruel dispossession as is mourning subsequent to trauma. The social mechanisms required for reparations amount to a highly relevant social historiography that establishes the connections between past and present that critics like Michaels would otherwise fail to see. And in the case of *Beloved,* reparation and the work of mourning—namely, working-through—are part and parcel of the same process. Here Dominick LaCapra's description of "working through" (which is rarely cited in trauma-theory readings of *Beloved,* but prominent in critical race and new-realist accounts of race and ethnicity) as a process involving "hybridized narrative," and "acting out" for the sake of achieving "critical distance on experience," is most helpful (*Representing* 199–200). LaCapra is refreshingly skeptical of the quasi-mystical analyses of mourning in Holocaust literature, as well as fetishistic narratives of melancholy. Establishing working-through as a historical process, part of but also separate from mourning, LaCapra points to how critical race narratives not only describe, but can also reinscribe legal and political constructions of what we otherwise loosely refer to as "historical consciousness."

The novel models one form of reparation near the end, when a group of women who had previously condemned Sethe, first for living so well so soon after manumission, and then for the excess of both her love and her crime directed at her children, come to exorcise the ghost that is sucking Sethe dry. Ella, who leads the women, was especially appalled by Sethe's "sin" but her sense of justice is keen enough to know that "what's fair ain't necessarily right" (256). This act of rescue is a reparation in the sense of "restoration," a term also suggested by the circularity of the word *claim*—restoring the self to the self. And if we recall *claim*'s gloss as a "shout, an affirmation" and note that the women prayed, sang, and "hollered" (257) for Sethe, we might say that in this way they claim Sethe on her behalf, an act advanced by Paul D's assertion to Sethe that "you your own best thing" (273).[20] At the same time, the women intervene and protect Bodwin, Sethe's former benefactor, whom she mistakes for schoolteacher. Bodwin is riding to 124 Bluestone, his childhood home, thinking about the treasure he once buried there, "precious things he wanted to protect" (259). The language here is suggestive of how different readers react to Bodwin, either as the strident abolitionist he sees himself as, or as yet another racist, paternalistic rather than domineering, but ultimately substitutable for schoolteacher. Are his "precious things" in fact Sethe and her family, the freed slaves to whom he gave a house but for whom he could not or would not shelter? Or do we read this as a search for his own childhood innocence of the brutal politics of slavery, his own "best thing"? It seems telling that Bodwin could suffer Sethe's vengeance despite the fact that he is not directly the cause of her misery. Michaels has critiqued the notion of haunting, seizing on Sethe's explanation to Denver that even "you who was never there" could be claimed by the burdens of the past, but Sethe's attack on Bodwin makes clear that history is not a neat package of linear cause and effect, and that we are subjects in the psychological and semantic fields of others.

If the experience of reading *Beloved* described by Avery Gordon and Kathleen Brogan is going to amount to a reckoning beyond haunting, and if we are ever to look up from the open grave constituted by the book in our hands, it is up to the reader to establish "critical distance" between past and present. Revising history means reconstructing a view of the past as well as recharting the future. To "make history come out right this time" (Peterson) means to acknowledge just what it is that characters in the novel and the novel itself claim of us. The problematically plural "us" or "we" invoked on behalf of the novel's readers is even more vexed when it comes to the topic of reparations for slavery and segregation. Any reader can imagine some of the more prominent objections to reparations based on America's spectacular racial and ethnic variety and histories, and it is precisely these objections that show us how to extend Brogan's and Gordon's suggestion that all readers identify, willingly or not, with some character or some aspect of *Beloved*. The predictable reactions, "Yeah, I'm white, but I didn't own any slaves and neither did my Turkish immigrant grandparents" or "Toni Morrison—she's black and she's got more money than God! What does she need reparations for?" point out how the discourse of reparations is political but also personal and ultimately ethical—by what logic do *I* owe *you*, or *you* owe *me*?

At the broadest levels of political redress, answers to this question can remain overly general and unsatisfying, but the ethics of narrative encounter produces an intimate as well as compelling answer. Adam Zachary Newton's Levinas-inspired thesis on narrative ethics explains a reader-text relation of "facing" where the humanity of the voice of the text preconditions the reading experience as ethical. Newton cites Levinas and interpolates his philosophy into thinking about literature:

> "The approach to the face is the most basic mode of responsibility. As such, the face of the other is verticality and uprightness; it spells a relation of rectitude. The face is not in front of me but above me . . . In the relation to the face I am exposed as a usurper of the place of the other" [Levinas].

> One of my claims here is that certain kinds of textuality parallel this description of ethical encounter in several obvious ways . . . narrative situations create an immediacy and force, framing relations of provocation, call, and response that bind narrator and listener, author and character, or reader and text. (*Narrative* 13)

Beloved's hauntology hails us all, situating us in a subjective yet ethical relation with the book's story, but also our own. From there it is easy to see that braiding the history embedded in *Beloved* with the genealogies of its readers produces an aggregate reading of America, moving us from ethics to politics. A national discussion on the efficacy and limits of apology, forgiveness, compensation, and broadly conceived social redress begins when readers turn from the private encounter with the novel to the public history the text produces. The desire for historically corrective justice transcends but also sustains a free State as well as a state of freedom.[21] Working for justice is the "difficult freedom" Emmanuel Levinas describes that involves continually wrestling with history in order to achieve the present.

Perhaps the strongest case for a reparations-based analysis of *Beloved* is suggested by the word *reconciliation,* one of reparation's glosses. Reconciliation is a friendly word—conciliation being the state of friendly congress—but it bears nothing less than the weight of history, as it is deployed both ethically and politically, in South Africa, for example.[22] Again, avoiding a discussion of the process of such a program, we might consider at least the intended result and compare that against our wish-fulfilling dream-readings of *Beloved.* A state of reconciliation may be achieved through recognition or a formal apology. Material compensation is not tied to symmetrical restoration of what was lost, but rather serves a future-oriented project of reconciliation. Indeed, reconciliation is both pragmatically political as well as ethical, meaning the (re)establishment of a state affairs sufficient for forward progress by reconciling parties into the future.[23] Susan Dwyer's conception of reconciliation as a form of "narrative incorporation" is especially helpful for thinking about how literature might participate in this process: reconciliation means revising our sense of the past based on a full disclosure of what happened, who participated, and how; coherently linking that past to the crises or schisms of the present; and using that narrative to produce a political program for forward progress (102).[24] I suggest that such a narrative is the fullest and most fruitful kind of "historical consciousness" for readers of *Beloved.* The critics I cited here agree that Morrison's novel initiates this narrative by linking past and present, and I am arguing that we take the novel most seriously when we further the narrative through reconciliation ourselves.

Reconciliation does not demand total compensation for loss, which with slavery is infinite. As James Hans astutely observes, among the central insights of *Beloved* is Baby Suggs's maxim, "good is knowing when to stop" (87), which can be read as an injunction against infinite *ressentiment* (Hans 101). What can be claimed is ultimately unclaimable. Reparation is, after all, a derivation of "repair" or *re-pare,* return to the homeland. In this way, reparation is a concept that negates itself, but for the fact that Morrison provides a language and a conversation starter adequate for understanding what was lost and what can be gained. Ella's asymmetrical formula, "what's fair ain't necessarily right," releases the present from an infinite debt to the past and hinges it to a future based on a politics and ethics of responsibility and respect. Both Baby Suggs's and Ella's comments suggest a utilitarian conception of justice over an ideal justice: "knowing when to stop" and "right" replace an infinite "good" or "fair." At least we can talk about it. *Beloved* has been called a slave narrative, a rememory, and a "counter-history," re-envisioning our past. But it is also our present. The novel we read is the text that reads us, as the saying goes. To the extent that we make reparation a consequence of reading, the book is either our traumatic past or we are its reconciling future.

PART TWO··· The Location of Cultures

4··· BORDERS, DIASPORA, AND EXILE

In 1882 Emma Lazarus, the Jewish American poet most famous for con-tributing the epitaph at the base of the Statue of Liberty, published a pastoral poem about Jewish refugees in America titled "In Exile."[1] "In Exile" celebrates the relative refuge found by Russian Jewish immigrants who escaped from the pogroms of Eastern Europe. "Strange faces theirs, wherthough the Orient sun / Gleams" Lazarus writes. Stranger still, these Jews are not Talmudic scholars, or even tailors or peddlers like so many Jewish immigrants. But then, the Jews in Lazarus's poem are not settled in New York, but in Texas, yearning for

> Freedom to love the law that Moses brought,
>   To sing the songs of David, and to think
> The thoughts Gabirol to Spinoza taught,
>   Freedom to dig the common earth, to drink
> The Universal air—for this they sought
>   Refuge o'er wave and continent, to link
> Egypt with Texas in their mystic chain,
> And truth's perpetual lamp forbid to wane. (179)

The poem describes a unique moment in Jewish history, but it also tells us more about America than it might presume, and more about the consequences of American diasporas than we could learn by reading only Jewish history. If we take note of the poem's date we realize that Texas, after years of contest and occupation, nonetheless comprises a part of the frontier that will stoke the national imagination. Lazarus invokes the rhetoric of biblical destiny for American settlement, an American poetic mainstay since Puritan times, but wonderfully reappropriated in "In Exile." Whereas Puritan and, later, American Romantic writers and poets invoked the conceit of Hebraic covenation and liberation while eliding actual Jewish history—"dead nations never rise again," wrote Longfellow— Lazarus reappropriates the Exodus story and revises America's "errand in the wilderness" at the same time. America *is* the destined refuge for the Hebrews—actual Jews and not lately styled religious missionaries. That said, Lazarus's revision is nonetheless a buttressing of American Manifest Destiny, for it contributes to the myth of the open frontier and the romantic transformation that land might have upon people, as ancient Hebrews become American pioneers. While easterners moved across the "frontier," grabbing land and accruing capital, Mexicans dwelling in the region— suddenly granted U.S. citizenship after 1848—faced the loss of national identity, and vulnerability to a tangle of U.S. land-grant laws that would eventually facilitate the nearly complete usurpation of land from all Mexicans in the region (Limerick, *Legacy* 236–40).

Interesting, too, we note that Lazarus describes her pioneers in typical racialized terms, common to her time, their faces strange and oriental. But their faces did not stay strange for long, presumably becoming tawny and steely, like the (stereo)typical American pioneer. That is, these oriental Jews became Americans. How did this take place? To what extent did the Jewish assimilation depend on U.S. imperialism? Clearly the presence of darker-skinned Mexicans and mounting atmosphere of unrest preceding the Mexican Revolution quickened the pace of U.S. acceptance of Jews as Americans, especially in imperially contested regions. But the juxtaposition of Jews among other nonnormative cultures—a juxtaposition that all cultural groups in America more or less share—certainly had a significant effect on Jewish self-perception, and on future articulations of the American-Jewish sense of home and diaspora as well.

Juxtaposing two national phenomena like the arrival of immigrants and the settlement of the West does not mean that one is the cause of the other, but puts the two in conversation. The synchronic occurrence of each tells us something about the other, and much about what both have in common, namely the impact of U.S. history on ethnic identity. The arrival of waves of German Jews in the United States in the mid-nineteenth century, and then Eastern European Jews at the turn of the century, upset nascent Jewish American theologies of exile, while the sheer increase in bodies gave significant gravity to the Jewish diaspora in America. The arrival of immigrants fueled a growing desire to open up and settle more land; meanwhile, in the newly acquired U.S. borderlands a new "alien" population, speaking its own language, following a different set of land laws and agricultural customs, came in conflict with American goals for westward expansion and land development.

This brief look at the context of Lazarus's poem then is not a case study of how Jews encroached on Mexicans, but an epigram of how issues of identity and exile can be exclusionary. Thus, asking the following questions of both Jewish American and Chicano history will yield different answers in some cases, similar ones in others: What does it mean to be in exile? When does exile end and how is it different from diaspora? And what does it mean to be in exile, or diasporic, in postcolonial America? I write "postcolonial America" with all its suggestive ambivalence implied. Indeed, the United States was a still recently decolonized nation in the mid-nineteenth century, and its projected imago, America bordered north and south, extending sea to sea, was a key premise for the American Dream. More to the point, it was a colonizing, conquering empire as well, repressing a broader culture of the Americas. We read the moment following U.S. conquest of Mexico as postcolonial in two senses then, and this becomes further complicated by the politics of migration, as displaced people from Europe came to settle among dislocated, newly termed citizens of the United States.

It would be inaccurate to read Lazarus's poem as emblematic of Jewish migration to the United States. Comparatively few Jews settled in the West in the nineteenth century, and certainly not enough to be a primary force in displacing Mexicans from Texas.[2] Rather, the poem provides an occasion for problematizing tropes of diaspora and displacement, and to foreground especially America as a site where ethnic identities, predicated on displacement, remain unsettled. At the same time Jews were enjoying freedom in Texas, Mexicans were experiencing the shock of dispossession subsequent to colonization. The clash of perspectives on Texas reflects the paradox of America and highlights the postmodernity of the postcolonial moment we now live in. America is a place of both refuge and oppression, an exiling nation and a place of peace for exiles, replicated in the gaze of each in radically distinct ways. In particular, at the start of a new century we are faced with not just the question of colonizer or refuge, but the historical legacy of each as a fact. On the one hand there is the history of American solace and comfort where the immigrant can remake him- or herself. And there is the other reality, America as an "undoing world," to use Tony Kushner's term, America as the colonizing force that creates the hegemony across Latin America, thereby forcing the migrations it then accepts, either compelling individuals to mold to a version of success, or abjecting those that don't fit the narrative—illegals, criminals, welfare leeches, and worse.

Lazarus's poem exemplifies the search for tropes to adequately express the relationship of immigrants or racial others to America. Lazarus posits the American pastoral as the genre of return and renewal for immigrants, a romanticized portrait for sure, but not incommensurate with the broader Jewish American attempt at defining diaspora. Indeed, the poetics of diaspora are often willfully romantic, sentimental, and finally hopeful. The anxious debate in the nineteenth century about whether or not American Jews were in *galut* (exile) or merely dispersed is typical of the kinds of identity construction all ethnic groups in America work through at some point in their history. Currently, Chicano critical discourse has transitioned from an identity predicated on the trope of Aztlán—a nationalist, atavistic, and patriarchal identity that yet offers a powerful resistance ethic—to the trope of the border. For Chicanos, the border has recently become the critical trope par excellence, denoting as it does the liminal relationship most Chicanos feel to two countries at once, not to mention the contingent legal status each country grants them. Border culture, like Jewish diaspora culture, is rooted in a past of multiple displacements, and "home" for the Chicano as well as for the diasporic American Jew is less a real place and more a place in memory, a subject for theory, a work of art.

This chapter, then, places a nuanced reading of current critical debate on Jewish American diasporic identity alongside critical and literary writing about Chicano and Latino exile and displacement. Questions of nationalism, the itinerary of identity as it crosses borders, and especially an understanding of what America signifies when yoked to an ethnic prefix—that is, Jewish American, or Mexican American—are common to both groups. Of course, Jews are not now faced with the prospect of deportation, wage exploitation, or social racism, while immigrants from south of the border and Americans of Mexican and Central American descent do indeed live with these threats. But the differences between Jewish and Chicano history will be productive for advancing a general reading of the space of the nation in literature. Jews are finally a white ethnic group in America, while Chicanos have been construed (legally and culturally) in racial terms, but I aim to examine the history and narratives behind these designations.

In comparing the literature and criticism of Jews and Chicanos, I will use the term *ethnicity* in favor of race, not with the aim of eliding the racial formation of Chicano culture, but to call attention to the mutual construction of ethnic others and America. Ethnicity—cultural difference—not only indicates a minority group, but interpellates a dominant other, a dialectic where neither position is stable but always shifting in response to the gaze of the other. There is cause to be concerned about an overly easy collapse of racial designations into the category of ethnicity, of course. Despite recent scholarship that indicates that white European immigrants to America in the late nineteenth and early twentieth centuries were indeed typed as racially distinct, even "colored," it is also quite clear that these same immigrants or their children gained their white status in differential relation to African Americans, Native Americans, Asians immigrants, and Mexican Americans. Thus, though we may say that Jews, Italians, or Irish were considered racially different upon arrival in America, America itself fundamentally altered its concepts of race through federal legislation, liberal social reform, land-grant policies, union construction, and (crucially) literary imagination in order to reinscribe the white/colored racial dichotomy. Any comparison of the cultures of white ethnics and racial minorities in America must be not only mindful of these differences but intellectually engaged with them.

My comparison of the two literary identities will move along an axis of place and displacement, space and nationality. Jewish American theorizing on diaspora, especially turn-of-the-century, premodern-Zionist writing that attempted to reconcile America as a benevolent place of exile, will prove helpful for thinking about current questions of spatial designations in Chicano critical discourse and ethnic American literature in general. Having arrived at a theoretical model for critically reading "border" narratives, I'll turn to an exemplary work of literature, Helena María Viramontes's much-reviewed short story "The Cariboo Cafe."

Early Jewish communities in America sought either integration into the mainstream or mutual recognition from fellow Americans as full and equal citizens. In the late eighteenth century, the Hebrew Congregation of Newport, Rhode Island, sent a letter of allegiance and support to the newly elected George Washington, and received in return his pledge to give "to bigotry no sanction, to persecution no assistance" so long as the Jews "demean themselves as good citizens" (Isaacs and Olitzky 4). Washington's implied contingency clause was real enough, for in 1862 General Ulysses Grant issued an order to all his commanders in the Mississippi area forbidding Jewish employees from entering the Treasury Department. "The Jews," he wrote "as a class violating every regulation of trade established by the Treasury Department . . . are hereby expelled from the department within twenty four hours" (the order was rescinded by Lincoln) (16). Still, America was a relatively felicitous refuge, and eventually the vexed question arose among Jews: Are we at home here?

The question of home versus diaspora[3] turned on the increasing comfort and prosperity of Jewish communities, and the rise of the American Reform movement, which generally favored assimilation of Jews into American society. Reform Judaism adopted a christologized theodicy of exile, suggesting a "fortunate fall,"[4] which spread Jews to all corners of the world, including, happily, America. Relatively prosperous and unmolested, a Jew in America indeed "could believe he had found a new Zion, and Reform Rabbis were fond of saying so" (Eisen, *Chosen* 20). Early Jewish American leaders, such as Rabbi Isaac Mayer Wise (1819–1900) and Isaac Harby (1788–1828), adopted the transcendental, romanticist view of America. Romantic Christian appropriation of Jewish prophetic language for America—the New Jerusalem—was matched by American Jewish reformers who saw America as a home from exile. According to Michael Meyer, "For Emerson, as for Jewish Reformers, revelation was not limited to the past. America would be different from Europe because it would reach forward not backward" (226).

At the turn of the century, waves of Jewish immigrants from Eastern Europe, the institutionalization of anti-Semitism in America, and, chiefly, the rise of a viable political attempt by European Jews to settle Palestine all further complicated Jewish relations to America. Beginning in the early 1900s, Zionism in particular forced Jews to rethink their position in the diaspora. If Israel—the Jewish people, but also the proto-state developing in the Middle East—was indeed the Jewish homeland, what was

America? No consensus was (or has been) reached on this question, given the multivoiced, even factional nature of the Jewish communities of the United States, but the growing Reform movement (the most popular Jewish sect in the United States) decided to support the settlement of Palestine, though not necessarily advocating the resettlement of America's Jews. Leaders of the Reform movement in 1937 supported "the promise of renewed life for *many* of our brethren" (my emphasis; Isaacs and Olitzky 63). The hedge here represents a dialectical Zionism that did not entirely come to fruition but would have posited Israel as the necessary center of Jewish civilization, with the diaspora as the equally necessary and equally contributing periphery. "Many" would settle in Palestine, but many would not, supporting it and drawing from it, living . . . abroad? or at home? Though now the question is only theoretical—most American Jews feel perfectly at home—it became exceptionally pressing and urgent during the 1930s and '40s, and following the Holocaust, a critical mass of Jews around the world supported the creation of a Jewish state. The question, briefly put down in the nineteenth century, arises again: where is the Jew at home?

Jacob Neusner expresses the paradox of the American Jewish community's support for Zionism after the Shoah. American Jewish Zionists affirm Israel as the Jewish homeland and tacitly confirm their own state of exile on the one hand; on the other hand, there is little urgency to emigrate, nor does exile in America live up to the profound historical or theological exiles of Jews throughout the ages. As Neusner puts it, "it would be pretentious to elevate the banal affairs of a bored, and boring, ethnic group, unsure of its identity and unclear about its collective purpose and meaning, to a datum of either metaphysical or even merely historical hermeneutics" (104). Neusner's caustically stated point might not characterize all American Jewry, but it does seem to reflect a central majority of Jews who, having lost touch with culture, custom, and religion, support Israel as the sole means of maintaining Jewish identity. Neusner's critique of American Jewish diaspora consciousness raises a question for ethnic studies at large: Does the rubric of diaspora have certain parameters for all ethnic Americans? Or is each diaspora—African, Asian, Mexican, Jewish—different? Or do white diasporas—such as Jewish, Irish, Italian—really exist as such? If so, do they interrogate the primacy of an American home in the same way as other diasporas?

The paradox of American Jewish Zionism can be read as a hedged expression of Jewish affiliation on the one hand, but it also provides an occasion for theorizing and problematizing nationalism and identity for ethnic groups at large. To be Jewish in America might afford a distance from which to critique American ideology, especially regarding the assimilation of ethnicity into the mainstream, and to affiliate with Israel need not be an affirmation of nationalism, for there are other models of the renewal of Jewish peoplehood not solely based on the centrality of land.[5] For example, Ahad Ha'am (born Asher Ginsberg, 1856–1927), proposed a Zionism based less on nationalism and more on cultural awakening. Ahad Ha'am was skeptical of the Zionists' ability to coax land from the Turks, and he anticipated conflict with Arabs already living in Palestine. Instead of a nation in Palestine, Ahad Ha'am proposed a cultural settlement that would renew Jewish theology, education, and language. His most noteworthy innovation for today is his philosophy of the dialectical relationship between Israel and the diaspora:

> The Palestinian settlement should be grounded in a gathering not so much of the dispersed people as of the scattered energies of the Jewish people. It was to serve as a place of refuge for the Jewish culture, a center from which the influence would radiate to the Dispersion. In Palestine Judaism would be regenerated, not by means of revolutionary reforms, but by steady evolution, in adjustment to the very exigencies of the new life. (Margolis and Marx 713)

Israel would be the center for spiritual renewal of Judaism, but not the center of Judaism itself. Out from Palestine would radiate Jewish culture and education, but the Middle East would remain decentered; instead, the diaspora would remain the center of Jewish civilization (a notion that oddly deconstructs the concept of centeredness). The diaspora would be expected to invest money, intellectual energy, and idealism into Palestine, thereby sustaining Jewish civilization, which diaspora Jews need to maintain their Jewish identity (Margolis 713).

In recent years, versions of Ahad Ha'am's Zionism have emerged as philosophies of "post-Zionism," which advocate a nonnationalistic, dialectical model of Jewish identity. Writing just after the signing of the Oslo peace accords, historian Norman Cantor speculates on the future of Israel-diaspora relations: "First, as the age of political Zionism lapses, there will be a reversion to the cultural Zionism advocated in the second and third decades of this century by Asher Ginsberg (Ahad Ha'am)" (12). Cantor advances a vision of increased investment by American Jews in Israeli universities, to which they will later send their children. American born and raised, Jewish undergrads would receive their Jewish "finishing" in Israel.[6] During the same year Cantor's article appeared, *Critical Inquiry* published a piece by Daniel Boyarin and Jonathan Boyarin which also called for a decentering of Zionism in Jewish life. Here the authors "propose Diaspora as a theoretical and historical model to replace national self-determination" (711). The authors argue that diaspora is more fundamentally the condition of Jewish civilization, while nationalism is "a subversion of rabbinic Judaism" (719).

Beyond partaking of the philosophy of Ahad Ha'am, the Boyarins offer a radical revision of the role of peoplehood for Jews around the world. Beginning with the premise that the nation of Israel constructs the present-day diasporic-Jewish notion of self, the authors seek to untangle Jewish consciousness from nationalism. At the center of Jewishness in the diaspora, the nation of Israel normalizes Jews, assimilates them into the Western discourse of nationalism, thereby rendering the Jewish religious impulse ("to be a light unto the nations") moot. For the Boyarins, the decentering of Zionism is intended to heighten the influence of Jews in the world rather than diminish it. Here the constructive work of imagination becomes crucial again. As the authors see it, Western religions have assimilated Jewish monotheism, and diaspora Jews are assimilating Western nationalism. In contrast, the Boyarins imagine a revised diaspora without assimilation, where Jewish difference is manifested for didactic effect within the host country: "Indeed, we would suggest that Diaspora, and not monotheism, may be the most important contribution that Judaism has to make to the world. . . . Assimilating the lesson of Diaspora, namely that peoples and lands are not naturally and organically connected, could help prevent bloodshed such as that occurring in Eastern Europe today" (722). Immediately, we may notice how much the Boyarins' theory contradicts the romantic nationalism of not only Zionism but of early Jewish responses to life in America as well; Jewish difference and nation-lessness would work to undermine conventional nationalist thinking, predicated as it is on sameness and borders. Diaspora Judaism, working within other nations, would deconstruct border-based nationalism and effect a messianic "peace among nations." Diaspora, more than a way of life for Jews, would be a theoretical alternative that other ethnic groups could draw on—similar in effect to borderlands theory in Chicano critical discourse. According to the Boyarins' formulation, America is home precisely because it is diasporic; neither the "homeland" nor the Jewish nation, America is a place where Jews can be comfortably uncomfortable, physically and socially safe, not pejoratively marked as interlopers exactly, but different all the same. Or, to recall our earlier terms, racial difference would give way to an ethnicity where difference is at once obdurate and deconstructive in a mutually interpellating dialectic.

The Boyarins' proposal is both theoretically challenging and ethically satisfying, and it merits serious thought, yet it rests on an assumption that seems untenable to me. Diaspora is as much about geographic dispersal as it is about self-perception—the perception of any individual Jew within the country he or she lives in. The history of diaspora Judaism, until as recently as 1988 with the fracture of Soviet Union, has been predicated on enforced exile; presently, however, it is doubtful that most Jews recognize their "dispersed" condition. Jewish difference (a concept that enjoys a resurgence as a postmodern trope) is waning in daily life, while assimilation and tolerance are increasing. Can there be a diaspora without an exile model? If an ethnic group is dispersed and remains so voluntarily, is it still diasporic? Still ethnic?

To add a third term to the questioning here, it seems clear that comfortable *class* standing has something to do with the waning sense of Jewish exile, and so we must consider to what extent Jewish diaspora theories are predominantly ideological artifacts of middle-class living? Where Neusner sees American Jewish cultural anxieties as "bored and boring," we might more aptly term them *bourgeois.* The fact is, many Jews feel at home living where they are, outside of Israel, because their class standing is so high.[7] We may well ask, then, whether diaspora isn't finally a middle-class descriptor, referencing sentimental interests in a putative home. If this is the case, all the more reason why politically sincere (and avidly leftist) intellectuals like the Boyarins would want to revitalize an ethics of diaspora, focusing emotional and ethical energy not on the homeland but on jeremiads among the hosts.

The Boyarins' idea gains support for this project (though the source might not advance their purpose), from none other than Philip Roth's comic/pathetic character Pipik in *Operation Shylock,* also published in

1993. Moshe Pipik is cast as the fictionalized Philip Roth's double, and as such he is both a foil for and a key to Roth's own imagination. Pipik (whose "real" name in the novel is also Philip Roth) usurps the famous author's identity and the two confront each other in Jerusalem where Roth has come to write and Pipik has come to espouse "Diasporism." Pipik explains his life's mission to Roth in terms uncannily similar to the Boyarins': "Diasporism seeks to promote the dispersion of the Jews in the West, particularly the resettlement of Israeli Jews of European background in the European countries where there were sizable Jewish populations before World War Two" (45). Here the terms, if not the ethical thrust, are similar to those in the Boyarins' essay. Pipik also acknowledges "the exhaustion of Zionism as a political and ideological force" (45). One of the funniest and most-often-quoted lines from Roth's novel rings as a hilarious send-up of the Boyarins' didactic project. Roth, chiasmatically assuming the identity of his own impersonator, finds himself praising "the greatest Diasporist of all, the father of the new Diasporist movement, Irving Berlin": "People ask where I got the idea [for Diasporism]. Well, I got it listening to the radio. The radio was playing 'Easter Parade' and I thought, But this is Jewish genius on par with the Ten Commandments. God gave Moses the Ten Commandments and then he gave Irving Berlin 'Easter Parade' and 'White Christmas'" (157).

In Roth's imagination, diasporic Irving Berlin is on par with Moses; for the Boyarins, Mosaic-Monotheism is superseded only by the diaspora. The didactic power that the Boyarins would attribute to a diaspora movement, Roth grants to Irving Berlin's "shlock": "Easter [Berlin] turns into a fashion show and Christmas into a holiday about snow. Gone is the gore and murder of Christ—down with the crucifix and up with the bonnet! *He turns their religion into schlock.* But nicely! Nicely!" (157). Just as the Boyarins' diaspora movement results in a "dissociation of ethnicities and political hegemonies," so does Roth's Diasporism effect a "Christianity cleansed of Jew hatred," both resulting in a more tolerant and pluralistic West (Boyarin and Boyarin, "Diaspora" 723; Roth, *Operation Shylock* 157).

The Boyarins' idealism and Roth's lampooning comedy are both powerful expressions of a desire for an alternative Jewish identity. The Boyarins value an identity that is collective and empowered, but not in power, an "identity in which there are only slaves but no masters" (711). This is

perhaps too easily said when one is not a slave, but as a theoretical construct it resonates the Rothian vision of the resettlement of Jews in non-
Jewish countries, thereby creating a minority that is also minoritarian.
Indeed, Roth's Irving Berlin is a counterhegemonic or "minor" artist, in
Deleuze and Guattari's use of the term, in just this sense, working inside
the majority language and tropology to alter dominate ideologies of
difference. Pipik himself is certainly not "bored and boring": In addition
to espousing Diasporism, Pipik runs an "anti-Semites anonymous" clinic,
"converting" Jew-haters into more tolerant Americans. Pipik, in effect,
does the leg work for the Boyarins, helping goyish America accept, even
value the Jewish other in its midst. In *Operation Shylock* Roth's America
is not a home for Jews, but Jews are uniquely woven through and belonging to it.

To be at home but diasporic at the same time is a theoretical goal for
Jews, perhaps, but the formulation is not all celebratory, nor entirely a
cerebral exercise, for it is a formula for social and economic survival.
Indeed, while the "diaspora at home" model is close cousin to nineteenth-
century European Jewish reformist sentiments that advocate that one be
a Jew at home but a *mensch* (a man) in public, it was not long ago that
Jews were almost entirely eliminated from Central Europe, and even more
recently Soviet Jews were persecuted for practicing Judaism. Critically,
Jews in America, though their grandparents may have emigrated from
Europe, are "dispersed" from Israel, the mother country offering refuge
as a last resort. Thus, American Jewish investment (psychic, financial, cultural) in Israel is a strategic hedge on a possibly dire future, predicated on
the premise that America may one day be less "homely" than it presently
is. In America, whether in the relative comfort Jews enjoy, or the challenging, even dangerous circumstances Chicanos and Latinos encounter,
diasporic populations "are enmeshed in circuits of social, economic, and
cultural ties encompassing the mother country and the country of settlement" (Lavie and Swedenburg 14). Presently, for many Jews Israel is a
source of pride and joy, but if pressed they will admit the primary basis
for their Zionism: "If, God forbid, it were to ever happen again . . . ," a
sentiment sanctioned more or less explicitly in Israel's own Law of Return
which accepts all Jewish immigrants as citizens.

How does this compare with the diasporic condition of other ethnic
Americans? Israel is indeed a psychical and strategic homeland for Jews,

but is this the same kind of relation Chicanos have with Mexico? During the Depression Mexicans living in California and Texas were forced (by a combination of economic necessity and legal coercion) to repatriate to Mexico, thereby forcing crises of national identification among the repatriates (Sanchez chap. 10). The old-newcomers were regarded with a certain amount of veneration for bringing Western culture and know-how on the one hand, but they were also derided for having lost touch with authentic Mexican culture. Indeed, even today Mexican Americans have an ambivalent relation with both Mexico and the United States, regarded by the mainstreams of both as a cultural other, speaking an inferior dialect, with an alien set of values. This, of course, necessitates a critique of national in-between-ness, not quite the same as Jewish thinking on diaspora, and Chicano border theory has certainly provided this. But if Jewish theories of diaspora have theoretical weaknesses or blindspots, what would a critical review of Chicano border theory show us? Is each theory only effective for understanding the respective ethnicity? Or can each be rethought, separately but also in terms of each other, to articulate an effective critical trope available to multiethnic literature scholars? This would be no scholastic exercise, but a difficult evaluation of differing responses to the United States by its ethnic others.

As Lazarus's poem at the beginning of this chapter indicates, the imaginative construction of diaspora for Jews was part of a widespread cultural articulation of "the American Dream," a dream that was authorized by the mainstream, but given a voice by European ethnic immigrants. Adding to the paradox, although the Jews in Lazarus's poem are "in exile" as the title suggests, the migration of European ethnic Americans to the borderlands had a whitening effect: Immigrants of non-Anglo-Saxon Europe who were otherwise considered racially inferior to whites were transformed into the new white vanguard by settling among a Mexican population construed as savage and "other" (Jacobson 206).[8] Furthermore, the dream of America as a happy refuge for European ethnic immigrants occludes the realities of the border, the presence of an indigenous population, or the legacy of slavery. A revision of Chicano border theory, which attempts to account for the cultural and legal alienation of non-immigrant ethnic Americans, alongside a revised theory of diaspora may finally build a theoretical bridge for reading the culture of all ethnic Americans. Such a project ultimately exceeds the scope of this chapter, but in writing about it, and implicitly modeling the critical comparisons I am calling for, I hope to prompt further inquiry in that direction.

The concept of the borderland has become so significant for Chicanas and antipatriarchal Chicanos because it intervenes in what was a once-dominant symbology of Chicano politics, the trope of the reconstructed Aztec nation, *Aztlán*. Constructed against the hegemony of colonization in the Americas, Aztlán is the trope for the regathering of Chicano national identity. The trope of the nation, of course, necessarily invokes inclusions and exclusions, and activates the chauvinisms—patriarchal, heterosexist—of its constituents, thereby excluding those like Gloria Anzaldúa, a lesbian feminist. For Anzaldúa, Chicano/as need a place without rigid identity strictures, one that expresses the multiple, even contradictory natures of its inhabitants: "I, like other queer people, am two in one body, both male and female. I am the embodiment of the *hieros gamos:* the coming together of opposite qualities within" (19). With Anzaldúa, contradictions beget contradictions: "As a *mestiza* I have no country, my homeland cast me out, yet all countries are mine because I am every woman's sister or potential lover" (80). Thus it is that Anzaldúa is between countries, living on a border that is porous, across which she can and will travel. For Anzaldúa, *mestizaje* is a way of translating the self into and through the various cultures one always already potentially inhabits. However, though the mestiza "learns to be an Indian in Mexican culture, to be Mexican from an Anglo point of view" (78–79), this is a grim choice, foregrounding the racializing conundrum produced by the U.S. colonization of northern Mexico and the subsequent border—a thousand-mile-long open wound (3)—it produced. To be either Mexican or Indian is to have to adapt oneself to the racializing gaze of the other, and though this may be a "Derridean deconstructive gesture" (Alarcón 48), it does little to defang racist nationalism inflicted on those who dwell on the border. It is one thing for the Boyarins to deconstruct nationalist-based identity when a Jewish nation with a "Law of Return" does exist, and Jews by and large do not face persecution in the United States. But a deconstructive psychoanalysis of the scopic construction of Chicano identity won't counter America's own "law of return"—especially since 9/11—the effort to round up "illegal" immigrants and deport them, nor does it help calm the hysteria in California that led to the passage of

Proposition 187 and the anti–Spanish language legislation, Proposition 227.

Anzaldúa, Guillermo Gomez-Peña, and José David Saldívar, are among the many who argue for the transnationality of identity, and the argument has gained great favor among academics, especially people of color, and "hybridized" border-dwellers. But border theory is dependent on a nuanced, dialectical reading of history, and Americans tend to resist history, especially the history of U.S. imperialism. Ironically, or perhaps not, this resistance is evident even with regard to contemporary U.S. foreign policy in South and Central America. Throughout the 1980s, during the Reagan and first Bush administrations, the United States exerted a military hegemony over the region, working to undo democratic elections on the one hand (in Nicaragua), while supporting dictators on the other (Chile). U.S. foreign policy during the 1980s (though not only then) could itself be termed a politics of the borderlands, acknowledging the porousness, even the interconnectedness of the region. Although a malignant and cynical version to be sure, such a borderlands foreign policy, already implied in *Borderlands/La Frontera,* structures our relation to the border as much as the postmodernity of the border region.

Similarly, circuits of economic exchange routinely traverse the border, as the very term *migrant worker* suggests. In California in particular, many so-called illegal immigrants defy older versions of immigration—the permanent, one-way trip across the Atlantic—traveling back and forth between the United States and Mexico depending on the growing seasons, the economy, even local festivals in the home community. The border, more than a region, is the condition of a large Latino diaspora, not only its locus but also the terms on which a diasporic community negotiates its relations with home and host countries. Roger Rouse, writing on migrant workers who regularly travel hundreds of miles between Northern California and Michoacan, Mexico, describes the negotiation this way:

Indeed, through the continuous circulation of people, money, goods, and information, the various settlements [in home and host countries] have become so closely woven together that, in an important sense, they have come to constitute a single community spread across a variety of sites, something I refer to as a "transnational migrant circuit." . . . Ties such as those between Aguililla and Redwood City, places two thousand miles

apart, prompt us to ask how wide this border has become and how peculiar we should consider its characteristics. (14–15)

I would add this question: is *border* the right term just now? Though I'm
not prepared to discard it, it needs to be seriously rethought, to cover dialectical relationships of economic and military push-pull.

Anzaldúa and others claim the border as "home" (even if ambivalently), but the very concept of home now needs to be thought through
in terms of diasporic negotiations of home and exile. As Rouse puts it,

> In the United States, as well as in Mexico, the *place* of the putative com-
> munity—whether regional or national—is becoming little more than a *site*
> in which transnationally organized circuits of capital, labor, and communi-
> cations intersect with one another and with local ways of life. In these cir-
> cumstances, it becomes increasingly difficult to delimit a singular national
> identity. (16–17)

Communities of migrant workers may dwell in the borderlands, but the
border itself is displaced, spread out, diasporic. The implications for reading ethnic American literature are at least twofold. First, we see their relevance of theorizing diaspora for reading ethnicity, even inflecting diaspora into border theory; Chicanos dwell in America, to be sure, but
America harbors a "greater Mexico." Second, ethnic Americans are not
the only ones subject to a diasporic reading; rather, America at large is the
site of diaspora, all the more so when we consider that the border—the
nation's outer limits and contact zone with its "outsiders"—is displaced
into American cultural centers, including Chicago, New York, and Los
Angeles. This is not the sentimental diaspora criticized by Neusner above,
but the revisionist version suggested by the Boyarins and Roth, where the
otherness of the ethnic American may challenge the separation of citizens
and "aliens," the inside and outside of the nation.

Helena María Viramontes's short story "The Cariboo Cafe," exposes
the intertwining of U.S. foreign and economic policy with the politics of
the border. The story narrates the lives of border crossers, but here the
border crossing of the protagonists is matched, even instigated by the
border crossing of U.S. foreign policy. Adding to the transnational circuits of migrant workers suggested by Rouse, the story narrates the similar oscillations of U.S. military and economic policies, thereby further
complicating our growing theory of the border. Not only do migrants

cross the border, but industry and the military do as well, projecting the border from the inside to the outside of the nation.

"The Cariboo Cafe" is parsed in separate disjointed sections, following a series of characters whose lives become tragically tangled. In the first section Sonya (around six years old) and her baby brother, Macky, are inadvertently locked out of their parents' apartment, somewhere north of the Mexican border. The parents, illegal immigrants, are both at work and have warned the children never to venture far from the apartment, never trust the "polie" for they are *la migra* in disguise, and never talk to strangers. Section 1 ends with the children lost, wandering a warehouse district, approaching a strange lady who seems to offer help.

Section 2 introduces the owner and operator of the Cariboo Cafe, a man down on his luck, unable to afford any wait-help, or even a dishwasher. Coping poorly with the breakup of his family, the café owner finds himself increasingly a peer of the junkies, drunks, and homeless who loiter in his café. Among the other liminal figures who enter are a strange woman and two children, clearly not her own. Watching the nightly news, the café owner learns that the children have been reported missing, possibly kidnapped, but upholding his own rule to never talk to the "polie," he declines to inform them of what he knows.

In the final section, the putative kidnapper, a washerwoman by trade, narrates her own story in a hazy jumble of memory and motive. A native of Nicaragua,[9] the woman suffers the loss of her own child, a victim during the U.S.-sponsored Contra rebellion of the eighties. Unable to bear living in her home, she migrates north, first to Mexico, eventually to Los Angeles where she works as a washerwoman. Still suffering the trauma of loss, still in a haze of grief, she encounters the wandering Sonya and Macky and perceives the young boy as her own lost child.

"The Cariboo Cafe" begins with a nearly anonymous and prototypical scene of illegal-immigrant border crossing which gives us much initial insight into Viramontes's vision of the space of America: "They arrived in the secrecy of night, as displaced people often do, stopping over for a week, a month, eventually staying a lifetime. The plan was simple. Mother would work, too, until they saved enough to move into a finer future where the toilet was one's own and the children needn't be frightened. In the meantime, they played in the back alleys, among the broken glass, wise to the ways of the streets" (65). This opening passage represents the underbelly of the American Dream, as seen from the perspective of the immigrant. Not entering by way of Ellis Island, but "in the secrecy of the night," not as hopeful immigrants, but as displaced people, people out of place who must dwell in the "meanwhile" while striving for a "finer future." Crossing the border does not garner one entrance into America, as the "inside" of America is reserved for insiders only.

In addition to the inside and outside of the nation, then, there is the liminal space of "meanwhile," that condition of dangerous stasis that separates the haves and the have-nots of the country. This space of "meanwhile" (described more below) is essentially the space of the border described by Chicano theorists previously mentioned, but by changing the terms we may dislocate the border from its geographical specificity and perhaps increase our understanding of the broad effects of liminality, not in order to do away with border theory, but to add to our understanding of how the nation implicates itself in the production of border liminality.

In "The Cariboo Cafe" the white café owner also occupies this liminal time-space, as do a series of characters who enter and exit the café, including transients, junkies, and the police. Just as the immigrants view a toilet of one's own as a signifier for arrival in America, so too is the café owner fighting a losing battle for control of his own toilet. The toilet, a trope for technology and hygiene, but also suggesting class status, privacy, and freedom from surveillance, signals a pared-down version of the American Dream.[10] At one point, a familiar junkie comes into the café to use the bathroom and overdoses, passing out and virtually erupting from both ends, coating the bathroom with the foul detritus of his toxic life. The café owner has no choice but to clean the mess himself, and in doing so he becomes figuratively linked to the Nicaraguan washerwoman in particular, and experiences the immigrant's exposure to a toxic environment in general.

Later the same day, the café owner's toilet is again taken over, this time when a nearby sweatshop is invaded by the INS, and some workers flee into the café, hiding in the bathroom. When the police enter the café for the second time that day, the owner is in a double bind. Previously, when they came around looking for the junkie, the café owner rejected their accusation that he was a drug dealer, but when they enter again he chooses between covering for the workers at his own risk or exposing them to the police, thus aligning himself with powers he had previously repudiated. Feeling guilty, he confesses to the reader, "I was all confused, you know. . . . I guess that's why I pointed [the cops] to the bathroom" (72). Pointing to the bathroom points him out as a subject of police surveillance and coercion, and underscores his status as a liminal figure. Later in the story, the café owner's confusion with the police is paralleled by the washerwoman's mad attack on them when they try to arrest her for kidnapping. Critically, her resistance revises the café owner's acquiescence, but we learn that with both, anger toward the coercive authorities springs from a similar well, for he too has lost a son, missing in action in the Vietnam War.

Viramontes is careful not to draw a dividing line between Latinos and Anglos here, even though the café owner has exposed the undocumented workers to the police. In fact, she shows us that he acts without agency, forced to submit to the law or have his café shut down. As he says, describing his interrogation by the police, "I had the cops looking up my ass" (71). Here, as José Limón suggests in another context, the themes of "anality, pollution, and bodily penetration" link the café owner, the junkie, and the migrant workers in a "body politic symbolically conscious of its socially penetrable status" (Limón, *Dancing with the Devil* 131). The café owner's bodily exposure parallels the surveillance of undocumented immigrants, and Viramontes likewise invokes images of corporeal disfigurement (as a synecdoche for oppressive labor conditions) to link the café owner with the liminal figures who come to the café. The café owner describes himself as "burning [his] goddamn balls off with spitting grease" and is fascinated with the body of a young woman named Delia who comes around: "That Delia's got these unique titties. One is bigger than the other. Like an orange and a grapefruit. I kid you not. They're like that on account of when she was real young she had some babies, and they all sucked only one favorite tittie" (69). The café owner's fascination with the woman's breasts, and the hyperbolic imbalance in life they suggest, mirror his own imbalance since his wife—the more diplomatic and shrewd Nell—left him, as well as his own role as one who feeds and sustains (albeit with meager resources) the workers and transients of his neighborhood.

The café owner is not the primary protagonist of the story, but he is crucial for reading how Viramontes imagines this borderzone world. Border conflict is often figured as a manichean space contested by "haves" and "have-nots," laborers and owners, or more generally, Anglo Americans and Latino immigrants. With "The Cariboo Cafe," however, difference and putative privilege (parceled out dialectically) give way as all the border-dwellers are caught up not just in the same space, but, metaphorically speaking, in the same time, the "meanwhile" between a past and future. Not just a contested space, or a site for oppression of one group by another, the border is described as a place that draws all its inhabitants into similar economic, social, and physical marginality. The border is not just the edge, or the outer limits of the country. The border is within America, a *version* of America. It is critical to read the café owner as a border-dweller along with the undocumented workers in order to implicate the United States in the manufacture of the border as oppressive site. Rather than a potential cite of alien transgression that must be policed, we see the borderlands are in fact produced by just this surveillance that enforces liminality. Nor is America passive with respect to its borderzones. Rather, it generates them, or is implicated in their development, as the café owner's forced complicity with the police makes clear.

Indeed, in "The Cariboo Cafe" Viramontes very shrewdly demonstrates the way official U.S. narratives and policy—that is, foreign policy— during the 1980s project an America beyond the official border and incorporate Latin America into the U.S. imagination. The tragic washerwoman of "The Cariboo Cafe" is Viramontes's figure for the displacing effects of U.S. foreign policy abroad. Not affiliated with the military, not a political instigator or a social organizer, the washerwoman, nameless throughout the story, is a common citizen, caught up in her country's civil war. Her story is simple: she sent her young son out for mangoes one morning and he did not come back. Viramontes is careful not to align the washerwoman with a political bent; in the story it is just as likely that her son was murdered—they suggest he was a spy—by the Sandinista police as by the U.S.-backed Contras. All she knows is that the civil war, fomented by forces outside her country, has somehow taken her son, and she is spiritually homeless: "These four walls are no longer my house; the earth beneath it, no longer my home" (75). The woman's sense of homelessness develops while she is still in Nicaragua, not yet homeless, but living an "unhomely" life nonetheless. Her diaspora begins at home, and her movement northward is not into but through a liminal space of political and economic disenfranchisement. National origins matter for a number of reasons, certainly, but they do not indicate an essential "home" in this story. Just as the washerwoman is alienated in her native country, so too is the café owner not at home north of the border.

Significantly, there is almost no mention of the border in "The Cariboo Cafe," and no depiction of the washerwoman's border crossing. In fact, concrete determinations of place are mostly absent throughout the text. Though not explicitly stated, we infer she is Nicaraguan by her reference to the Contras. But where in the United States does the story take place? Again, the terrain—railroad tracks, a warehouse district, the garment factories—suggest a heterotopic metropolis, likely Los Angeles, but even this is not certain. The confusion is compounded by the hallucinatory perspective of the washerwoman in the third section of the story, who herself does not always seem to know where she is. At a crucial point in the story, when she spots Macky and confuses him for her son, the washerwoman effects a recrossing of the border, a dash across a busy street to Macky on the other side: "I jumped the curb, dashed out into the street, but the street is becoming wider and wider. I've lost him once and can't lose him again and to hell with the screeching tires and the horns and the headlights barely touching my hips" (76). Her dash for "her son" is effectively a crossing back into her past, back into Central America, the site of the initial trauma. The washerwoman is back in Central America at this point, or has brought Central America with her, superimposing it onto the equally dangerous terrain of this unnamed northern city.

Viramontes's technique for representing her displaced protagonist, then, effects a displacement, or dislocation of the reader. Because we are unable to locate characters according to their environment, we are unable to "place" them as well. Though we know that certain characters are nominally "illegal" workers, they seem no more out of place than those who we would assume are "legal"—the café owner, the junkies, and so on. The ruling police are present in time and space—death asserts itself—but even they and the terror they bring are imported, in the washerwoman's mind, from Central America. The story then, as much as it is about displacement, is itself a "displacing" narrative act, asking readers to suspend judgments regarding class, caste, and legal definitions of home.

Border theory, up until now, has primarily described the conditions of diasporic people in the United States, or people whose national affiliations are ambivalent because they are born in a liminal borderzone.

With "The Cariboo Cafe" we see that the borderzone reaches far beyond the border, displacing people on the very ground on which they live. The term *border* here might even seem itself misplaced, inappropriate given the distance between Central America and the United States; nor should we forget the agency of the Nicaraguans in their own civil war, advanced by but not exclusively staged by the United States. Viramontes's story helps us see that the border is as much a physical place as psychic reality for the dominant U.S. majority, popularly perceived as a bulwark that needs to be guarded at all costs. The border, is after all, the tool for U.S. foreign policy in the Americas, and Viramontes's story is finally about the internationalist effects of border-crossing—the United States crossing its own border, the washerwoman crossing into the United States, caught up in "the dialectics of our America."[11] The washerwoman's final and deadly battle with the police confirms her own sense that the border is a wide-open, nonnationalistic zone, as she conflates the local police with her native country's military.

In a multiperspectival story such as "The Cariboo Cafe" rigid determinations of proprietary place and space, authority and resistance give way to a phenomenology of experience which, though difficult to articulate, may be, if clarified, exceptionally useful for thinking about the border as both subject and object of ethnic American literature. As we have seen, individuals in the same space can find themselves in entirely different places, constructed and perceiving others based not so much on any actual physical border, but on an ethics of spatiality they carry "within." And though I write "within," it is not so much an internal mechanism, a way of thinking on, or a political attitude regarding the border that aligns, say, the washerwoman's son and Macky, or the police in California and the military in Central America; instead, characters in the story *embody* a border-ethicopolitic that results from the subject's physical *and* psychic experiences with the border. The washerwoman, for example, is a border crosser in legal fact, but after her son is "disappeared," space for her is conditioned by the binary of presence and absence, rather than north and south. Where her son is, she is at home. The café owner, not a border crosser in legal fact, does cross legal borders, and his working conditions—opening and closing the café, and running it in between with no help, sleeping in a back room after hours—align him with the *maquiladoras,* the illegal garment workers he feeds.

To pursue this border/body relation and thus propose a model for thinking about the border and how it constructs a diasporic consciousness, I want to suggest the metaphor of a Mobius strip, a three-dimensional, horizontal figure eight. Elizabeth Grosz uses the Mobius strip as a metaphor for the body's border, namely skin, to structure her philosophy of the body, and though the border is our primary subject here, it becomes increasingly apparent that borders and bodies have more than a little in common. Grosz explain,

> [The body's skin] is the twisting Mobius strip, the torsion or pivot around which the subject is generated. The double sensation [of touching oneself] creates a kind of *interface* of the inside and the outside, the pivotal point at which inside will become separated from the outside and active will be converted into passive (a line of border which is not unlike the boundary established by the duplicating structure of the mirror, which similarly hinges on the pivotal plane represented by the tain of the mirror). (36)

If we inserted "border" for "Mobius strip" in Grosz's first sentence, we would have an accurate account of the dynamic consequences of the border in the Chicano literature we have looked at so far: The border, crossed or not, generates a subjectivity for each character, locating each both inside and outside official boundaries; or, better yet, each character embodies the dynamic folding of inside and outside that the border represents. Thus we see how an individual can be displaced while at "home": not only can the map include and exclude a nation's subjects, but so can its policies—legal and economic, foreign and domestic. Extending our earlier considerations of diaspora, we see that to be diasporic is not just to be on foreign soil, but to be foreign to the land in which one dwells; whether in conscious opposition to, or from subtle (and not so subtle) rejection by the state, diaspora is the condition of living inside-out/outside-in the space that would be home.

Furthermore, I want to double the efficacy of the Mobius-strip metaphor to argue that the United States itself, acting as self-contained "America" while operating across the Americas folds the inside out, the outside in. "America" here refers not to the United States so much as the imaginary-order version the United States projects. "America," extending from sea to shining sea, and bordered north and south is the image of the United States whole and self-contained, self-possessed, wrapped in a skin, the skin of its borders. In Grosz's formulation the skin of the body folds inward like a Mobius strip, and I want to posit here that the United States, projected in ideology and military policy as "America," is likewise generated by the twisting, torsional border. The border, like a skin, is the inside's contact zone with the outside, but it also folds the outside in: Immigrant workers, Latino culture, imported agriculture, military recruits; Jewish refugees, Yiddish culture, the Holocaust—all pass through portals in the border and become part of "America" itself.

The metaphor is not intended to exhaust all possible readings of the border, but does, I hope, account for the implicating, enfolding, paradoxically inside-out relation between the United States and its others, be they immigrants, ethnic groups within, or dissidents abroad. Reduced to stark literalism, the border would define who (and what and where) was inside the United States and who outside; the literature we read in this chapter shows us, on the contrary, that these neat distinctions will not hold up. The washerwoman, still in Nicaragua, is implicated in U.S. ideological processes and into the United States itself; The café owner lives on the margins of the law; even Roth's Moshe Pipik, father of Diasporism, posits himself as an outsider but requires an inside position to do so. The border, read as a site of diaspora, helps us read ethnic American literature as a construct of both the ethnic group's experiences and America's ever changing relationship to its ethnic others.

I have put theories of diaspora and the border into conversation in this chapter to see what they might say to each other about the respective literatures. Criticism and literature on Jewish diaspora, read without context, seems overly theoretical and (to put it playfully) lacks an "edge." Border theory provides that edge, the sense of what is at stake in diaspora, not just for Jews but for a general theory of the literary construction of American. Reading diaspora in both Jewish and Chicano literature, we find an America grappling with (if not necessarily recognizing) the outside turned in, the inside harboring outposts of the third world. I have tried to displace or disperse border theory from the border itself, reading it as a dividing line of social difference. The border as we see it does not separate America from its others but draws them in and deposits them as part and parcel of the nation. Enfolding the other is not the same as embracing the other, of course, and so I read the border as still a dangerous place to be different. Nonetheless, I recognize that my torqued border, troped as the Mobius strip, loses some of the specificity of experience described by Anzaldúa and others. Mine is not an attempt to revise or replace Anzaldúa's version of the borderlands; I do not wish to widen and thereby whiten it. Rather, as I hope I have made clear, I am borrowing the insights and tropes of Chicano literature and criticism, already intact, to help define ethnic American literature at large. Diaspora and border theories are particularly useful because they do more than just respond to America; they describe it, give an account of its internal workings, and thereby suggest a way of thinking about America useful for literature studies in general. By "dispersing" the border—that is, theorizing it in terms of diaspora—we see that the relation between ethnic Americans and the mainstream is less manichean and more implicate. This does not mean, in some glossy way, that all Americans or even all ethnic Americans have vital interests in common, or "common ground," as it were. Rather a border-based theory of implicate relations becomes a starting point for social criticism, providing the vocabulary for a dialogue on how ethnic Americans are "othered" in the first place, and how they may counter-discursively interrogate specular America.

5··· OUTING ETHNICITY, "UNDOING" NATIONALISM

Gloria Anzaldúa's celebrated work *Borderlands/La Frontera* (1987) broaches a set of contradictions and challenges for thinking expansively about the place of gender and sexuality in American ethnic life. Anzaldúa's hybrid work of history, memory, and poetry is an attempt to embody the contradictions of identity which are usually policed, prohibited, or castigated: A Mexican identified American, a woman identified woman, a mixture of races and histories, at home in the north and the south, though neither is fully home—these are the contradictory aspects of identity for Anzaldúa.

In laying out the contradictions, Anzaldúa also lays bare the intellectual and political impasse for fully embodying them. Two central dilemmas comprise the borderlands of identity, but they mutually implicate one another and, combined, they create havoc for notions of purity, authenticity, and the possibility of neat allegiances. The first is the problem of living on the metaphorical border of racial and sexual identities, where the term *Chicana* is a self-conscious political gesture of resistance to binary identities, signaling the dispossession from both Mexican and U.S. national heritages, yet the possibility of claiming both. The other dilemma is of reconciling gender and sexual nonconformity with an essentially conservative culture. In fact, cultures in general are conservative, for they require a large measure of self-replication by their constituents, and as much as those constituents are nurtured by the culture, the culture itself is predicated on the notion that its members will nourish it. Consider, for example, the central role of memory and ritual in many cultures, holidays that restage historical events, pilgrimages to holy sites, and those embedded presumptions that shame multicultural mixing or other forms of heterodox betrayal. The politics of betrayal are doubly complicated, then, for gay and lesbian Chicanos and Chicanas, because gay, lesbian, or queer is not simply a third term or identity in-between "anglo" and "Mexican," but a term that transgresses and is in turn policed asymmetrically by the two different cultures at the same time.

The dilemma sketched here suggests the extreme difficulty and even danger of such a radical in-betweeness, but remarkably, Anzaldúa's trope of the borderlands is widely and commonly appropriated as a celebration of difference rather than an acknowledgment of the pressures of cultural conformity. As mentioned in the previous chapter, critics working outside the field of Chicano/a studies have been quick to point to "the borderlands" as the answer to essentialist paradigms of identity, without importing the antecedent history that produces the trope in the first place. And history *does* precede the trope, quite literally, for Anzaldúa precedes her poetic depiction of the borderlands with nearly one hundred pages of historical and personal reflections, critical essays, and scholarly notes. Without the history, we have only the poems, which by themselves are inviting, inclusive, and, surprisingly *liberal.* For example, in one of her commonly cited poems, "To live in the Borderlands means You," the first stanza places "you" in an environmental and social context, explaining that to live in the borderlands is to be "caught in the crossfire between camps / while carrying all five races on your back" (194). But the last stanza reverses the priority from place to person: "To survive the Borderlands / you must live *sin fronteras* / be a crossroads" (194). Human being— embodied, experiential being-in-conflict—is not only the consequence of living in the borderlands, but also a strategy for cultural negotiation.

The emphasis on the body as the site of contradictions suggests that the body is the experiential zone of oppression as well as the site for liberation. But liberation, how? And into what? As debates in feminist theory illustrate, the personal may be political, but revolutionary politics require revolutionary connections among diverse persons with often competing interests. With Anzaldúa's "new *mestiza*" those competing interests are embodied in one individual, and the struggle to avoid self-canceling fragmentation may demonstrate a method for a wider politics of coalition building. So far, however, Anzaldúa's work has been widely appropriated as a celebration of individual liberation and transformation, or rightly defended as a representation of Chicano history. Yet, self-concern and liberalism more generally are problematic starting points for Chicano identity for two reasons. First, *Chicanidad,* with its Marxist roots, is a collective identity with the goal of protecting and propagating the culture through a politics of cultural rights and recognition. The second reason is the reverse of the first: liberalism is the starting point for assimilation into American identity, where ethnic cultures are private and domestic, and public individuality is presumed to be culturally neutral.

I begin with Anzaldúa's work because it poignantly describes and locates the crises, conflicts, and potentiality of identity politics which other writers more explicitly take up and attempt to activate. The works examined in this chapter, by Arturo Islas, Cherríe Moraga, and Tony Kushner, amplify Anzaldúa's by pointing to both the traps and liberatory potential in identity politics. Specifically, Islas's novel is a narrative account of "being a crossroads," and the shortcomings of liberalism as a strategy for managing such an identity. Moraga and Kushner take up the same topic and broach theories of nationalism—reconceptualized according to cultural experience—in order to posit a political response that permits a borderlands identity and produces a culture wherein such an identity can flourish.

As with the prior chapter, I do not aim for a comprehensive survey of how nationalism is deployed across ethnic cultures; instead, I examine how U.S. nationalism restricts cultural difference, and how gay ethnic writers attempt to critique and reconstruct the nationalist ideal. Islas's novel represents how ethnicity, as opposed to nationalism, mandates an allegiance to local or ethnic sexual norms, while gays and lesbians who straddle cultural boundaries are perilously abjected from the quasi-national protection of cultural community. Cherríe Moraga attempts to reconstruct a version of nationalism that is both radical and wary of the policing tendencies of nationalist agendas, thereby making it capacious enough to accommodate sexual as well as ethnic, racial, or tribal difference. Moraga's nationalism is a revision of the Chicano movement's quest to reclaim the land of Aztlán—the U.S. southwest—where the Aztec culture is believed to have originated before migrating south to what is now Mexico City. Moraga's nationalism is unique because it does not rely on a myth of autochthony, but on experience, the experience of oppression and social powerlessness. This is lived, embodied experience, as the body is both the site of oppression and the starting point for self-conscious political resistance. However, though Moraga's method intends to be expansive and inclusive, her experiential-based model of nationalism results in a tautological body politic that reifies the differences between insiders and outsiders. As a strategy of resistance, it works; but for pragmatist politics, experience-based identity knows only itself and does not interrogate or reconfigure social and political power at large.

I respond with an analysis of a comparable queer-nationalist thesis in the work of Tony Kushner. Kushner's vision is transcendent and not based in materialism as Moraga's is, and his radical nation is utopic: it is the United States itself. Though his citizens declare their experience, it is their self-conscious awareness of the social construction of experience itself which enables their coming together. The difference between Kushner and Moraga mirrors a theoretical impasse between those who would advocate a neo-realist, experience-based foundation for identity and postmodernists who critique the concept of identity itself. I conclude by exploring how both methods require and enable one another for the sake of a literature of social critique.

Arturo Islas's novel *The Rain God* (1984) explores how ethnicity is troubled by gender and sexual difference, and how both are policed by nationalism. *The Rain God*'s plot conflicts are produced by border crossings—sexual, gender, economic, and national—and its tragedies result from the conflict between competing cultural allegiances and an individual's allegiance to the self. Characters embody the crossroads of cultures, but are unable to link this experience to form a wider border community because the novel's sanctioned communities are predicated on a liberated, free individualism. The novel thus depicts the twofold bargain of pluralist ethnicity: pluralism presumes public and private spheres, a structure that necessarily denormalizes the private, ethnic home. And ethnicity, from the point of view of the ethnic culture, must police itself for betrayals of cultural confidence or ruptures of private into public. Moreover, the bargain presumes a liberal individual cultural agent, capable of reading the codes of his culture and freely performing or masking them as the situation requires. But does this free-agent citizen exist? Or can he?

This is the novel's central question. It is narrated through the perspective of Miguel Chico, or Mickie, a second-generation Mexican American, a member of the Angel family, and son of the patriarch Miguel Grande. Miguel Grande is the favorite son of the family matriarch, Mama Chona, an immigrant who left Mexico during the revolution in 1910. The Angel clan continually negotiates with the border's cultural ambiguities, as they collectively move from the lower to the middle economic class. The ascension requires muting visible displays of Mexican social difference and repressing the embarrassment of homosexuality. The bargain that the novel's younger characters strike with the wider society parallels Mama Chona's own insistence on her Spanish colonial heritage, and she similarly demands her family deny any vestiges of Indian history. Consequently, for Mama Chona and her family, "impure" sexuality, including miscegenation or homosexuality, is abjected, and characters quite literally pretend it does not exist.

The promise of individual liberation in *The Rain God* is belied by the history that precedes and determines the novel's events, including the exile of the family matriarch who comes to the United States not as an immigrant looking to "melt" in, but as a Mexican citizen displaced northward by the war into what was already a cultural borderlands, rather than a pure U.S. cultural zone.[1] Events preceding the novel's present time establish a paradigmatic set of contradictions that are formative for all future boundary crossing in the novel. Distinctly, the name of the family matriarch refers to a pre-Colombian Mexican culture, and the subsequent *mestizaje* of Spanish and Indian cultures. Mama Chona's full name is "Encarnacion Olmeca de Angel." Her name codes her as the incarnation of both the Olmec, or indigenous Indian past, and the Catholic-European culture syncretized with native religion over the centuries since the conquest. Each member of the Angel family responds differently to their embodied *mestizaje*. Mama Chona outwardly denies her mixed ancestry, urging her children to identify with European Spanish culture. Miguel Grande, on the other hand, though a self-identified Chicano, wishfully believes in a limited type of assimilation along with full status for Mexicans in America. Only Miguel Chico, or Mickie, the novel's narrative consciousness, understands and acknowledges that his family embodies self-canceling cultural contradictions, and his task is to make sense of these and fully claim them.

Mama Chona's equation of racial purity and religious purity descends from Mexican culture, where *mestizaje,* or racial mixedness, is a sexually as well as racially charged concept, recalling the figure of La Malinche, the Indian woman who was coerced into serving as Hernan Cortes's informant and concubine in 1519 and who became Mexico's mythic race traitor.[2] Alternatively, the Mexican avatar of the Virgin Mary, the Virgen de Guadalupe, or the "Brown Mary," is the chaste symbol of the Catholic embrace of the indigenous Mexicans, which also implicitly condones the Mexican syncretism of European and indigenous religions. Though Mama Chona and her children all have dark skin, long noses, and high cheekbones, she insists repeatedly, they are not "indios," indicating a hoped-for racial and sexual purity. Her sidestepping of her racial ancestry, and her anxiety over any kind of sexuality, is belied by her body's own sexual insistence: she dies of a prolapsed uterus, her "monster" that slips from between her legs even as she denies its existence. Likewise, Miguel Grande's ravenous sexual appetite, and Felix's desire to fondle the young men he hires at the factory where he is a foreman, contradict Mama Chona's sexual ethic, and furthermore suggest a sexual component of Chicano culture at odds with American sexual norms.

Sexual norms may be subtly embedded in long-standing cultural traditions, but the boundaries between Mexican and American sexual norms can be sorted out. Tomás Almaguer has summarized the structural differences between Mexican and U.S. sexuality succinctly: "Each sexual system confers meaning to homosexuality by giving different weight to . . . sexual object choice and sexual aim" (256–57). In European-American society "the structured meaning of homosexuality . . . rests on the sexual object choice one makes," with same-sex desire confirming one's homosexuality (257). However, "the Mexican/Latin-American sexual system . . . confers meaning to homosexual practices according to sexual aim— i.e., the act one wants to perform with another person (of either biological sex)" (257). Generally speaking (for there are exceptions), in Mexico male same-sex relations occur between *activos* and *passivos,* those who are "insertors" and are not themselves penetrated, and those who are penetrated, and the separation of these two categories makes all the difference (Almaguer 257, Alonso and Koreck 116). Social stigma is directed only at the male passivo, or *joto.* According to Alonso and Koreck, "[male] *jotos* are perceived as having male bodies but they are symbolically construed as women in numerous contexts. For example, *jotos* dress as women on festive occasions, wear make-up . . . [and] are interstitial beings who transgress and confound the power-laden categories of gender" (117).

This cross-construction of gender and sexuality works in two directions. To be a joto is to be like a woman (the regulated antithesis of macho patriarchy), and women are expected to be passive receptors of male will. Meanwhile the activo, also called *macho,* or *chingone* (fucker/penetrater), is regarded as a normal male (Almaguer 257). And, according to Alonso and Koreck,

> in rural northern Mexico . . . the active penetrating role in sexual intercourse is seen as a source of honor and power, an index of the attributes of masculinity, including virility. This is why the active role in *macho-joto* relations carries no stigma. Indeed . . . , men who have sex with both *jotos* and women are not distinguished from those who only have sex with females, for they are also *chingones.* (117)

Though there is a growing body of research on Mexican and Chicano sexuality, it is also clear that sexual norms are in transition as Mexico's economy and hemispheric relationship with the United States changes, and it would be erroneous to transport this research entirely intact into a study of Chicano culture.[3] In *The Rain God* it is precisely the negotiation of differing cultural norms that defines cultural identity in the novel, and characters in *The Rain God* are continually moving in and out of American, Mexican, and Chicano cultural boundaries as they revise their personal sense of family, religion, language, and clearly gender and sexuality.

In the assimilation model, which Miguel Grande assumes, the family polices its own local cultural allegiances, but also anxiously internalizes the norms of the public sphere, making it a doubly repressive site of identity. Miguel Grande's heterosexism combines a Mexican denigration of jotos with an American intolerance for same-sex expressions of affection. He adopts, at least outwardly, the sexual attitude that forbids and shames any aspect of male-male desire or physical relations, or any behavior that is deemed unmasculine. In one telling scene, when Miguel Grande discovers that his wife and their housekeeper, María, are allowing the young Mickie to play with dolls and dress in women's clothes, Miguel Grande erupts in a fit of heterosexist rage. He accuses his wife of turning their son into a joto, and Mickie is required to formally apologize to his father for his "effeminate" behavior, thereby reaffirming the heterosexual law of the father (16). Miguel Grande's retribution also asserts his domination over the women in his family, reestablishing their role as passive receptors of his patriarchal law. We will look more closely at Mickie's own negotiations of family, nationality, and sexuality later, but for now we note that the term *joto* exposes not just sexual difference, but the primacy of the male gender in the Chicano family.

Still, as much as Miguel Grande would assert his dominance through displays of machismo, his attempts to assimilate into U.S. culture require that he recognize (and play into) U.S. standards of gender performance. In effect, Miguel Grande is caught between dueling sexual systems that require him to repress and deny aspects of masculinity on the one hand, and performatively affirm machismo on the other, with the play between the two undercutting the efficacy of both national and sexual norms in either culture. Within Mexican culture, Miguel Grande is a macho, an aggressive male who attempts to dominate those around him, especially sexually, either by symbolic emasculation or penetration, wielding power as the family patriarch, bullying subordinates on the police force, and carrying on affairs with other women with little discretion. These acts constitute a performative assertion of masculinity: they are displays of aggression or domination staged for the view of an affirming Chicano community. Unlike illicit sex, which is potentially a private act kept secret between two people, Miguel Grande's affairs are staged in plain view of his family and community. Most brazenly, he has an affair with Lola, his wife's best friend, and derives satisfaction especially from the visibility of the relationship to all but his naive wife: "Any man, Miguel reasoned, must envy the joy and excitement in his heart when he walked into places with a woman on each arm. On one side, his wife and the mother of his sons. On the other, the woman who brought ecstasy to his everyday life" (75). His sexual excesses and the particular way he thinks of his wife and his mistress are all typical of a Mexican patriarchal ambivalence toward women which would have them be sexually pure (yet bountiful as the Virgin Mary) like his wife, on the one hand, yet passive and available for violation (as La Malinche) like his mistress on the other hand (Alonso and Koreck 117).

Miguel Grande's hypermasculinity is not precisely a *Mexican* cultural trait, nor is his homophobia squarely *American,* for he is ambivalently within both sexual rubrics at the same time, negotiating them both, at times parlaying the one into a firmer grasp on the other. This is not to say that his actions and attitudes are not misogynistic and homophobic, for they surely are; but he uses (or is caught in between, at various times) the already-in-place codes from *both* cultures for negotiating his assimilation. His reflection on his sexual prowess, after all, is dependent on the gaze of his approving, or "envying," peers, and he is especially preoccupied by that gaze around the time he is campaigning for police chief. His supposed display of virility, springing perhaps from Mexican sexual culture, is finally performed before an American audience, including his peers on the police force and in the city, when he makes his bid to gain power in an American institution. After all, as police chief, wouldn't he be the ultimate chingon, yet with a firm hold on an American patriarchal institution?

Miguel Grande's desire for dominance in America is finally subverted when the codes of sexuality he adheres to are themselves policed and penalized by American sexual normativity. First, his affair with Lola unravels. To his Anglo peers, his uxorious affair confirms the stereotype of a hot-blooded, sexually licentious Mexican; to his Chicano friends and relatives, mismanaging the affair threatens the stability of his own family, the ultimate betrayal of Mexican culture. In a telling comment, Miguel Grande anticipates his own reversal: "'Asshole,' he said to himself, 'you've screwed yourself'" (79). The motif of self-penetration suggests how he has figuratively transformed himself from a chingon to a *chingado,* from a dominant male to a submissive, powerless joto. By calling himself "asshole" Miguel Grande acknowledges the reconstruction of his identity: pride, power, and the approving gaze give way to shame, censure, and social control.[4]

The second sexual scandal that disrupts Miguel Grande's bid for police chief occurs when his younger brother, Felix, is murdered after he sexually flirts with a seemingly willing Army soldier and offers to drive him back to his base. On the way, Felix puts his hand on the soldier's knee, is told "don't do that," and before he can apologize he is pummeled by a rain of blows to his body and his face (137). The murder is committed in a canyon that marks the U.S.-Mexico border, and we see that in *The Rain God* negotiations of sexuality are ultimately negotiations of national cultures. The border that divides the two nations symbolizes cultural differences regarding sexual propriety, and the borderland the characters inhabit is beset by ambivalent and ambiguous codes of sexual conduct.

Presumably, in a homogenous Mexican locale, Felix's initial advances would be understood as a passivo courting an activo, not a sexually threatening scenario. On the other hand, an Anglo gay man would probably recognize the danger in propositioning an eighteen-year-old army recruit from Tennessee. But on the border, with cultures and codes mixed together, judging the meaning of an affable conversation or a friendly smile becomes a difficult and deadly task. Brutally sorting out the cultural conflicts is the force of the law and nationalism. American sexual codes and the regime of American heterosexuality are finally asserted by the army soldier, upheld by prosecutors who refuse to try the murder, and hegemonically confirmed by Felix's family who accept the shame heaped on them and agree to bury the case with their dead. Because of Miguel Grande's prominence on the police force, Felix's murder scandalizes the Angel clan at large, marking the family as both Mexican and queer. The killing disrupts Mexican assimilation by hyperbolizing cultural difference and thus reasserts the dichotomies, gay-straight, Mexican-Anglo.

Are we surprised, then, that for all his hints that he is gay, Mickie—Miguel Grande's son and Felix's nephew—stays in the closet? Recognizing all the cultural ambiguity, familial hypocrisy, and general repression of homosexuality on the border, he moves to San Francisco and cloaks his life in secrets. The logic of the closet is the corollary to the logic of assimilation, as both split, repress, or deny the body. Miguel Grande, who helps hide Felix's sexuality after the murder, tacitly approves of Mickie's choice to escape. Mickie's repression also links him to his grandmother, and the comparison is not lost on him. At the beginning of the novel he is gazing at a photograph of the two together, hand in hand, striding along the border (marked by a street running through town), "in flight from this world to the next" (4). Like Mama Chona, Mickie is a border-crosser, in flight from a culture which menaces him, denying his sexuality to his family yet bound to the family by his critical love.

By linking Mickie and Mama Chona, the novel makes an exceptional statement about family. Despite the enormous chasm opened up by Mickie's decision to live in San Francisco, despite his critical, superior attitude toward the family, and despite his homosexuality, he is finally bound to his grandmother and the family at large. Not, however, because of some transcendent love or familial essence. There is real love in the family, but it is the shared secrets, the sexual shame, and the mutual experience of cultural in-betweeness that finally make the family a home. On her death bed Mama Chona whispers the fraught words *"la familia"* to him, and he must work out the meaning of the term. Mama Chona's death is the physical realization of her desire to expunge sexuality from her life, and Mickie, with his colostomy bag strapped to his side, wonders if he faces the same fate. Near the end of the novel he has a dream in which he acknowledges his grandmother's passing, and he claims her legacy. In the dream his own monster, a multivalent figure representing sexual repression, his illness, and his family, comes to him, embraces him, and attempts to seduce him into death. The two stand on a bridge and the monster whispers into his ear, "Jump!" (160). His monster seems to suggest Mama Chona's fate for him: abstinence, sterility, death. And in the dream he does jump, but he takes the monster over the bridge with him. The dream's end allows for multiple readings, but clearly his embrace of the monster symbolizes the difficulty of reconciling with his family. To remain part of la familia he must continue to repress his sexuality, a move akin to death. But the monster itself is la familia, telling him, "I am what you believe and what you don't believe, I am the loved and the unloved, I approve and turn away, I am judge and the advocate" (159). Accepting the monster's challenge to jump, Miguel Chico accepts the hold la familia has on him, despite the necessary ensuing repression.

Family in *The Rain God* is bound by common, self-inflicted wounds. The family comprises a community for its members, but it is a community under siege, not a stable ground for participating in a broader culture. This perilous bond is metaphorized in Mickie's dream of embracing his "monster." Literally without firm ground, without a land or space to fully inhabit as a legitimate citizen, Mickie can only hold on tightly to what he loves and fall. The bridge and the space below are fluid and antibinary, but certainly not the sort of felicitous borderlands dwelling theorized by Anzaldúa. What's more, the shared experiential reality of living in between cultures and exceeding the sexual codes of each makes the family itself a target of persecution, and the family subsequently takes on the role of self-policing culture.

Writing to recuperate this crushing cultural borderland, Cherríe Moraga and Tony Kushner both imagine a new sort of nation, based on a reconstructed family. In her writing, Moraga seeks and ultimately produces a new family, but consequently leaves her old family behind. Kushner, in a postmodern gesture, reconstructs the notion of family through gender performativity rather than the normative biological gender roles.[5]

Though Kushner's postmodernism is not politically oppositional like Moraga's experiential-based politics, it is culturally more broad-reaching, able to do things performatively in the world around, obviating the need for the separate nationalism Moraga calls for. The two examples of gay ethnic culture respond differently to separate sets of challenges and are not to be conflated here as part of one general (that is, deracinated) ethnic gay culture. But the comparison is fruitful for demonstrating that the common goal for both writers is not just the expansion of the respective ethnic culture for the inclusion and tolerance of gays and lesbians; indeed, "tolerance" would suggest the endurance of hierarchies of value for those who conform to the norms of group identity.[6] Instead, Moraga and Kushner use the rhetoric and symbols of their ethnic culture to deconstruct the logic of heterosexism and patriarchy, redefining what it might mean to be Chicano, Jewish, and American. Regionally localized, interpolating a populist audience, all the while locating themselves at the center of a reconstructed ethnic nation, Moraga and Kushner in their work posit strikingly similar representations of an ideal within or of America. I proceed by exploring the origins of Cherríe Moraga's advocacy for the new nation, "Queer Aztlán," and though I find shortcomings with her experience-based theory, I attempt to shore these up with Tony Kushner's performative nationalism, performed in his collaboration with the klezmer band the Klezmatics.

Cherríe Moraga's autobiographical essays in *Loving in the War Years* (1983) and *The Last Generation* (1993) describe her personal and intellectual journey toward self-expression and activism, leading up to her retheorization of the Chicano nation, "Queer Aztlán." Moraga's story as a lesbian is different by degree and kind from what Islas describes in his novel about gay Chicano men, for she wrestles with the repression of sexual difference and patriarchal gender roles in Chicano life. Moraga comments on the difference between her writing, which openly announces and nurtures her sexual identity, and the writing of those in the closet like Islas: "I remember my friend, Arturo Islas, the novelist. I think of how his writing begged to boldly announce his gayness. Instead, we learned it through vague references about 'sinners' and tortured alcoholic characters who wanted nothing more than to 'die dancing' beneath a lightning charged sky" (*Last* 163).

Unlike Islas's gay male characters, who constantly seek some protection and solace within the family, Moraga recognized early on that as a Mexican American woman, she was being trained to relinquish sexual freedom and personal volition for the sake of family conventions. Repressing her lesbian inclinations for a stake in a family structure meant bargaining away one aspect of her identity only to confine another. Consequently, as with Islas, the family is a paradigmatic object of struggle and identification throughout Moraga's work. In Islas's novel, Mickie embraces his family and jumps into an antinationalist space—over the bridge, into the canyon—a gesture only ambivalently suggesting a leap into freedom, and more likely death. In contrast, Moraga is propelled by her desire for liberation, and eventually commits to cultural nationalism.

Moraga depicts her trajectory by juxtaposing her writing against the expectations and prejudices of her family in the introduction to *Loving in the War Years: "Can you go home? Do your parents know? Have they read your work?* These are the questions I am most often asked by Chicanos, especially students. It's as if they are hungry to know if it's possible to have both—your own life and the life of the familia. I explain to them that sadly, this is a book my family will never see" (iv). Sad indeed, her remarks point to how theorizing on culture may transform the theorist more than the culture, particularly when the family itself is the object of her theory. This is the logic of Moraga's title, *The Last Generation,* which indicates how a culture pivots on a generation's self-awareness as cultural agents. Different from culture, however, the normatively or hyperbolically gendered family constantly reproduces its own self-sustaining logic. Simply put, as revolutionary as her writing is, can Moraga's work change her own family? I invoke her family here as a synecdoche for self-normalizing traditional family values, so the breadth of the question is much wider: how can a radical reconceptualization of gender and sexuality within ethnicity appeal to those who have a stake in the conservative stability of the family, the culture, or the nation? Moraga's strategy is to work at the level of the Chicano Nation, and following our analysis of Islas, we see why: A retheorized nationalism can create a safe cultural space for gay and lesbian Chicanos, something Islas's characters and the novelist himself desperately lacked. But nationalism always creates insiders and outsiders, so the task is to reformulate a thesis of Chicano identity that can be broadly appealing and inclusive, and that does not replicate the chauvinistic logic of borders that it attacks in the first place.

Moraga did not initially embrace revolution or cultural reformulation. Instead, she explains, "I made a series of choices which I thought would allow me greater freedom of movement in the future" (*Loving* 99). Realizing that resisting sex roles was far easier for her to do apart from her family than within it, Moraga explains, "I gradually became anglicized because I thought it was the only option available to me toward gaining autonomy as a person without being sexually stigmatized" (99). "Autonomy" is not the same as individuality, or liberation from all identity, and even as such, Moraga recognized that personal "autonomy" detached from cultural identity was a myth: "That is not to say that Anglo culture does not stigmatize its women for 'gender-transgressions'—only that its stigmatizing did not hold the personal power over me which Chicano culture did" (*Loving* 99). Moraga suggests that there is no "ethnicity-free" zone, no place or culture where she might emerge as a lesbian, plain and simple. In contrast to someone like Richard Rodriguez, whose recent work argues for the muddying or "browning" of identity categories in order to produce a postethnic climate for radical individualism, Moraga recognizes that ideologies precede and enforce certain sets of identity values.[7] Movement out of one culture means a movement into another, which involves different and more or less coercive negotiations with embodied identity.

Moraga's personal growth and acceptance of her lesbian identity took place at the same time that the Chicano student movement was articulating its demands for cultural rights and recognition, winning important victories for public-school funding, Spanish-language curriculum, and Chicano studies courses and faculty in universities throughout the West. The movement was oriented around Aztlán, and this nationalism gave Chicanos a basis for postcolonial politics and a metaphor for collective identity. For Moraga, the movement was politically inspiring, yet agonizingly frustrating, for it was both radical and conservative, oriented around cultural liberation but committed to the traditional Chicano family:

> The preservation of the Chicano familia became the Movimiento's mandate and within this constricted "familia" structure, Chicano políticos ensured that the patriarchal father figures remained in charge both in their private and political lives. Women were, at most, allowed to [perform] the "three f's" . . . : "feeding, fighting, and fucking." (*Last* 157)

"El Plan Espiritual De Aztlán," read by Corky Gonzalez in 1969 at the Denver Chicano Youth Conference, explains that "nationalism as the key [to *La Raza Unida*] transcends all religious, political, class, and economic factions or boundaries. Nationalism is the common denominator that all members of La Raza can agree upon" (quoted in Barrera 38). Nationalism is the common denominator because it is the common goal for Chicanos: the end of economic, social, and environmental oppression through collective autonomy.

The means of attaining the goal is family loyalty, as the La Raza Unida Party Platform preamble states, "we are the people who have been made aware of the needs of the many through our suffering, who have learned the significance of *carnalismo,* the strength of *la familia* and the importance of people working together" (quoted in Barrera 41). *Carnalismo* refers to an ideological brotherhood, but it invokes the brotherhood of familial patriarchy from which it springs. Likewise, *la familia* suggests the general condition of the Mexican American home, where women serve men, sisters serve their brothers. Nationalist movements typically produce a "regime of the brother" (MacCannell), where "the individual is both abstract (i.e., characterized by no qualities) and implicitly masculine; women's exclusion from democracy is not accidental but structural" (Sedinger 55). At the height of the movement, Moraga was a self-described "closeted, light-skinned, mixed-blood Mexican American, disguised in my father's English last name" (*Last* 145). She yearned to escape all such excluding structures. Leaving her family only to join the movement would recommit her to the family role she was escaping rather than offer cultural liberation.

The last essay in *Loving in the War Years,* "A Long Line of Vendidas," is Moraga's attempt to untangle the threads of gender, racial, and national identity that comprise her experience shuttling between two cultures, while resisting the roles established for women in Chicano culture:

> You are a traitor to your race if you do not put the man first. The potential
> accusation of "traitor" or "vendida" is what hangs above the heads and
> beats in the hearts of most Chicanas seeking to develop our own
> autonomous sense of ourselves, particularly through sexuality. Even if a
> Chicana knew no Mexican history, the concept of betraying one's race
> through sex and sexual politics is as common as corn. (103)

Moraga's sexual "betrayal" is overdetermined and structured by the legend of La Malinche, the figure synonymous with female sexual shame and betrayal in Mexican culture.

With "A Long Line of Vendidas" and continued in "Queer Aztlán," Moraga seeks to locate within the legend a feminist ethic and politics that would align Chicana feminism with the earlier Chicano movement's goal of radical social justice. Referring to her mixed race, but also to domestic gender oppression, Moraga writes "to be a woman fully necessitated my claming the race of my [Mexican] mother. My brother's sex was white. Mine, brown" (*Loving* 94). In literal terms, Moraga and her brother could both pass as Anglo, but as a woman Moraga recognized that she was oppressed nonetheless. To pass as Anglo, then, would align her with a dominant culture of oppression, while to identify with her Mexican heritage allowed her to assert her social activism. Moraga is working with an ironic set of identity subversions, aligning sexual transgression against Chicano patriarchy with social activism and progress, while gender and sexual oppression within the movement is linked with Anglo hegemony and dominance. Her gender, and even her sexuality, mark her as Chicana and align her with the Chicano movement's social goals; conversely, patriarchy within la familia, troped as her "brother's sex," betrays the movement's goals by reinscribing oppression of Chicanas.

If Moraga's critique was solely her intellectual response to sexism and racism in Chicano and Anglo culture, it would be a compelling analysis but not a replicable basis for social activism. However, Moraga's thinking is based on her experience, and it is responsive to the experiences of other women of color, gays, lesbians, and transgendereds, and the working poor who are the victims of economic and environmental racism. In this way, Moraga's work extends to and encompasses a wide range of experiences all under the banner of a reconstructed Chicano Nation. The theorist and critic Paula Moya cites Moraga's theory as an example of a "new realist" construction of identity, which grounds identity in the experience of one's "social location," rather than postmodern invention. Moya explains,

> Moraga does not merely "choose" to be a woman of color, nor does she
> mentally "construct" the racialized aspect of her heritage (her Mexican
> ancestry) on which she identifies as a woman of color. Of course—
> inasmuch as the identity "woman of color" is a political construct, and is

only one among a range of identities defensible within a realist framework available to her—Moraga does have a choice. But her choice is not arbitrary or idealist; it is not unconnected to those social categories (race, class, gender, sexuality) that constitute her social location and influence her experience of the world. . . . [A]s a result of her expanded, and more accurate, understanding of the social world, Moraga's self-conception and her identity change. Moraga's new-found identity, "woman of color," is more epistemically and politically salient than her former identity—implicitly white "woman"—insofar as it more accurately refers to the complexity and multiplicity of Moraga's social location. (93)

In contrast to Islas's gay characters who are depicted as living in-between identities, and whose borderlands locale mandates multiple repressions of authentic self-expression, Moraga's theory of the borderlands claims her body's longings, physical markings, history, and consequently the experience of oppression based on the body—gender, race, and sexual discrimination. Moya's discussion of Moraga is helpful for thinking through what we mean when we claim an identity, and she shows us how Moraga's activism fits within the history of feminist consciousness-raising. Moya shows that Moraga is "reading" her experience and working to find some kind of community that permits all aspects of her self, and identification is a strategy for coalition-building and activism.

Again, read against Islas's work, we see that claiming one's experiences as part of one's identity may literally be life-saving, and it is evident that life becomes safer for Moraga through her experiential journey toward self-knowledge. Furthermore, this safety is extended to others with a common experience through the politics of nationalism under the banner of "Queer Aztlán." As a nationalism, Queer Aztlán links Chicano claims on the American southwest territory with indigenous Native American claims on the land, building a coalition among people with a common set of experiences: colonialism, loss of language rights, usurpation of property, and social and environmental racism. Similarly, her claim on the land, Aztlán, is not based on a myth of autochthony, but on the experience of abuse and degradation: "The nationalism I seek is one that decolonizes the brown and female body as it decolonizes the brown and female earth" (*Last Generation* 150). The *experience* of colonialism, gender oppression, and racism link with the environmental abuse of the land. It is also rooted in alternative formations of community, including socialism and the tribal model of native American nations: "In an ideal world, tribal members are responsive and responsible to one another and the natural environment, . . . 'Familia' is not dependent upon male-dominance or heterosexual coupling" (166–67). Though "tribe" and "familia" are synonyms for an imagined community, Moraga insists on "nation" for strategic reasons: "I cling to the word 'nation' because without the specific naming of the nation, the nation will be lost" (150). Lost not only through dispersal but through the sorts of cultural bargains Islas describes.

Moraga's version of the nation is similar to the Jewish concept of a diasporic "nation": A displaced people, bound together by a common culture and ethics. For both Jews and Chicanos, the nation is a gathering place rather than excluding force, and especially given that Moraga is describing a diasporic, or virtual nation, her work produces something more like common cultural memory than national citizenry. As we saw the Boyarins argue against Zionism and for a diasporic nation in the previous chapter, we see here Moraga's nationalism revises and expands the goals of the original Chicano movement. Moraga wants to "retain our radical naming," that is, maintain a counterhegemonic, antiassimilationist, and resistance-based political movement, while "expand[ing] it to meet a broader and wiser revolution" (150).

Presuming we have access to our experiences, what is difficult to pin down in Moraga's work, and in Moya's theorizing of experience based on Moraga, is how to articulate them so that they lead to a "wiser" revolutionary social activism. Symptomatic of the problem, Moya summarizes Moraga's theorizing in surprisingly weak terms: "Moraga's conception of Queer Aztlán is a non-relativist realist claim that it is wrong to discriminate unfairly against people on the basis of race, gender, and sexuality" (78). Perhaps, but is that all there is? How do such realist claims appeal outward to a wider public, perhaps inclined toward discrimination? After all, discrimination does not happen by accident. Privileged groups of people have a stake in discriminating, just as the victims of oppression have a stake in battling discrimination. Rather than diminishing the importance of Moraga's work, I mean to call attention to the difficulty of seeing it realized as revolutionary beyond the point of view of those inclined to agree with her in the first place.

Though Moraga draws together as broad a coalition of the victims of racism, colonialism, sexism and heterosexism, and environmental degradation as can be united through recourse to experience, the logic of the nation itself implies another nation, the nation of oppressors: those who benefit from exploitation and oppression; or more insidious, those who have become so used to their social privilege that they experience any rise in the status of minorities as an impingement on their rights and recognition. For example, legal scholar Carol Swain notes of the rise in hate crimes on college campuses over the last two decades in the United States: "Most of the experts on hate crime believe that the reported violence on college campuses is a reaction to increased campus diversity" (325). Such reactions are matched anecdotally in the stories told by white civil service workers convinced they were passed over for promotion so that a "diverse" employee could be promoted, or by white law school applicants charging "reverse discrimination" as a consequence of affirmative action policies in admissions. These sorts of anecdotes and their regressive conclusions of "reverse racism" are based on the logic of experience, and as Swain points out, those who are convinced they are the victims of diversity or minority comeuppance will band together to protect what they perceive to be their own interests.

Activism and ethics based on experience helps sharpen a group's perceived interest, but the strategy does not address competing claims based on experience. Ramón Saldívar frames the problem here in terms of the reasonable question,

> what counts, objectively, as better or worse? What serves as the dependent or independent variable in such a test? What is the "control" element? And what counts as a *wrong*, not to say *un-real*, judgment or identity? . . . I wonder how in everyday lived experience one may *reliably* distinguish between experiences that produce dynamic and negotiated judgment and experiences that simply produce *false consciousness*. ("Response" 853)[8]

When claims about reality are based on experience, how do you convince someone who disagrees with you—based on his own reading of experience—that he is wrong and needs to change his mind? And in just what way is he wrong? Imagine a white person, born into privilege—admitted to Yale because he is a legacy, let's say. Imagine he is floated through failed business dealings because of his access to power—his father is the president, let's say. He succeeds to the presidency himself—in part because a regional campaign manager was also the secretary of state in charge of voting procedures in a key swing state, perhaps. This person's experience surely normalizes and confirms for him the correctness of his own privilege, does it not?

More to the point, and no less realistic, is the experience of the families of gays and lesbians, families like Moraga's: *Can you go home? Do your parents know?* While for many, a child's coming out is precisely the experience that changes the way they read reality, and folds them into the broader queer nation, it is also sadly true that homophobia has once again found its voice in this country. The current vice-president is the father of a lesbian daughter, yet is comfortable with his party's gay-bashing domestic and foreign policy agendas. In the post-9/11 era of the new American Nationalism, where we live in a "homeland" rather than a republic, and where leaders take their directive as much from heaven as from the polis, alternative nationalisms can only be a starting point for building coalitions and political resistance. Alongside work like Moraga's, we still need political and artistic practices that broadly interrogate the presumptions and strategies of discrimination.

Moya specifically attacks the postmodern theorizing of Judith Butler, Donna Harraway, and Barbara Herrnstein Smith, arguing that these theorists undermine our access to and thus the efficacy of our experience, but I contend that postmodern critiques of identity like Butler's famous deconstruction of "gender" are the necessary complement to work like Moraga's.[9] After two generations of theory and critique, college freshman are now largely comfortable with the premise that "race" is a social and historical construction. Likewise, I am convinced that strategies of gender parody and deconstruction are similarly effective for undermining regimes of conformity with gender and sexual identity.[10]

In this final section, I turn to one last example of a gay American writer with a strong claim on ethnicity, who also writes toward reconfiguring the nation's embodiment of gender and sexual normativity. In an evocative and compact song lyric, written in collaboration with the klezmer band the Klezmatics, Tony Kushner suggests how newfound voicings of experience like Moraga's can participate in interrogating the fundamental myths of identity in the nation at large.

Tony Kushner's work reaches well beyond Jewish themes, yet he has been influenced by and responsive to European and American Jewish cultural life. His stunning play *Angels in America* (1993) is subtitled "A Gay Fantasia on National Themes," appropriate for the way the play yokes contemporary gay life to U.S. postwar social history, arguing finally that the former is part of the latter. But the play is no less a *Jewish* fantasia or, better yet, a Jewish-gay fantasia, given that the ethical ruminations of the play, not to mention the play's epistemology of death and redemption, pass through the Jewish character Louis Ironson.[11] Kushner's subsequent work is more strongly focused on Jewish traditions and themes, and includes an adaptation of An-ski's classic *A Dybbuk,* and the collection of essays that he edited with Alissa Solomon, *Wrestling with Zion* (2003). *A Dybbuk* is set in an eighteenth-century European Jewish shtetl, and tells the story of a woman possessed by the ghost of her one-time lover, a student of Kaballah, and her subsequent rabbinical dis-possession. Though rich with traditional overtones and rabbinical pronouncements, the play is finally about transgressive love, and the bonding among men and boys in the traditional study houses. Thus Kushner, working within the tradition, is able to tease out the transgressive.

In 1995 Kushner collaborated with the popular klezmer band the Klezmatics to create a performance for the Los Angeles klezmer-fest, "Klezmania." Titled "It's an Undoing World or Why Should It Be Easy When It Can Be Hard," the performance marks Kushner's growing interest in *yiddishkeit* (Yiddish-Jewish culture) and its revision by Jewish gays and lesbians in recent years. As we saw Moraga do with "Queer Aztlán," Kushner imagines an American landscape where oppressed minorities find common ground and come together to claim national belonging. This claming is highlighted in the title song, "An Undoing World," and the broader context of Jewish queer culture attempts to open up within the new yiddishkeit a safe space for the cooperation of multiple subject-identities, including gays and lesbians, victims of AIDS, and refugees from war strife. The Klezmatics, with their frequently gay-themed klezmer music, are part of a broad and diffuse reassimilation of Jewish gays and lesbians *back into* Jewish culture. The challenges Moraga has with directing her work beyond an intellectual elite are met and perhaps bridged by the pop/camp culture of contemporary (or even traditional) klezmer music.

In the liner notes to the Klezmatics' 1997 album *Possessed,* Tony Kushner testifies to the affective nature of the band's music: "*oy so gorgeous,* so sexy, so full of August Mystery, I decided to reinvent the kind of Jew I am upon hearing it." What Kushner finds so attractive in the Klezmatics' music, besides its melodic beauty, is its mixture of traditional yiddishkeit and contemporary left-wing politics, especially the band's Queer Nation–inspired brazen homoeroticism and "out" approach to sexuality and ethnicity in general. On stage, horn player Frank London (who is not gay) is given to shouting, "Sing along with us, whether you're religious or leftist, whether you're a bride or a groom! We're all sisters! We're all brothers! We're all here! We're all Gay!"[12] Several, though not all, of the band's members are gay, and the band's identity is bound up in the New York yiddishkeit revival scene, a broad movement which, like Kushner, is reinventing New York secular Jewish culture.

Though the band's members are diverse, and their interests eclectic, they are united in their goal to claim Yiddish-Jewish culture as their own, and to subsequently refashion it as part of contemporary left-wing political and social culture. The overt representation of the band's gay members is part of their overall expression of Jewish culture. As London puts it, "I hate the 'don't ask, don't tell' attitude. It's never served the Jews well" (Morris). The ethic of being "out" and the links between cultural and sexual identity parallel Moraga's comparison of her gender with her ethnicity and signal a coalition resistant to hegemony and assimilation.

Besides publicly claiming their sexual diversity, the band works within the klezmer tradition to queer old standards. On *Possessed*, for example, a traditional song about mixed gender dancing (a violation of Orthodox Jewish mores) ironizes the implicit homoeroticism of same-gender restrictions, "with a female, with a female, / Truly a major transgression." On an earlier album, *Jews with Horns* (1995), a traditional party tune is given new lyrics, and sung by gay lead singer Lorin Sklamberg, narrates male homosexual love:

A regular delight right now
I'll sing a song for you
Though the melody is old,
The words are all brand new
Our grandpas used to sing it
And our grandmas sang it too . . .
A man so Greek in his physique in
New York I adore
I met a man in a hat with a tan . . . [13]

Rather than binarizing the traditional past against a radical present, the song interpellates an audience of all ages and of varying degrees of religiosity. No mere rhetorical shift, the song's reconstructed lyrics appeal to a considerably mixed audience of old and young, all of who can find occasion to sing along. While it is tempting to label such lyrics "subversive," that might miss the very basic naturalness of the songs. Klezmer is loud, ironic, playful, and exuberant to begin with. The Klezmatics' gay-themed songs are not slyly coded, subtle revisions, but the out-and-out inhabiting of what is finally party music.

The Klezmatics' reclamation of Yiddish culture marks a reversal of a larger Jewish cultural phenomenon during the late 1950s and early 1960s, when young Jews searching for alternatives to what they saw as a conservative and patriarchal religion turned to Eastern and New Age religions or secular social activism. For many during this time, American Judaism was either too restrictive or too assimilationist. During the 1950s through 1960s major Jewish institutions like the American Jewish Committee, and its journal of social criticism, *Commentary*, turned politically conservative, and by 1968 the editors and contributors to *Commentary*, including Norman Podhoretz, Nathan Glazer, and Martin Himmelfarb were openly hostile to the implementation of civil rights victories for African Americans and other minorities through policies like affirmative action.[14]

At the heart of the political realignment was an American Jewish fear of the power of group identities in public life; a politics of group identity had long been used to exclude Jews from free participation in public life, and the Jewish commitment to pluralism, based on liberal public sphere individualism seemed in jeopardy as a consequence of the new racial and ethnic social movements. Leftist Jews committed to social justice, especially feminists, and gays and lesbians were alienated from the Jewish mainstream and struggled for decades to establish a stable cultural basis for social activism.[15]

For the Klezmatics and many of its like-minded fans and fellow yiddishkeit enthusiasts, Yiddish is a linguistic and cultural alternative to traditional religious Judaism. "Yiddishism," writes the band's founding fiddler Alicia Svigals, "looks to Ashkenazic Yiddish culture as the source of a rich Jewish identity and proposes to salvage that culture—its language, literature and most important for our purposes, its music—but for the most part discards religious observance" (Svigals 44).[16] Furthermore, Yiddish is a domestic language, the language of home, mothers, and children. In contrast, Hebrew has traditionally been the language of liturgy, prayer and finally exclusion. For Sklamberg, Yiddish has "a coziness" that he "finds very comfortable." "In Yiddish," he says, "the term for a gay man is *faygeleh*. That doesn't sound particularly harsh. It's kind of a sweet word that's never said with much rancor. When you hear old people using it, it's usually with just a shrug" (Morris).

In *Unheroic Conduct* Daniel Boyarin explains that "*Yiddishkayt . . .* exalts for men an 'ethics of the household and a sphere of the domestic' as a secular continuation of the rabbinic opposition to European romantic 'masculinism'" (37). This might initially seem like an intellectual's attempt to colonize a nostalgic safe-space of female domesticity, but Boyarin recognizes that sexual norms are regulations of national norms and national identity. Writing parallel to Islas and Moraga, Boyarin is aware that part of the process of claiming cultural rights in the United States involves fully inhabiting one's local or ethnic culture, which by itself requires some measure of cultural reconfiguration. In this case, Yiddish music, Yiddish poetry and theater, Yiddish humor, and most critically Yiddish social activism in Europe and America in the late nineteenth and early twentieth centuries have rendered the language familiar and familial, and cannily counterhegemonic and serviceable for social critique. By turning to Yiddish culture, contemporary Jewish gays and lesbians like Kushner and the Klezmatics' members are not supplanting traditional yiddishkeit with subversive politics so much as allowing Yiddish culture to speak in and back to a postmodern world.

Tony Kushner's contribution to the Klezmatics' *Possessed* is quite prominent, but I am most interested here in the single song, "An Undoing World." The title suggests not just Jewish or gay, but universal misfortune, the "undoing" of bonds, cultures, and love, by nameless forces with reconciliation coming in the form of art and narrative. The lyrics begin with the conceit of a couple in a dance, intertwined "merely" by "melody," finally separated by the vicissitudes of the fickle heart. The lyric "merely melody" casts doubt on the efficacy of the song itself, or more generally culture, for bringing people—Jews, gays and straight, the singer and the listener—together, and the lines are echoed by the lone flute with its wide vibrato which wavers in pitch, a note not at home, contrasting klezmer's rich jazz sound.[17] As the song continues, the conceit of heartbreak is transformed into heart failure and death, homelessness, cultural attrition, and ethnic warfare—a catalogue of "undoing." The result is a "dispossession by attrition . . . the permanent condition / That the wretched modern world endures." "Dispossession" primarily connotes the loss of self, and the notion that one loses one's self as a result of cultural, social, or mortal attrition corresponds with Moraga's anxiety over the disappearance of "the last generation." "Dispossession" also picks up resonance in the second half of the album, which consists of songs for Kushner's adaptation of *A Dybbuk*. The homoeroticism of the play, and the play's representation of the severe "undoing" of homosocial bonds through the exorcism of the dybbuk, allegorizes how the social construction of "proper" love and marriage disrupts homosocial/sexual bonding.

The middle stanza of "An Undoing World" is a lyrical reworking of Emma Lazarus's "The New Colossus," also popularly known as the "Statue of Liberty Sonnet." His revision of her poem exposes the gender assumptions implicit in national self-fashioning. The original poem projects a national ideal-image of the nation as a nurturing mother, welcoming home her children, a conceit that is partly prophetic and partly phantasmatic. Certainly Lazarus, the author of the immigrant-pastoral poem "In Exile," did not imagine colonized Mexicans in Texas or the subsequent generations of Mexican immigrants when she declared America open for the world's "tired, poor, and hungry." What is clear, however, is that Lazarus was intentionally configuring the emblem of the nation as a surrogate mother, providing a national metaphor that facilitated European Jewish acceptance in the United States. "The New Colossus" describes the statue as "Mother of Exiles" and America is subsequently a homeland for diasporic peoples from the world over.

Furthermore, the statue is a national but not a classically nationalist emblem. The Statue of Liberty in Lazarus's poem is "Not like the brazen giant of Greek fame"—that is, the Greek Colossus of Rhodes—but is instead "a mighty woman with a torch, whose flame / Is the imprisoned lightning, and her name / Mother of Exiles." Lazarus's explicit break with Greek and masculine models and her substitution of Hebrew biblical imagery marks her poem as a revision of national symbolism; or, as Maeera Shreiber puts it, the poem reverses a series of binaries implicated in nationalist agendas: "Greek Hellenism (the Colossus) thus gives way to Hebraism, masculinity to femininity, a colonizing nation to a 'tribe' of wanderers, and place gives way to displacement" (46).[18] Rather than the classic, patriarchal, and exclusive version of the nation-state, Lazarus's poem and her reading of the statue—the nation's emblem—imagines an America that is inclusive, predicated on displacement, itself destabilized by gender reversals within the symbolic order.

According to Shreiber, "in 'The New Colossus' the feminine ultimately problematizes both Americaness and Jewishness" (47); but a critical question remains, how to problematize the feminine, or gender and sexuality more generally? Gathering in the poor and the wretched must also mean gathering in those exiled from their families. The statue, Mother of exiles, may reverse the binary of male/female in the national agenda, but does not necessarily destabilize it. But in "An Undoing World" Kushner, while building on Lazarus's revision, recasts the statue yet again, not just as *Mother,* but *Queen:*

> Copper-plaited, nailed together, buffeted by ocean weather
> Stands the Queen of Exiles and our mother she may be.
> Hollow-breasted broken-hearted watching for her dear departed
> For her children cast upon the sea.

To use Shreiber's words, Kushner's statue is "out there . . . occupying a liminal status," the status of gender-deconstructing drag-queen. Kushner's image points to the performativity of gender, calling attention to artificial garb ("copper-plaited"), as well as the exterior agency necessary for sustaining gender performance; that she is "nailed together" recalls the literal process of artisanal construction, and allegorizes the social construction of gender categories. By calling attention to the performativity of gender, "An Undoing World" simultaneously announces the statue as a "woman," while undermining the inherent value of the given gender category. Like Moraga, Kushner inhabits the sartorial shell of nationalism with a new body politic, in this case the nation-in-drag.

Kushner's Queen "*may* be" "our mother," but this is no stereotypical *yiddishe mama.* To begin with, she is silent, mutely watching for her children. Also, mothers in ethnic narratives are typically conduits for assimilation, but the "Queen of Exiles" has her back turned on the nation and gathers her children under the sign of alterity. Further, as her constructed quality indicates, she is not a "natural" mother, but the potential surrogate for us all: "Darling never dream another woman might / have been your mother / Someday you may be a refugee." Kushner's drag-mother is emblematic of a type of surrogate guardian-figure, positively represented in Jennie Livingston's film *Paris Is Burning* (1990). In this film about the subculture of New York City drag-balls, drag-queen mothers watch out for their "children," gay men who have been rejected by their original families and communities and who have congregated in communal homes in Harlem. The "children" attach themselves to self-styled "houses" and each house is united by common codes of style and performance, regularly displayed at the drag-balls. With the song "An Undoing World," the entire United States becomes a "house," the house of exiles, including gays and lesbians, and ethnic immigrants, where identities are performed. The statue, "Queen of Exiles," stands as the guardian and representative type for her "children." Not just the tired, poor, and hungry, but the socially ostracized, politically persecuted, or religiously rejected are invited to congregate as part of a new family, Americans. There is an obvious contradiction between the nation's being and what Kushner hopes it becomes, but then at the same moment that gays and lesbians were marrying at break-neck speed in Boston and San Francisco in 2003, the U.S. Congress was debating a constitutional amendment enfranchising heterosexuality as our national sex-choice.

Kushner's lyric is not nationalist in the way Moraga's essays and poetry are, and he has nothing like Moraga's banner of "Queer Aztlán," to signal an oppositional coalition resistant to American hegemony. On the other hand, his reconstruction of the Statue of Liberty as a drag-queen borrows from the parodic strategies of the political group Queer Nation, which was active in the early 1990s, a keen move that marks the dominant nation itself as the location of minority resistance and struggle. In contrast to Queer Nation, which all too often lifted the veils of repression only to reveal the white male face of gay America, Kushner, like Moraga, yokes the oppression of gays to that of minorities, the poor, and immigrant-refugees.[19] Though these diverse groups have entirely different social experiences in America, their oppression is similarly a dispossession and undoing of identity by the cultural bargains with assimilationist American culture. In contrast, Kushner imagines a gathering of the dispossessed, and a narration of their diversity that would stand counter to official narratives of assimilation.

Kushner links the experience of dispossession with the breakup of biological families, and the same affective longing for family haunts his work as it does Moraga's. We recall in *Angels in America,* for example, that protagonists Louis and Prior, though both essentially estranged from their families, cannot shake the presence of their familial and ethnic history in their current lives. Prior Walter is haunted by the "prior Walters" in the first half of the play, and at the end of "Perestroika" Ethel Rosenberg recites the Kaddish (the Jewish mourning prayer) through Louis over the dying Roy Cohn. With Kushner, identity is as much a choice as an affective reaction to one's familial and social past. We live not just in our positive and constructive choices, but as Islas and now Kushner show, in our shame, fear, and conflicting loves and desires. There is no essential American, on the one hand, but no essential minority either. Identity here means reading one's history as a subjective narrative rather than an objective experiential reality.

By the end of the song, a plurality of voices and perspectives unite to form a chorus, a grouping of different voices which communicates different experiences but a coherent and singular demand for recognition. This is not a pluralism where differences are muted—as they literally are in Lazarus's poem, where the immigrants do not speak—but a pluralism that interrogates the singularity of the nation.[20] In Islas, Moraga, and now Kushner, we see that an ethnic as well as an ethical hermeneutics is required to read the collection of narratives that comprise ethnicity, group identity, and finally America. In "An Undoing World" this task falls to the statue, Queen of Exiles, who, unlike Lazarus's "Mother of Exiles" does not speak, but rather, listens:

> Grant us shelter harbor solace safety
> Let us in!
> Let us tell you where we traveled
> How our hopes our lives unraveled
> How unwelcome everywhere we've been.

The power of song and narrative are ultimately affirmed in this stanza, as the lone voice from the beginning of the song is joined by a chorus, and the flute picks up the accompaniment of drums, horns, and fiddle. The chorus carries the music now, which sonically communicates the lyrical command. Though the refugees would presumably have separate tales to tell, their need for shelter and their desire for narration—a renarration of the nation—unites them as a collective. The song proffers a reimagined America where migrants and refugees do not assimilate or "melt" in. Rather, difference is maintained by subjective testimony.

At the end of chapter 2 we saw the efficacy of testimony affirmed by Alejandro Morales as a means of cultural survival. "An Undoing World" links testimony to the reimagining of the nation. The sorts of stories the speakers would tell their queen/mother—"how our hopes and lives unraveled"—are comparable to Felix's and Mickie's stories in *The Rain God,* and Moraga's own journey first from dispossession to self-possession and expression. Unlike Moraga, Kushner's version of story-telling requires an external witness. Contrary to Moya's reluctance to grant the efficacy of postmodernism, Kushner requires that his Queen expose the ideological nuts and bolts inherent in identity construction. The song may be "merely melody," but it turns out that even postmodern culture can illicit and sustain the experiences of the nation's exiled citizens. The family matriarch is conflated with the nation in "An Undoing World," but the family does not produce a new heterosexist or patriarchal logic. Indeed, in *Angels* heaven consists of "big dance palaces full of music and lights and racial impurity and gender confusion," in short, the eclipse of essential identity categories that then permit new identities to flourish (219). Or, as Homi Bhabha puts the point, "what is crucial to such a vision of the future is the belief that we must not merely change the *narratives* of our histories, but transform our sense of what it means to live, to be, in other times and different spaces, both human and historical" (256).

CONCLUSION: THE ETHICS OF ETHNICITY IN LITERATURE

This book began with the assumption that the idea of identity is vital for a consideration of works of literature where ontology and ethics meet up with local, sociopolitically constructed epistemologies and histories of the nation and its people. Attempts to move "beyond" or "post-" ethnicity place ethnic identities in a temporal framework, and rely on "progress" as the imaginary engine of history which would drive us to update our critical conceptions. For example, in 2003 the citizens of California voted down the "racial privacy initiative" (Proposition 54), a ballot proposition banning racial identification in state information-gathering enterprises. I have many friends on the Left who were at least tempted to vote for the bill with a sense of utopic arrival: at last, we no longer need these categories because we have outgrown them, socially, politically, and morally.

I sympathize with this optimism. When I taught at a sprawling state school in California, I had many classes where students took their own diversity, even their individual mixed-race background, for granted, giving the impression that the walls of race categories had indeed been breached or had become irrelevant. Could this be our nation's future? You need to squint your eyes and look in just the right direction to see this version of California—and it doesn't hurt to be looking down from a window, high up in an ivory-tower academic office either—but no such maneuvers permit one to miss the permanence of racial divisions that persist across America, and the subsequent inequality that comes with them throughout the country. At the North Carolina college where I now teach, most of the students are white (89%), and most of the custodial staff is black. At the hog-slaughter plants down the road from here, most of the workers are recent immigrants from Central America and Mexico.

Whether or not these groups of people self-identify in terms of race or ethnicity, some nexus of politics, economics, and culture, coming together along a trajectory we call "history," has produced these groupings. To turn away from them with good intentions and a real faith in the universality of the human condition is to negate the lived experience of that humanity in the world. More perniciously, I believe that some people who occupy a position of privilege have a stake in maintaining such divisions, and act to support them, consciously or unconsciously. It is not a coincidence that we ended up with a racially stratified society, and dropping the language of race and identity from our critical vocabulary will not change the fact that America has historically organized its labor force and meted out social opportunities in racial terms.

To the extent that literature and other aspects of culture can teach us about how lives are raced, and to the extent that ethnicity provides a language through which people can observe and express their own experiences within such a society, an analysis of ethnic literature must begin by taking the question of how ethnic identification works, especially how it relies upon or draws energy from literature. Literary and critical writing about ethnicity does not statically represent ethnicity; rather, it produces a discourse with which we can speak of and therefore understand what ethnicity is, where it comes from, and what it is for.

If we reject attempts to throw over the concept of "identity" based not primarily on a theoretical and intellectual intervention but through recourse to the lived experience of people with identities, we need to proceed nonetheless with a theory of identity in hand. Though most of my honors English students are white and most of our school's basketball players are black, it is still not clear what "white" and "black" mean as identities to these students, or if "identity" is even the right starting place for thinking about their lives as narrations of racial and ethnic experience. What we need is a thesis about identity that would suggest how identities are produced by histories, and that accounts for the widely accepted premise that individuals have a degree of choice, from revision to dissent, with regards to their identities. How to think about what identity is and how it functions in relation to how people experience identity, while side-stepping the logical problems identity's critics have noted is the task of this chapter.

This problem appears at the end of the book rather than the beginning so as to relieve this study of ethnic literature from the false burden of contending with the problem of identity. Starting with identity would suggest that we better get identity right, or—*poof!*—ethnic literature will disappear. Because ethnic identity is a matrix produced by other sets of concerns organized here under the headings "history" and "geography," it is more urgent to pursue through comparison how points within a given matrix produce cultural problems that necessitate a theory of identity in the first place.

This chapter has a dialectically unfolding method: it begins with some questions about how to approach identity in general, followed by an examination of how an ethics of identity in multicultural literature study implies a utilitarian conception of identity in general.

This is an "ethical" chapter according to the title, but *ethics* here means something less than transcendent. Following Geoffrey Harpham, I consider the ethics of ethnic literary criticism to descend from the imperative to "act on principle," whatever the principle; or in the case of ethnic literature, whatever the cultural, historical, and spatial assumptions a given group of people holds (3). "Ethics," Harpham suggests, "can . . . be construed as a principle of commonality between practices and discourses often considered to be independent from each other and from the world of action" (5). For "discourses" I would substitute literature, and for "practices," criticism. Following Harpham, I posit that the two are indeed dependent on each other and interact with the world around. "Getting it right," to borrow from Harpham one last time, means allowing criticism and theory to attend to the specific imperatives of individual cultures, but also using criticism to speak back to and across cultures, thereby establishing some agency for critical practice in the production of "ethnic American literature."

Homi Bhabha theorizes identity by first examining traditional modes of self-identification, then locating those within a postcolonial framework. As Bhabha sees it, the postcolonial subject faces the horns of a dilemma: either to adopt the persistent Western myth of the self-evident, transcendent, and autonomous self, or to identify along a continuum within the binary of nature/culture, where culture is synonymous with European Enlightenment. Though Bhabha's critique is directed toward the postcolonial situation, we might grant that the contemporary Native American, Jewish American, African American, Asian American, or Chicano shares more than a little in common with the postcolonial subject, when it comes to the question of a liberatory post–civil rights identity. Nostalgia, historiography, even the very structures of language within which the postcolonial or post–civil rights subject exists, bundle and bury him or her in a tangle of associations and influences that we generally call "the dominant culture."

For ethnic Americans who are aware of the legacies of oppression embedded in identities but who would nonetheless seize a moment of agency enabled by identity, the task is not only to round out a cultural point of view but to critically examine conventions of identification in the first place. As Bhabha puts it, "in the postcolonial text the problem of identity returns as a persistent questioning of the frame, the space of representation, where the image—missing person, invisible eye, Oriental stereotype—is confronted with its difference, its Other. This is neither the glassy essence of Nature . . . nor the leaden voice of 'ideological interpretation'" (46). In fact, the encounter with identity since the rise of multicultural consciousness in the 1970s is finally not an encounter at all, but a coming upon an absence, the absence at once of the authentic ethnic or subaltern subject, along with the strategic effacement of the dominant ruling class. It is not merely that the two are in dialectical relation with one another, and hence each exists as the mirror opposite of the other. Instead, because the poetic, social, and political inscription of each is radically undermined by subaltern identification, the moment of identification is freighted with the overthrow of an entire linguistic and symbolic order. To articulate a theory of the subject which neither relies upon the dominant other's perspective nor partakes of the other's metaphysics involves an entire questioning of the frame of questioning: "We are no longer confronted with an ontological problem of being but with the discursive strategy of the moment of interrogation, a moment in which the demand for identification becomes, primarily, a response to other questions of signification and desire, culture and politics" (Bhabha 50).[1]

This final chapter examines how Chicano and Jewish American theorists of ethnic identity have outlined the context for identification, how they recognize the problems inherent in the project but build a utilitarian concept nonetheless. Bhabha's theory is a starting point because he has stated the problem that vexes ethnic scholars, be they postcolonial, post–civil rights, or multicultural Americans. The theorists we will look at similarly phrase the question of identity as a questioning of the very frame of the question, the attempt to articulate the absent self in the presence of some prevailing epistemology of identity. Indeed, this is a basic premise running throughout this book: Our writers and critics can be read as writing against certain legacies, tendencies, trajectories, or mappings of culture across history and geography. The previous chapters show how we might nudge this cultural questioning into a critical method and also a viable critical vocabulary that works broadly but also in particular and local ways. No single theory or praxis of ethnic criticism works with all the literature we call "ethnic," but they start in similar places, and scholarship might proceed with the dialectical approach I model here.

Historicism and poststructuralism suggest two strategies for a critique of ethnic American literature.[2] As I understand the imperatives of each and put them into play so far, I see historicism generating a context for a productive scholarly encounter with emergent culture, while poststructuralism provides an impulse for skepticism toward normalizing tendencies in Western thought. Historicizing cultures allows us to see that persistent problems of ethical and political justice inform, even produce cultural memories and social, political, and legislative formations of race and ethnicity.[3] A poststructuralist critique of identity is similarly useful for observing how and why ethnicity resists absorption into a dominant cultural imaginary.[4]

Two quotations will help indicate how historicism and poststructuralism produce useful problems for the articulation of ethnic identity. Although we will look at others in this chapter, I choose to start with Jonathan Boyarin and Cherríe Moraga because both have written nearly single-mindedly on the subject of ethnic identity. The authors confront the challenges contemporary American culture poses toward maintaining anything like an authentic and recognizably different ethnic culture, and both write to account for gender, sexuality, and the instability of cultural contingency. Recognizing the limitations of their respective ethnic identities, and of the concept of identity in general, they similarly reject a monolithic (often conservative and patriarchal) ethnic group boundary.

And, crucially, both authors recognize that identities are necessarily inco-
herent temporal indexes of the historicity of individuals within broader
group affiliations.

In *Thinking in Jewish,* Jonathan Boyarin writes:

> By hereby coining (I think) the phrase *critical post-Judaism,* I mean to
> name an already existing but unidentified commonalty, a way of being
> Jewish "otherwise than Being." This is not quite a school of thought, nor
> yet does it exist only in thought. This kind of identity formation is not
> enabled solely through its own intellectual passion and inventiveness, but
> on the contrary, only within or at the margins of academic institutions and
> academic cultures. . . . As a post-Judaism, it is marginal to the would be
> "Jewish community" monolith. As criticism, it is subject to the centrifugal
> pressures. It finds its creative tension in an unstable mixture of accommo-
> dation and resistance to the centrifugal spin toward the margins, and it
> need not be its members' only Jewish world. (170)

Boyarin writes with a kind of scholarly élan, at ease with the instability
and marginality he is writing on, as comfortable with the ivory tower as
with an ethics of resistance toward academic intellectual hegemony. The
"post-" in post-Judaism indicates not so much the end of Judaism or even
a movement beyond it, but a rejection of Euro-American historicity of
Judaism that requires Judaism and Jews to be at once integral to while
marginal within the dominant cultural matrix. Though Boyarin seems
overly couched in academia in this selection, grinding out an identity of
and for academics, the quote is culled from an ethnographic reflection on
the author's marginal life amid Hasidic Jews while living in New York.
The selection above ends with the reminder that one can have more than
one identity, and for Boyarin a Jewish academic should feel compelled to
spread out among other various Jewish circles, which may inform a critical post-Jewish identity, and may also be stretched to accommodate the
post-Jewish Jew, the radically different among the different.

Boyarin proposes a deconstructive approach to Jewish critical identity, and though it belies his attempt to connect academic Judaism to
something like a common lay Jewish community, it is nonetheless exemplary of the academic Jewish multicultural moment. The move beyond
being acknowledges or even accepts a poststructuralist deconstruction of
ethnic ontology, but locates ethnicity prior to ontology, in the ethical condition of humanity. The diffusion of identity, the practice of reading

against the grain of history, even the critique of ethnic and cultural categories in the university are all common strategies among Jewish scholars who are rightfully skeptical of the academic tradition that privileges a Western mimetic identity on the one hand, but who are enthusiastic for the potential of a multicultural ethic of marginal critique.[5] This amounts to a constantly self-referential and -reflexive Jewish criticism, where "Jewish" and "criticism" are tandem, reinforcing concepts and practices. There is a sense, however, that very little is at stake in such a project, at least relative to comparable multicultural articulations of identity. In Boyarin's writing, and with Jewish theorists we will review below, Jewish difference is theorized as something quite close to Derridean *différance,* the endless deferral of identity in favor of identity *associations,* or complex utterances of Jewish identity that at once break from (and break up) calcified models of Jewish subjectivity while deconstructing ethnicity at large. While it makes sense to deconstruct the inscription of a given identity—to apply the tag "post-" to Judaism—this occurs in a broader context where identities and cultures have abundant textual histories already.

Writing from a strikingly different position, we find in the work of Cherríe Moraga an attempt to negotiate similar straits: a theory of identity at once grounded in history while skeptical of historiography, a recognition of the gap between the academy (writing) and the ethnic community. In contrast to Boyarin's formal theoretical bent, Moraga begins with a historical reference to the Spanish conquest of the Aztecs, locating ethnicity in the material history of empire and subjugation. In her introduction to *The Last Generation,* Moraga writes

> In 1524, just three years after the Spanish Conquest of the Aztec Empire, the Nahuatle sages, the tlamatinime, came before the missionary friars in defense of their religion. "Our gods are already dead," they stated. "Let us perish now." Their codices lay smoldering in heaps of ash.
>
> I write with the same knowledge, the same sadness, recognizing the full impact of the colonial "experiment" on the lives of Chicanos, mestizos, and Native Americans. Our codices—dead leaves unwritten—lie smoldering in the ashes of disregard, censure, and erasure. *The Last Generation* emerges from those ashes. I write it against time, out of a sense of urgency that Chicanos are a disappearing tribe, out of a sense of this disappearance in my own familia. (2)

For Moraga, "dead leaves unwritten" signal not just a dying culture, but one never fully articulated; this is the condition of emergent cultures in the United States.[6] The formulation of Moraga's critique—"from those ashes"—suggests the possibility of renewal in the act of naming the present cultural moment. For though her ancestors were conquered and colonized, and though the present generation of Americans of Mexican descent increasingly participate in a hegemonic negotiation with mainstream American culture, it is precisely the struggle between past and present, dominant and minority, which defines the contemporary Chicano subject. Though she titles her book *The Last Generation,* it could very well be called "The *First* Generation," a generation of Chicanos, culturally (re)constructed by a set of ethics resistant to the internal colonization of dominant U.S. culture.

Still, Moraga and other Chicano theorists face an uphill battle against "disregard, censure, and erasure," an elision that occurs at least as much within the academy as without. Like Boyarin, Moraga is writing in the postethnic moment, though her view of things stands in contrast to Boyarin's. With Moraga, Chicano difference includes the history of Chicano oppression and resistance, as well as hegemony. Rather than a deconstruction of a previously regarded stable ethnic construct, Moraga's Chicano subjectivity speaks to the internal difference of the Chicano in America. Significantly, whereas Boyarin's model of post-Judaism is synchronic—the post-Jewish Jew is not a product of history so much as history's construct, where history supplies the terms, ethics, or models for a contemporary expression of Jewish life—Moraga's is diachronic, the summation of a five-hundred-year history which is only now being articulated as such.

The very different theoretical approaches notwithstanding, the claims made and the tasks set out by Boyarin and Moraga are more alike than different, for despite the enfranchisement of Jews in the academy (relative to Chicanos), and despite the Chicano impulse to historicize (against the deconstructive impulse in so much Jewish theorizing), both writers are working toward a theory of ethnic identity that at once acknowledges the authenticity of ethnic subjectivity (even when this is a psychoanalytically conceived split subject) while interrogating the frame of academic cultural questioning in the first place. The difference between the two quotes represents the broader multicultural moment we inhabit in the academy, where the different methodologies and dual aims are presently deeply ingrained in the formation of "ethnic studies." We are faced with the tension of dual demands: historicize identity on the one hand, but beware of nostalgia or essentialist constructions of identity on the other.

Within Jewish studies it is the second mandate that we find most compelling or urgent, given that Jewish historiography following the Holocaust has succeeded in locating the ongoing history of trauma in a broad theoretical matrix. In fact, outside of an academic community, Jewish history has taken a conventional, knowable shape, so much so that it is commonly appropriated for other purposes, as discussed in the first chapter. Boyarin's concern in *Thinking in Jewish,* however, is not just with a broad appropriation of Jewish history by non-Jews, but the uncritical hegemonic response to Jewish history by major Jewish organizations and by a conservative stripe of the Jewish community that uses Jewish history to solidify a hold on American capital.[7] The task for the critical Jewish intellectual, then, is twofold: to deconstruct the seemingly monolithic sensibility of Jewish history predicated on nostalgia and sentiment on the one hand, while reconstructing an oppositional stance that draws from Jewish ethics, yet resists the center-pull of the Jewish mainstream, hence a "post-Judaism."

Moraga's writing represents a moment in the development of Chicano thought that is simultaneous but by no means the same as the current moment of Jewish thought, still arriving at similar conclusions: the need for an identity or identity position that is grounded in history but not buried in it, politicized but not traditionally nationalistic, and conversant in the ethic of multicultural critique, but not hamstrung by it. It should be clear by now that with both Chicano and Jewish theory, I am splitting the scene of writing in two. I am concerned here with both the theoretical maneuvers being made as well as the social and cultural landscape in which they take place. Even this secondary component requires further splitting, for as both Moraga and Boyarin indicate above, the academic environment and the cultural life on the streets share only nominal commonalty. Rather than get caught up in the metaphysics of identify, or the sweep of globalist critique, I aim to locate the scene of identity formation in American academic productions of ethnic identity. Within academic accounts and descriptions of identity formation, "ethnicity" emerges through the tension of social forces and the textual inscription of those forces, and the practice of critical reading is central to both aspects.

Angie Chabram has written an important essay that explores the position of the Chicano critic in a poststructuralist critical milieu. Her essay, "Conceptualizing Chicano Cultural Discourse," presents interviews with some of the principal contributors to the seminal collection *Criticism in the Borderlands: Studies in Chicano Literature, Culture, and Ideology,* including the book's editors, Héctor Calderón and José David Saldívar. In these interviews we learn of the early conflicts Chicano scholars encountered in the academy between theory and perceived experience, encounters that would later shape their critical studies. For example, of his early days at Yale, Héctor Calderón tells Chabram, "I walked into an auditorium to hear Derrida speak, and I remember having people point out Geoffrey Hartman and Paul de Man, J. Hillis Miller. And the atmosphere was sort of: 'Here is the word.' The final answer was about to be given, and these critics were gathered to hear it" (132).

But Calderón finds "the word" (ironically, poststructuralism) at once totalizing and exclusive, unable to accommodate his perception of Chicano identity:

> Another thing that bothered me about Yale, offended me even, was this notion that history does not exist. You know . . . That you can't write history anymore. That even the subject doesn't exist. Again, that seemed to exclude a whole group of people who were very much involved with history. . . . The Chicano Movement itself was not only making history at that moment, but it was a process in history, and there did not seem to be space for thinking about that within a frame work that says: "there's no subject, there's no history." (132)

José David Saldívar, who also earned his Ph.D. at Yale and is the coeditor of *Criticism in the Borderlands,* puts a finer point on it: "It seems a bit ironic that just when all these [mainstream] critics are talking about the end of the subject . . . that we should have Chicanos . . . finally beginning to see themselves as subjects, as capable of action instead of just being acted upon" (132). Saldívar's claims for Chicano agency do not necessarily counterpoint the poststructuralist critique of identity; instead, he critiques the academic framing of knowledge that would leave Chicano roots-based culture outside the field of vision or discussion. As Calderón and Saldívar depict it, the Chicano at Yale in the late 1970s is the invisible other within the very structure of cultural understanding.

Indeed, Saldívar's and Calderón's (and many others') complaints are what Bhabha calls a "moment of interrogation" in which "the demand for identification becomes, primarily, a response to other questions of signification and desire, culture and politics" (Bhabha 50). On the one hand, Saldívar and Calderón are coming out of a culture in which "the possibility of a Chicano readership in the late sixties and early seventies was itself a revolutionary idea" (Calderón and Saldívar 111): gaining a foothold in the academy and access to its ideas represents a social and historical shift. On the other hand, as these two critics point out, the ideas the academy has to offer would sever the self-defined ethnic scholar from his identity, the very cultural starting point whose ethos promoted attendance at Yale in the first place. Access to the academy by no means leads to counterhegemonic action, for the ground rules of literary scholarship, it turns out, comprise a static point in the structure of self-knowledge, at best ignoring or historicizing Chicano life, at worst undercutting any possibility of a counterhegemonic historiography. The task for the Chicano scholar, then, is to work within the discursive and theoretical parameters of the academy, all the while challenging assumptions about literary value and the place of ethnic literature in the canon. Early, formative Chicano criticism studies roots-based culture, such as folklore, *corridos,* popular art, and literature, while reworking the insights of poststructuralism. As Luis Leal puts it, "The Chicano has to create a new synthesis out of history, tradition, and his everyday confrontation with the ever-changing culture in which he lives" (Leal 4).

It is noteworthy that the "Yale School" Calderón and Saldívar speak against was so dominated by poststructuralist theorists who are Jewish, such as Geoffrey Hartman, Harold Bloom, and Derrida himself. In *White Mythologies* Robert Young reminds us that French poststructuralism was a theoretical corollary to the social uprisings of the late 1960s (including the student revolt and the Algerian War of Independence), and that both social and philosophical upheaval comprised a devastating critique of Western epistemology. It is no surprise that postwar European theorists and philosophers included so many Jews interested in challenging European logocentrism, including Hélène Cixous, Levinas, and Derrida.

Similarly, American deconstruction has been an attractive theory for American Jewish scholars. Especially in its early days when deconstruction was set in opposition against formalist New Criticism and its attendant conservative/Christian ideology, deconstruction offered those on the margins an approach to the professionally legitimizing canon without having to subscribe to canonical or Christological norms. Still, though one can speak of a common mode or school of Chicano criticism, there is not one group of texts to point to and say, "this is Jewish criticism," or the Jewish theoretical model. As the interviews above indicate, many of the most significant Chicano scholars whose works are influential today came out of the same generation, even attended the same universities, resulting in a similar critical and theoretical point of view. In contrast, Jewish scholars influential today are coming out of a wide variety of backgrounds and generations. Still, if there is a comparison to be found between Jewish theorists and their Chicano counterparts, it is in their mutual interrogation of academic epistemologies. And while for Chicanos and other minority scholars the tide appears to be turning—consider the recent significant expansion of American studies curricula to reflect the multiculturalism and multinationalism of the Americas—Jewish scholars increasingly find themselves left out of the picture, either linked to a monolithic construction of Europe, or more insidiously, philosophically regarded as the locus of repressive Western values, the Jew in Judeo-Christian thinking.

The critical collection *Insider/Outsider: Jews and Multiculturalism* (1998, edited by Biale, Galchinsky, and Heschel) attempts to reflect on the problematic of Jewish history and culture within the multicultural academy. Two essays in particular express a common Jewish critique of multiculturalism. Susannah Heschel's "Jewish Studies as Counter History" calls for a reradicalization of Jewish studies in the academy in order to fully realize its potential and locate it on the same plane as multiculturalism, while Amy Newman's "The Idea of Judaism in Feminism and Afrocentrism" surveys the monological construction of Judaism as a foil within multiculturalism. Heschel's essay traces the early development of Jewish studies in German universities in the late nineteenth century. After Emancipation, Jews were admitted to universities with increasing frequency, and Jewish studies developed its potential as a radical counter to European constructions of Jewish history and culture. Following Spivak, Heschel reads nineteenth-century Jews as the subaltern of Europe and recalls "that the very construction of the subaltern carries the seeds of its undoing" (105).

The task for Jewish studies scholars, then, was to locate the idea of Judaism in the construction of European Christianity in order to demonstrate how European culture depended on its other to maintain its vision of cultural stability and superiority, not to mention universality. Early Jewish studies scholars "saw the study of Judaism as not simply an addition to the general curriculum [of European history] but as a revision of that curriculum, an effort to resist and even overthrow the standard portrayal of Western history" (Heschel 102).

Jewish studies scholars struck at the heart of Christian religious historiography, which construed the advent of Christianity as the reclamation or recuperation of a debased and corrupt Judaism. What European religious scholars called "Judaism" was the discursive lacuna into which Christianity appeared. But this is also the point where the Jewish scholar could unravel the cultural construction:

> In the particular case of the Christian repression of Judaism through its construction of "Judaism," the subaltern Jewish voice begins by insinuating itself as necessary to the Christian, even while claiming that the Christian is not necessary to the Jewish. It is not the Jew who desires Christianity, but the Christian who requires a myth of Jewish desire in order to legitimate Christianity. (105)

Keeping in mind Bhabha's method of questioning the framework of knowledge, Heschel's subjects do not merely reconstruct the image of the Jew, but expose the flawed internal logic of identity construction to begin with. Reviewing the work of Abraham Geiger's Jewish historiography of Jesus for example, Heschel explains that

> by reversing the position of the observer, from Christians writing about Judaism to a Jew writing about Christianity, Geiger reversed the power relations of the viewer and the viewed. Until now, the gaze of scholarship had been a Christian gaze and Judaism appeared occasionally as the object viewed. In Geiger's writings, the gaze is Jewish, and Christianity is transformed into a semiotic representation within Judaism. (111)

Though Geiger maintained an anti-Christian polemic throughout his career, Heschel shows that his strategy is finally effective not so much for reconstructing a Jewish identity, nor critiquing a Christian one, but for destabilizing hegemonic ideologies of dominance and otherness. For Heschel this is a potential model for Jewish studies within a multicultural academy. Jewish studies might be one of "a variety of gazes that will unsettle and throw into question the complacency of academic categories and analyses" (112).

And indeed, as Amy Newman describes it in her essay, multiculturalism itself can stand for scrutiny, especially as premises of radical Afrocentrism and feminism rely on just the kinds of Jewish historiography Heschel's subjects defy. Newman's essay, "The Idea of Judaism in Feminism and Afrocentrism," seeks first to expose the false construction of Judaism that would link it monologically to Western culture (whatever that might be) and then to show how this false construction has led some feminists and Afrocentric scholars to blame Jewish culture for the misogyny and cultural racism inherent in Western culture. Newman responds with her own counterhistory and concludes that a reevaluation of the term *Judaism* itself is needed, for over the course of two thousand years and even within the last century, Judaism has been refracted into dozens of different stripes: "the term 'Judaism,' as conventionally used in both popular and academic discourse, has no external referent" (167). This is more than an antiessentialist dis-location of culture, following, say, Said's critique of Orientalism. In Said's work, and in postcolonial criticism in general, the critic's task is ultimately to open up a space for self-representation of colonized or formerly colonized peoples. With Newman and Heschel, however, the task is to end *mis*representation, or the monological association of Judaism with whatever is ethically distasteful in the (academic) construction of "Western culture." Quoting Jacob Neusner, Newman writes,

> "When people use the word 'Judaism,'" Neusner explains, "they use it only in the singular, and they assume that the word refers to a single religion, or religious tradition, extending (if not from Creation) from Sinai to the present." But, he continues, "when we treat as uniform and harmonious—as testimony to a single 'Judaism'—the extant corpus of documentary evidence for Judaism in its formative centuries, we misunderstand what we have in hand." (167)

In Neusner's advisory we hear a direct contrast to Moraga's earlier pronouncement on the urgency for a rearticulation of Chicano ethnic identity. Judaism and Chicano culture have long histories, but for Newman and Neusner this prevents the formulation of anything like a statement of *common* culture.

Whereas Moraga seeks to gather in internal difference or *mestizaje* produced by colonization, and Calderón and Saldívar attempt to inscribe the previously unnamed subject, Newman suggests that it is precisely the Jewish history of colonization and dispersion that prevents such a cultural construction, and this history retroactively and omni-chronically assigns the "post" across Jewish history. But then, there is seemingly no need to create a space for Jews to talk about Jews, for this they have already done, and for millennia, in liturgy, commentary, poetry, philosophy, and literature.

We are back at square one, and hence the problem with the multicultural academy as it now exists: There is something out there we could call Jewish culture or Jewish literature, but it is so various and refracted, spanning centuries, borders, and national cultures, that it is hard to imagine where Jewish studies might fit in an academic multiculture that (despite its rhetoric) longs for borders, bodies, and chairs to identify a given ethnic corpus. Neusner's quote begs the question, what *do* we have in hand when we speak of Judaism or Jewish studies? If it is merely counterhistory, or the gaze of the other locked onto hegemonic cultural constructions, is this really Jewish or just the function of deconstructive difference? We find ourselves following the path of Lyotard (*Heidegger and the "jews"*) or Deleuze and Guattari (*Kafka: Toward a Minor Literature*), using Jewish difference as a deconstructing trope, or a general agent of social change, all the while leaving out what Lyotard refers to as "real Jews."[8]

The problem with Heschel's piece in particular is that while it effectively questions the framing of knowledge and cultural study within the academy, and especially argues for the efficacy of Jewish "counterhistory," there is little suggestion of what would finally be Jewish about Jewish studies. With Heschel's observations, we are indeed "post-" Judaism, especially the hegemonically constructed Judaism of European enlightenment, for which Jewish history is a negative pole in a binary dialectic of Western idealism. But if Jewish religious culture is to be philosophically liberated from the occluding phrase "Judeo-Christian (culture, values, society, etc.)," on what grounds will it finally stand alone?

In Jonathan Boyarin's formulation, critical post-Judaism indicates a continual engagement with Judaism's changing face in the world. Judaism itself undergoes critique, but can be read as a critical practice. Ambivalently, Boyarin turns to the model of messianic Hasidim whose networks are ethnically local and global at the same time, interior and hermetic in lifestyle, transnational and postmodern in their mission to bring the Messiah into the world. The Hasidim, Boyarin writes, "simultaneously subvert and exploit 'modernization,'" and in this sense they are both postmodern and post-Jewish, not beyond either but critically revising the normative tendencies of both. But if Judaism ought to constantly revise itself, the question persists "what in it remains Jewish?" (*Thinking* 200). This is Boyarin's question as well as my own, and at the end of *Thinking in Jewish* he hints at an answer that is oblique at best: "Let us not wipe away that question mark. Let us gather around it, and let us ask more questions, and then some more" (200). His answer is only somewhat satisfying to the eager, would-be post-Jewish scholar, as is the fact that the essay from which it comes was originally written by Boyarin in Yiddish, making it a praxis model for postmodern Jewish renewal, albeit of a distinctly Ashkenazi ethnic stripe, further occluding internal Jewish difference.

Boyarin is at his best when "thinking in Jewish" himself, which amounts to an amalgam of ethnography, theory, and cultural critique, but ethical earnestness does not always make good theory, nor does theory amount to an ethics of Jewish living. If a critical post-Judaism is finally a theoretical position or method, it is not clear that it will have value outside the academy or even within it alongside other ethnic studies agendas, rendering Jewish studies moot to a broader social milieu. A post-Jewish critique may be satisfying for one who regards him- or herself as Jewish (the result of heritage, affect, or ethical inquiry), but does not offer a model of the Jewish subject or of Jewish culture that would be recognizable either in or out of the multicultural academy.

Some have posed the solution not of changing the conception of Jewish culture or subjectivity, but of changing or critiquing academic multiculturalism. While Bhabha argued for making the presence of the invisible palpably rendered in the face of the visible, I do not think he meant for the subaltern to disappear altogether, or to persist as a dogged ghost of the past, but this seems to be an implicit result if not the outright tack taken by some Jewish scholars whose recent work on ethnicity suggests ethnicity's end in the academy. For example, entranced by David Hollinger's notion of a "Post Ethnic America," David Biale advocates the further diffusion of Jewish cultural identity: "[I]t is possible for a multiracial or multiethnic person to identify at one and the same time as both Irish and Italian, or both black and white, or even Jew and Christian. That is, in place of a new, monolithic identity to take the place of the ethnic or racial identities that make it up, one could imagine multiple identities held simultaneously and chosen as much as inherited" (30). Like Hollinger, Walter Benn Michaels, or even Werner Sollors, Biale writes with a breathless enthusiasm for "postethnicity" as he attempts to usher in an age of identity that is not only not monolithic, but so diffuse, apolitical, and uncritical as to be useless. Certainly one *could* identify as both black and white, Jew and Christian, but only if identity meant a superficial, uncritical choice before an apolitical social gaze. Following Sollors, who argues that ethnicity is a function of "consent" and "descent," Biale attempts to liberate ethnic identity from its current status as a social or political "given" and make it a choice, without critically questioning choice to begin with. To identify as a Chicano (to choose one of many possible examples) is itself a choice among many appellations, including Mexican American, Latino, or simply American.

Postidentity and postethnic critics are working with the equivalent of a critical "Ockham's razor," lopping off legacies of prejudice or cultural domination by severing identity from history. Benn Michaels especially has positioned his work as antiracist, aiming to slash through the traps of modernist-era thinking about identity. He and Hollinger both argue that our vocabulary for identity, including terms like *ethnicity, race,* and even *culture,* ultimately objectifies the would-be subjects of identity, turning people into objects of history rather than agents in their present moment. However, as Moya and Mohanty's "new realist" accounts of ethnic identity make clear, to choose to identify as "Chicano," say, is not simply to choose among a number of equally compelling identities. Rather, it is a statement of the inadequacy of the other choices, of the problematic of imperialism and hegemony implicit in the very term *American.* Furthermore, strategic identification involves reflecting on the experience of being identified by a social gaze that places gender, sexuality, and skin color in hierarchies of value. The question that so many Chicano critics pose is whether or not the individual subject is sufficiently liberated as to make such choices, or if "culture" is itself the product of actively choosing, where choosing alternately signifies resisting a passive nonchoice.

As Cherríe Moraga puts it, in a passage that follows the one quoted at the beginning of this chapter, "My tios' [uncles'] children have not taught their own children to be Mexicans. They have become 'Americans.' And we're all supposed to quietly accept this passing, this slow and painless death of a cultura, this invisible disappearance of a people. But I do not accept it. I write" (2). Passively becoming white versus actively writing a Chicano identity—this is the choice for Moraga, and more accurate, it seems to me, than Biale's choice of identities where all associations are value-free and on the same social plane, neither dominating the other or canceling the other out. As Kandice Chuh points out, "in conceiving of multiple kinds of differences, we must of course recognize that they do not exist independently of each other. Rather, they converge and conflict and thus participate in shaping each other" (148). This confusion and convergence amounts to a deconstruction of the linguistic signs of identity, but if we grant that there is no space outside of language wherein identities and narratives of identification exist, the signs of identity do not disappear, nor is it clear that it would be desirable if they do. Like Boyarin, who actively attempts to advance Jewish identity into theory, Moraga is aware that by writing she is not just choosing an identity, but performatively *making* one. For Moraga, writing herself into a reformed identity matrix necessitates a two-pronged critique of both American mainstream culture and Chicano oppositionalism, and as we saw in the previous chapter, the results are provocative for thinking about ethnicity in America in general.

To Biale's suggestion of multiple ethnicities, I would rephrase José David Saldívar's earlier comment and say that it seems ironic that just when we have truly interesting work within ethnic studies, especially by Jewish studies scholars, one would want undermine the efficacy of ethnicity. While I still recognize the problems inherent in Boyarin's post-Judaism, or Moraga's experiential culture-naming consciousness, I am not inclined to dismiss ethnic identity altogether, which would be the effect of Biale's formulation.

Recalling Boyarin's reminder that a critical post-Judaism need not be its members' only Jewish identity, it seems the choice of *what kind of Jew* one may be, or *what kind of Chicano,* is a far more interesting and pertinent question to the project of multiculturalism. In its banal and popular forms, multiculturalism means that it is much easier to discard an identity, or even to pair it with another, all for the purpose of "celebrating difference." But what if multiculturalism, and Jewish studies in particular, asks not, say, "can one identify as gay and Jewish?" but "what does it mean to be both at once?" Is there a way of thinking of "Jewish" that signals "gay" as well? What kinds of material and social conditions give rise to this yoking of identities and how can academic theorizing work on behalf of identities which enable the fullest realization of being human? A critical, revisionist ethnic culture might avail itself of more than one identity, not to produce some hybrid—a new identity that stands apart from the old— but to transform the way identities are conceived in the first place. To speak of a gay-Jewish experience may produce a progressive critique of both identities, but still leaves both intact, and separate. Better still would be a revision each of the terms *gay* and *Jewish,* which would obviate the need for the qualifying other.

In *Unheroic Conduct: The Rise of Heterosexuality and the Invention of the Jewish Man,* Daniel Boyarin (Jonathan's brother) locates an ethic of gender ambivalence in rabbinical Talmudic culture; but his real innovation is the invention of a contemporary ethic of Jewish feminism, which critiques male Jewish culture from a male point of view. Boyarin's discovery in Talmudic literature of a Jewish male ethic of pacifism and homoeroticism opens a place in Jewish tradition for a gay male Jew who is not hyphen bound, "imagined," or marginal, but the very center of Jewish ethics itself. Tony Kushner's praise for Boyarin's work is instructive: "Boyarin's readings . . . illuminate our current crises in such a way as to suggest, and it is a very Jewish suggestion, that such slim hope as exists for transformation and redemption can only be found through a countenancing and a settling of accounts with the past."[9] Here a "countenancing" with the past means rereading it and reinventing the present. Whether the past is always already the bedrock of the present, or whether the past is read as a synchronic accumulation of images, ethics, and identities, clearing space in the present for new identity constructions necessarily involves settling with or unsettling the past. Rather than reifying history, such a concept acknowledges the ever-belated construction of the past through present practice, while just this act has the effect of reshaping the present. For Daniel Boyarin, the process involves applying the pressure of contemporary social ethics to the textual legacy of the past, asking present-day questions and expecting answers from the rabbinical forefathers. The method is midrashic, and neither reifies the rabbinical perspective into some "voice of the father" nor does away with it altogether.

I will expand upon the paradigm of midrash for cultural construction in a moment, but first I pause to note that the general model of textual continuity as a component of ethnic identity is presented with a good deal of skepticism in contemporary Jewish literature. With Roth's *The Ghost Writer* and Ozick's *The Messiah of Stockholm,* Jewish characters are chiefly critical readers of the texts of their pasts who finally find only false constructions of their present selves. In fact, we recall that the textual legacy each protagonist encounters carries with it a sort of matrix for contemporary ethnic construction—primarily the elevation of historical trauma to the nexus of ethnic identity—and both Roth's and Ozick's reluctant heroes finally reject the legacy or matrix as false constructions of their present selves. Ethnicity per se is not rejected so much as dominant constructions of Jewish identity which hegemonically play into the nostalgia trade. The problem for protagonists in both novels is not that they believe the past cannot speak to the present, but that the present will not listen, as contemporary ideology imposes a set of values, predetermining any reading. Both writers seem to warily reject nostalgia, sentimentality, and the cult of victimhood in the construction of identity, but in the end, neither protagonist emerges with a stable sense of self.

Alejandro Morales's *The Rag Doll Plagues* (discussed in chapter 2) affirms the relevance of cultural legacies and suggests the empowerment of the individual as a *reader* of his or her past. Neither a historicizing student of the past nor a reader intent on imposing present desires on the past, Morales's historically recurring protagonist is a critical reviser, never totalizing the experiences of his Spanish/Chicano forefathers into a rigid ethnic model, but always synthesizing contemporary experience with the voice of the past, a practice akin to Boyarin's claims for midrash.

In an earlier study comparing midrash with contemporary literary theory, Boyarin reminds us that "all interpretation and historiography is *representation* of the past by the present, that is, that there is no such thing as value-free, true and objective rendering of documents" (*Intertextuality* 12). This much is evident in skepticism of Roth and Ozick's tales, but Boyarin's definition of midrash holds out for a still more positive construction of the process of reading and interpretation:

Were I to attempt to define midrash at this point, it would perhaps be radical intertextual reading of the canon, in which potentially every part refers to and is interpretable by every other part. The Torah, owing to its own intertextuality, is a severely gapped text, and the gaps are there to be filled by strong readers, which in this case does not mean readers fighting for originality, but readers fighting to find what they must in the holy text. Their own intertext—that is, the cultural codes which enable them to make meaning and find meaning, constrain the rabbis to fill in the gaps of the Torah's discourse with narratives which are emplotted in accordance with certain ideological structures. (*Intertextuality* 16)

For Boyarin, intertextuality is not just the presence of one text within another, but the very condition of ideology in the everyday, the cultural condition that compels us to ask the kinds of questions of the past that we do. Yet the very fact that we are compelled to look toward the past for answers to present questions—questions of ethics for Torah readers, but for ethnic scholars in general the pouring over of texts and histories that are made to speak to present conceptions of (any given) ethnicity—indicates, finally, the incoherence or the "gaps" in our present ideology—the problematics of ethnic identity construction. We read and interpret the gaps of the past because the gaps in our present text compel us to.

In the practice of critically reading the past, whether it be Moraga's reading of "dead leaves unwritten," Jonathan Boyarin's reading on his own body the inscription of his Judaism, or any countenancing with conventional history, something like a midrashic (re)construction of ethnic subjectivity occurs. Illustrating the reconstruction is the critical work of Chicano scholars Ramón Saldívar and José Limón and their readings of the work of anthropologist Américo Paredes. Writing a generation after Paredes, Saldívar and Limón find in his work the raw material for the future construction of Chicano ethnicity. Though Saldívar and Limón are not technically midrashic in their reading of Paredes, their methods and conclusions can be understood in the same terms Boyarin uses to describe midrash. What is common, finally, is a model of ethnic criticism that, while skeptical of a transcendent consciousness that would claim ethnic identity, nonetheless performs the work of identity construction through a consciousness that is passed through a self-reflexive criticism.

Since the mid 1980s, virtually every major statement on Chicano literature and culture includes a chapter or a section on the influence of

Américo Paredes' ethnography and narrative studies for Chicano criticism. In his seminal work, *With His Pistol in His Hand* (1958), and in
countless novels, stories, poems, and essays, Paredes historicized and tex-
tualized the oral and musical folk culture of Chicano communities in
South Texas, from the late 1800s onward. Paredes has since become the
subject of Chicano historiography himself, and two works in particular
offer a cogent statement of his influence through a rereading of his textual legacy.

One appears in Ramón Saldívar's work *Chicano Narrative: A Dialectics of Difference*. Early in the first chapter, Saldívar declares "*history* is the
subtext that we must recover because history itself is the subject of [Chi-
cano narrative's] discourse" (5). The privileging of history over the subjective experience begs the question of how to approach that history, how
to write it and how to read it if Chicanos are still in conflict with the
dominant culture, a question reminiscent of Bhabha's urge to interrogate
the framing of academic and official knowledge itself. Saldívar's answer is
to theorize the Chicano subject according to Theodore Adorno's model
of a negative dialectic which "negate[s] the possibility of an ultimate synthesis of subject and object in every conceivable concrete situation" (173).
"Identity," Saldívar continues, "is a contradiction": "In opposition to a
positive identity, fixed, namable, absolute, and self-satisfied in its stability . . . Adorno offers a negative dialectic that proposes a critique of
'every self-absolutizing particular,' even the absolute notion of the self as
an autonomous, independent entity" (174).[10] Ramón Saldívar's agitation
of a fixed identity directly contrasts (his brother) José David Saldívar's
rejection of the end of subject-hood, but his project of counterhegemonic criticism is the same: "An unfixed, decentered identity alters the pat-
tern by which a society must position the subject so that 'it shall freely
submit to its subjection'" (*Chicano Narrative* 174). Saldívar's dialectics of
difference locates the dominant identity ("society") on the same plane
as the marginalized ethnic subject. Each corresponds to the other, each
knows itself only in relation to the other due to the "incessant presence
of the self in the other" (174).

Saldívar comes close to a formulation comparable to Bhabha's at the
beginning of this chapter: the Chicano, as an autonomous ethnic subject,
has no voice and is effectively invisible within the dominant field of study.
Instead, he is only known in so far as he haunts the prevailing culture.

Saldívar stops short of extending his analysis of Chicano subjectivity to issues of mimicry and parody—the discursive condition for the postcolonial subject, according to Bhabha—but we can nonetheless follow this thread ourselves, reading the gaps in Saldívar's own text to come full circle in this one.

A particularly provocative footnote appears in *Chicano Narrative* which, when read hermeneutically, locates a reading strategy that at once follows Bhabha's model and Daniel Boyarin's. The footnote in question is appended to a poem Saldívar cites by Américo Paredes. The poem, "The Mexico-Texan," is cited because it "tells in brief the history of the Chicano in the Southwest" (11). The poem parodies an already parodic stereotypical Texano voice, and tells the story of the emblematic Texano's plight

> The Mexico-Texan he's one fonny man
> Who leeves in the regin tha's north of the Gran'
> of Mexican father he born in these part,
> And sometimes he rues it dip down in he's heart
> For the Mexico-Texan he no gotta lan
> He stomped on the neck on both sides of the Gran . . .
>   (Paredes, quoted in Saldívar, *Chicano Narrative* 11)

The poem, partaking of the colonists' voice, mocks that voice and asserts the plight of the colonized Texano, whose land has been usurped. Cloaked in derision, the poem is indeed "a brief history" of the Texano's plight, and can easily be heard as what Genaro Padilla calls a "whisper of resistance" (Padilla 44). Despite its potency, Saldívar leaves the poem and all its mimicry behind, moving onto a discussion of "history" in broad terms. But for the footnote, it would seem the poem had only "throw-away" value for Saldívar.

Here is what the footnote tells us: "the poem quickly caught on as an anonymous folk expression of popular resistance." The poem was written in 1934 and "was picked up and circulated fairly widely in ensuing years, verbally for the most part" (11). The poem, popular for its defiance, appears in a Latino news journal in 1937, and again in a Latino yearbook in 1939. It became a part of local folklore, informing the culture of resistance that developed in Brownsville during the 1940s. In a conversation with Américo Paredes, Saldívar learns the poem "was used in political campaigns, was reprinted a few times as anonymous, and entered oral tradition locally. [The poem was] collected in Brownsville as 'folk poetry' in the 1960's" (Paredes, quoted in Saldívar 11). Also, two recent critical works quote "The Mexico-Texan" to establish a folk-based political sensibility, and of course, the poem appears as a point of reference in Ramón Saldívar's theory of the dialectics of difference (11). The lengthy footnote, including the apparent conversation with Paredes, indicates that the poem is significant to Saldívar, but he closes the footnote only by mentioning the interesting way oral poems become written texts.

"The Mexico-Texan" has an uncanny itinerary from folk poem to political statement to critical exemplar. If with Jonathan Boyarin's theory of a critical post-Judaism we lacked a model or definition for what Judaism is, we find in Saldívar's study of Paredes a latent model for locating the dialectical and performative *readerly* nature of Chicano ethnicity. Likewise, the poem, and Saldívar's reading of it (or the reading we tease out of his footnote), is much closer to the model suggested by Daniel Boyarin. The movement of Paredes' poem from folkloric artifact of the political unconscious into the contemporary critical conscious is typical of the politicized, historically based Chicano critical movement, and illustrates the way ethnic folk culture informs political culture. True, the poem was a political act to begin with, but during the 1960s, Chicano activists asserted it as a "root metaphor" (McKenna, "Chicano" 193). It is during the movement that folk culture "becomes transformed from a genre of cultural performance to the status of a root metaphor for the paradigmatic contestation between the Anglo-American 'other' and Mexicans on this side of the border" (193). According to Terry Eagleton, a root metaphor is a "metaphor of the text . . . furnish[ing] the terms in which the text can know itself" (Eagleton 19). This seems a true if incomplete account of "The Mexico Texan," for though the poem has an enduring power, exerting an ethic of resistance across generations, each generation finally reads or wields the poem according to the contemporary cultural terms. Written as a folk parody, and likely as a means to express an identity (through mimicry and resistance), the poem is reread and essentially rewritten during the Chicano movement, for which Américo Paredes serves as something of an elder statesman.

The peripatetic itinerary of the poem replicates the spiraling influence of Paredes' seminal study of Chicano folklore, *With His Pistol in His Hand.* José Limón's thoughts on Paredes' book are significant for introducing a creative and key conceptualization of Chicano ethnicity because Limón privileges *reading* as the primary process by which the Chicano comes to know him- or herself. If Paredes' study indicates the early cultural products of an emerging ethnic community, Limón's reading of Paredes locates the precise origins of ethnicity, and it is with Paredes himself. Echoing Saldívar, Limón explains, "Paredes's scholarly anthropological study became a powerful influence on a new generation of Chicano writers, intellectuals and activists as they produced a new critical social discourse" during the 1960s (*Mexican Ballads* 65). As Limón sees it, a new generation of Chicanos just entering the universities, found *With His Pistol in His Hand* to be "a new kind of *corrido* [epic ballad], one whose complex relationship to the past enabled it to speak to the present" (65).

Limón argues that this community of young scholars (spread out at universities around the United States, though united by their marginalization as well as scholarly interest in Chicano culture) came to idealize Paredes himself, forming a corrido-like discourse around him: "When Chicano movement people gather and the conversation turns to the subject of Américo Paredes, one can often detect the gradual emergence of what I shall call an unsung proto-ballad/legendry of Américo Paredes. It is as if such conversations—a kind of Chicano movement oral tradition—construct the known life and career of this man into folklore" (Limón 1986 26). Building on this narrative in a later essay, Limón proceeds to draw further links between the legendry of Cortez and that of Paredes. He reviews Paredes' near-mythic life, blending a variety of voices into a narrative that quickly reveals itself a mirror of Paredes' own masterpiece about "a border ballad and its hero." Limón quite self-consciously invokes his mentor's own work to model his study of the significant influence Paredes has had on a huge number of Chicano scholars.[11] Not only does Limón document Paredes' influence on subsequent scholars, he also performs that influence by reperforming Paredes' original work. Both works move from cultural to political to critical product.

Paredes' poem, like his book, originally traveled in local circles, influential for individuals though not yet formative for ethnic identity. Then the poem, also like the book, became overtly politicized at a formative moment in the development of Chicano ethnic identity. Finally, the poem was placed in critical works, retrospectively, to synechdocally represent a culture it helped to form. Here we see that criticism, as Terry

Eagleton has noted, is bound to the culture which it critiques, serving to naturalize and institutionalize that culture: "In the need to incorporate new classes and fractions of classes into cultural unity, to establish a consensus of social taste, construct common traditions and disseminate uniform manners, criticism becomes one fulcrum of a whole set of ideological institutions: periodicals, coffee-houses, aesthetic and social treatises" (Eagleton 19).

But criticism does not just exist on the same plane, sharing the same space as other cultural practices, as Saldívar's footnote shows us. Criticism works to unify, consolidate, and naturalize culture, all the while calling attention to its own processes. It is difficult to say in retrospect how "The Mexico-Texan" influenced the formation of Chicano identity during the '40s or '60s. But contemporary critical writing has the power to retrospectively emblematize history with ethnicity by grafting onto history the lately regarded cultural artifact.[12]

To return to the midrashic model of ethnic criticism, the *readerly* model of ethnicity suggested here is not only dialectical, but performative. Cultures reproduce themselves through the experiential process of reading and responding to their gaps and inconsistencies—an anxious maintenance—as well as to accommodate an ever-changing climate of multicultural encounter. I am reminded of Thomas Hobbes's meditation on the repair of a ship at sea: What if the ship were repaired, during a journey across the ocean, plank by plank? Would the ship that arrives at port be the same one that originally embarked on its journey? Ducking the philosophical problem of difference and repetition for a moment, I would suggest that cultures are like the metaphorical ship at sea, ever reconstructing themselves, bearing with them the agents of their reconstruction, cutting through an environment that calls for continual though gradual maintenance. So we might reorient Boyarin's basis for midrash: fighting to find what they must and certainly filling in gaps takes on a whole new urgency aboard ship, and this suggests both the ethics and pragmatics of this sort of cultural maintenance. Like sailors on a ship, a culture bears its members through seas, either rough or calm. Similarly, a holy text produces a value system and an ontological conception of the world for its adherents, but this too means that believers must actively read both ancillary texts and the world at large to shore up against any leaks.

Ethnicity is widely acknowledged to be a *process,* and this chapter describes and illustrate that process rather than conducts an investigation into the content of ethnicity or culture itself.[13] Though the construction of an ethnic matrix described above may seem hopelessly relativistic, depending on a ever-shifting and prior conception of culture, relativism is part of the broader mechanics of critical praxis. Following both Daniel Boyarin and Ramón Saldívar, I suggest that a critique of ethnic culture is most honest and clear-sighted when its motivations are the explanation of the present day, its aims the exploration of fissures of difference among contemporaneous cultures. This may be a jargony way of describing what is already being done—Chicano criticism, say, which analyzes the syncretism of native and colonial motifs—but also points to the rigorous questioning of the very modes of inquiry that Bhabha has called for. This means locating "ethnic" tropes for cultural criticism, such as diaspora, the border, or Moraga's "Queer Aztlán," but it also means pursuing the critical assumptions and the political results of those tropes.

Comparisons across ethnicities, such as the ones I have made here, sharpen our understanding of the differences between ethnic cultures, all the while highlighting the points of relation between dominant and minority cultures. The diaspora/border comparison in chapter 4 may be a good example of this mode of critique as we see America and its ethnic others are at once mutually constitutive of one another, while holding quite different notions about what or where America is in the first place. The comparisons have the effect of highlighting the differences among Jewish, Chicano, and mainstream American spatial ontologies, but also critically questioning those given ontologies to begin with. Such questioning is not meant to be a cynic's project, intent on undermining the efficacy of native tropes of criticism. On the contrary, my broad task in this book is a critical questioning of the frameworks of understanding in order to revise them and thereby enhance their ability to describe the past and inscribe the future in culturally recognizable and ethically progressive terms. In keeping with points made so far, I should add that I draw those two goals—cultural continuity and progressivism—from the bulk of the literature examined in this book, though it is also important to note that what counts as "culture" or "progress" varies from writer to writer. Insofar as this continual questioning reverences the past by making it speak to the present, and so long as the present day responses to the past are attempts to "find what we must," the method is indeed midrashic.

At this point it is worth noting that Daniel Boyarin's work on midrash comes at a time when "midrash has been largely suppressed in Jewish hermeneutics, as much as it has been marginalized in the West" (*Intertextuality* xii). By writing on midrash, he not only introduces an otherwise occluded practice for Western readers, he builds a case for the further study of an otherwise veiled component of that broad term *Judaism*. In effect, Boyarin critically reads and then rearranges the normative conception of Judaism and Jewish thought. The result is not a contrast with or a break from Judaism but a discovery of Judaism's import in present day poststructuralist theory. Even my limited use of his theory here has the rippling effect of affirming and expanding the Jewishness of midrashic readings, and by applying midrash to a theory of ethnic literature and criticism strengthens a conception of Jewish critical practice. Still, ethnically specific as my critical model may be, there is no reason why it cannot remain Jewish all the while being a Jewish way of naming the practice of ethnic criticism at large. But calling it a "Jewish way" of reading foregrounds the specificity of the practice, which itself has manifold implications.

Midrash is not the dominant mode of Jewish hermeneutics (despite its academic cache), but following Daniel Boyarin, employing midrash as a trope and naming it as "Jewish" might add to the vitality of this reading strategy. As with Heschel and Neusner, I maintain that this is not the wholesale invention and importation of a lately stylized theory into an already existing monological culture, but a teasing out of what was already there to begin with, finding in the practice a relevant answer to contemporary questions about ethnicity, identity, and reading. Finally, by calling midrash a *Jewish* way of doing ethnic criticism, I hope to put at least some (but not too many) limits on the critical concept. While the critical trope of midrash is dynamic and suggestive for thinking about ethnic criticism at large, I hope that among the things it suggests would be other ways of doing similar things specific (and relevant) to other ethnicities.

Someone recently asked me if there was a Chicano equivalent to midrash. In my haste to seem knowing and full of answers, I suggested the prototypical Chicano ballad, the corrido. Like midrash, it is an oral story form, intertextual, ideological, responsive to contemporaneous ideological problems. But the comparison eventually petered out as the obvious differences began to glare through my hazy comparisons: The corrido is a kind of reportage, rather than religious interpretation, and it is artfully sung rather than hashed out in a *heder*. But then, it occurs to me now that José Limón, in his study of Américo Paredes—who himself did his seminal work on the corrido—uses the trope of the corrido to theorize the evolution of Paredes from folklorist into folklore subject himself. And though I have suggested that Limón's work is midrashic for all its intertextuality, Limón's own critical trope is the corrido, a ballad that sings the news of the present but only registers when pitched in the recognizable idiom of the recent (and ever-replicating) past. And this is an altogether *Chicano* way of naming the practice of ethnic criticism at large.

NOTES

INTRODUCTION

1. See Wells, "Federal Indian Policy," in Reeves, and McKee and Schlenker, *The Choctaws.*

2. See Galloway ("Choctaw Factionalism" 143) for more on the historical Redshoes.

3. This is the latest "crisis in the humanities" according to two panels, titled "The Future of the Humanities," at the 2004 MLA convention in Philadelphia. Louis Menand, Toni Morrison, and Gayatri Chakravorty Spivak, among others, spoke to the need to recover for humanities scholars the domain of humanistic inquiry in the wake of poststructuralist and postmodern theories.

4. Besides Palumbo-Liu's collection, see Robert Lee's *Multicultural American Literature,* Timothy Powell's *Ruthless Democracy,* and Jeff Karem's *The Romance of Authenticity.*

5. See *Outside the Subject,* esp. chap. 10, for example.

6. See Eisen, *Galut.*

7. For example, consider the meeting of two Chinese sisters separated for decades by the immigration of one to the United States in Maxine Hong Kingston's *Woman Warrior* (136).

8. See Gates, "Writing 'Race.'"

9. This is Richard Rodriguez's critique of multiculturalism in his memoir, *Brown.* Rodriguez, the *bête noire* of Chicano studies, has consistently, albeit deeply ironically, identified himself as a Hispanic, but has folded the implicit cosmopolitanism of "Hispanic" into his analysis of American culture. Among the many critiques of multiculturalism in print, Seyla Benhabib's essay, "The Liberal Imagination and the Four Dogmas of Multiculturalism" is comprehensive, reasonable, and sympathetic to the project.

10. See Gordon and Newfield for a useful survey of the multiple multiculturalisms, the plurality of pluralisms, some of which effectively resist the tendencies Lowe indicts, others which are complicit and warrant her critique.

11. Upon reading a draft of this book, Adrienne Pilon reminded me that "colored," too, has responded to historical vicissitudes, as Chicano and Asian American social movements indicate.

12. See in particular the work of Fred Gardaphe, including *Italian Signs, American Streets,* which draws heavily on Sollors and a semiotics of ethnic difference. Also in dialogue with contemporary ethnic studies is the work of Thomas Ferraro, including *Ethnic Passages: Literary Immigrants in the Twentieth Century.*

1. THE JEW WHO GOT AWAY

1. The topic has, of course, been debated for nearly a century in this country. *What Is Jewish Literature* is the title of an edited collection by Hana Wirth-Nesher (and a new edition is in the works), and the question is the subject of a notorious exchange of essays between Michael Kramer and a group of luminary interlocutors printed in *Prooftexts.*

2. Young's *Writing and Rewriting the Holocaust* (1988), Langer's *Admitting the Holocaust* and *Holocaust Testimonies,* Friedlander's *Probing the Limits of Representation,* and Felman and Laub's *Testimony,* all published within about a decade of each other, draw on deconstructive and postmodern theories of literature and representation. Each writer argues for the impossibility of a literature from within the camps (Langer), but Young and Felman are especially committed to the notion that the impossibility of representation is itself a kind of testimony to the rupture of history that is the Holocaust. Also see Hartman's collection, *Holocaust Remembrance,* Hungerford's excellent *The Holocaust of Texts,* and Michaels's essay, "You Who Never Was There," in Flanzbaum's collection, *The Americanization of the Holocaust* for examples of criticism that dissents from Young's and Felman's commitment to the conflation of memory and history. Throughout this book I cite several works by Dominick LaCapra, whose commitment to rethinking historiography through psychoanalysis and poststructuralism positions his work as a metacommentary on Friedlander, Young, Felman, Caruth, and others. LaCapra's work is distinguished by a deep skepticism for fetishizing both the Holocaust through theory and theory through the Holocaust. Rothberg's *Traumatic Realism* is a solid application of Holocaust-deduced theory to American literature. Hungerford's *The Holocaust of Texts* is an excellent cut across the grain of Holocaust theory, arguing that Holocaust theory leads to a "personification" and sacralization of the text.

3. It is painful but important to recognize how ideological tendencies in American culture and historiography have parlayed the Holocaust into a marketable event, a conservative narrative, and banal universal story. See Tim Cole's excellent *Selling the Holocaust.*

4. Much has been made of Fredrick Jackson Turner's famous "Frontier Thesis" (see Limerick). Ronald Reagan was fond of reaching *deep* into history to collapse different ethnic histories in America, asserting that anthropologists believe that American Indians migrated across the bearing strait 30,000 years ago, and therefore we are all immigrants from somewhere (see Rogin's *"Ronald Reagan," the*

Movie, especially chapters 5 through 8, for an excellent analysis of historiographi-cal elisions of ethnic plurality in the United States). Fukuyama's *The End of History* establishes liberal democracy as the end point of history. Also see D'Souza's *The End of Racism,* and *What's So Great about America,* as examples of historical revisionism that threads ethnic narratives into a master-story of American liberal-ism. Of course, readers of my generation were weaned on *School House Rock*'s "The Great American Melting Pot" (1973–80).

5. See Lowe 96.

6. I list and respond to these titles in chapter 3.

7. See Flanzbaum, Yudkin, Langer, Novick, and Cole for analyses of popular representations of the Holocaust. Besides the texts I cite in this chapter, I would add one more example of the popular value of the Holocaust in everyday life. I recently purchased a Jewish cookbook that lists one of its contributors with this stunning blurb: "Ben Moskovitz, a Holocaust survivor from Czechoslovakia, whose Star Bakery in Michigan bakes a fabulous chocolate babka *that is to die for*" (ital-ics added!). Less spectacular, but in the same vein, another baker proffers a recipe for "matzah she made while hiding from the Nazis." Though not necessarily about immigration, these comments cite the Holocaust as a value-added bonus to the recipes. The horrifically tragic (the Shoah) becomes the background for the plainly quotidian (food).

8. Brodkin's important ethnography, *How the Jews Became White Folks, and What That Says about America,* explores the rising material and cultural fortunes of Jews in America after WWII. Eisen's *The Chosen People in America* and the ear-lier *Galut* are excellent sociologically derived analyses of Jewish self-perception in mid-century and nineteenth- and early twentieth-century America, respectively. Eisen's *The Chosen People* relies in part on Sklare and Greenblum's important soci-ological study, *Jewish Identity on the Suburban Frontier.* At the Smithsonian Mu-seum of American History, the exhibit "Communities in a Changing Nation" sin-gles out the experiences of Jewish immigrants to the United States in the nineteenth century as a paradigmatic example of the process of immigration and assimilation by white ethnic communities.

9. According to Eisen, Jews in the mid-1950s were astoundingly well off mate-rially compared to the rest of the United States. Also, Jews were apprehensive about living among Gentiles: "[Jews] are welcomed as good citizens and good neighbors by people who nonetheless view them to some extent as intruders and upon whom, should 'push come to shove' (i.e., should anti-Semitism become widespread), the Jews could not rely. As a result, the Jews keep their distance. Eisen explains that the "ambassador mentality" was a common response, as Jews felt the need to be on their best behavior and the need to mute candor and frankness for the sake of mak-ing a good show (*Chosen* 128, 144).

10. For a sustained argument about the epistemology of narrative in Philip Roth's work, see Franco, "Being Black, Being Jewish, and Knowing the Difference: Philip Roth's *The Human Stain.*"

11. See Novick, especially chapter 5, for a discussion of the sorts of dilemmas American Jews faced in relating to the Holocaust. While I believe that Novick overstates his point for the sake of rhetoric, thereby overly aligning Jewish opinions with conventional American opinions, his history is nonetheless an important critique of contemporary Holocaust culture.

12. Ozick's *The Cannibal Galaxy,* Bellow's *Mr. Sammler's Planet,* and Malamud's "The Last Mohican" establish cosmopolitanism rather than Jewish theology as both the problem and the solution to encountering the Holocaust.

13. See Gilman's analysis of the implication of racial theory in the rise of cosmetic surgery in *Creating Beauty to Cure the Soul,* and the consequences for Jewish self-hatred in his *Jewish Self-Hatred: Anti-Semitism and the Hidden Language of the Jews.*

14. 1998 was the fiftieth anniversary of the publication of the diary and the year *Anne Frank* was restaged on Broadway. Also in the mid-1990s two important works were published that revealed that the problematic questions discussed above were actively contested by the various figures responsible for bringing Anne's story to public notice, including her father, Otto Frank, novelist Meyer Levin, Hollywood screenwriters Albert Hackett and Frances Goodrich (who adapted the diary for the stage), and the play's producer, Kermit Bloomgarden. Meyer Levin was among the first American journalists present after the liberation of Buchenwald in 1945, and he was subsequently compelled to bring a voice from the ashes to bare witness. When he became aware of Anne Frank's diary, published in French in 1950, he quickly contacted Otto Frank promising to sponsor the book in America and foster it along into a play or film. Frank and Levin had a falling out, however, over the nature of the play, and Levin would later find himself battling the play's writer and producer as well. The central conflict between the parties was over the nature of the story: Levin wanted to tell the story as he saw it in Buchenwald, one girl's experience in a primarily Jewish tragedy. The diary, for Levin, represented the century's greatest evil, directed at the world's perennial victims, the Jews. Otto Frank and the play's producers wanted to present a more universal story, one about hope in the face of adversity, and one that would ultimately posit the persistent goodness of people. The question persists, what does Anne Frank signify? See Graver's *An Obsession with Anne Frank* (1995), and Melnick's *The Stolen Legacy of Anne Frank* (1997).

15. Even here I am making a leap. It is never clear exactly where and to whom Lars was born, and it is quite possible that he is plainly a Swedish orphan, in no way connected to Jewish history. Thought of this way, Ozick's critique would echo my own to start the chapter: the Holocaust and Jewish history in general have become too easily available for cultural appropriation by ideologies with no vested interest in the particularity of the experience. On the other hand, to grant that Lars likely *is* Jewish, as so many of the novel's other characters turn out to be, and therefore was smuggled out of Eastern Europe confirms a critique parallel to Roth's: For Jews, the Holocaust has become an all explaining, all-signifying bedrock epistemology.

2. WORKING THROUGH THE ARCHIVE

1. For a very funny visual corollary to this truism, see the magazine *Heeb* (April 2005), and its photo essay, "Yarmulkes on Goyim."

2. In addition to Brogan and Peterson, see Tate's *Psychoanalysis and Black Novels* (1998), Cheng's *The Melancholy of Race* (2000), and Bouson's *Quiet as It's Kept* (2000), as well as many numerous studies of Jewish American literature.

3. See Santner's *Stranded Objects.* LaCapra's *Writing History, Writing Trauma* is less focused on cultural analysis and more directed toward theorizing the methods of such an analysis.

4. I first became aware of the phrase "the usable past" in Lois Parkinson-Zamora's 1997 book, *The Usable Past: The Imagination of History in Recent Fiction of the Americas.* Parkinson-Zamora cites Van Wyck Brook's "The Usable Past," published in Riesing's *The Unusable Past: Theory and the Study of American Literature.* See also Roskie's *The Jewish Search for a Usable Past* (1999), which similarly rests on a premise of the cultural efficacy of literary mourning.

5. In a helpful review article of Derrida's *Archive Fever,* Herman Rapaport explains, "[Derrida's] archives occur at the moment when there is a structural breakdown in memory. This contrasts rather sharply with Michel Foucault's view in *The Archaeology of Knowledge* that archives are, in essence, the textual systematization of their own enunciability and that, as such, they are predicated upon mnemonic reliability. Derrida's archive, in contrast, is mnemonically unreliable insofar as it is somewhat feverish, hallucinatory, fragmentary. . . . In short, where there is regularity and efficiency in Foucault's archive, there is trauma in Derrida's" (69). Rapaport's distinction usefully captures the two impulses inhabiting my sense of the Archive in Morales's work.

6. Morales, even more than most Chicano writers, is particularly influenced by Mexican and Latin American literature. He completed a dissertation on Spanish American literature at Rutgers, and is a professor of Spanish at the University of California Irvine. Most of Morales's fiction is set in Texas and Southern California (though his latest novel, *Waiting to Happen,* is set in Mexico City), but his baroque aesthetics, and alternating social realism and magical realism are heavily influenced by Latin American writers.

7. The collections *Modern Chicano Writers* (ed. Sommers and Ybarra-Fausto, 1979), and *The Identification and Analysis of Chicano Literature* (ed. Jiménez, 1979) make brief reference to Morales as a new, up-and-coming writer. *Contemporary Chicano Fiction: A Critical Survey* (ed. Lattin, 1986) has two chapters on Morales, suggesting a rise in his stature. It is telling, however, that by 1990, major works such as Ramón Saldívar's landmark *Chicano Narrative: A Dialectics of Difference* (1990), J. D. Saldívar and Calderón's collection, *Criticism in the Borderlands* (1991), or the recent study of Chicano urban fiction by Villas, *Barrio-Logos* (2000), offer virtually no reference to any of Morales's fiction (though Carl Gutierrez-Jones's *Rethinking the Borderlands* [1995] has an excellent section on Morales's *The Brick People*).

In 1995 the journal *Bilingual Review* published an issue devoted to Morales, later revised and published as an edited collection of essays, *Alejandro Morales: Past, Present, Future* Perfect (see Gurpegui). Jesús Rosales has published the only full-length original book on Morales, *La narrativa de Alejandro Morales: encuentro, historio, y compromiso social* (1999). Several recent dissertations on Morales hopefully promise more published work to come. Though Morales's first three novels (*Caras viejas y vino nuevo* [1975], *La verdad sin voz* [1979], and *Reto en el Paraíso* [1983]) are stylistically and thematically difficult, his historical novel, *The Brick People*—the first written in English—is uncharacteristically lucid and a good place to start for readers interested but unfamiliar with Morales. *The Rag Doll Plagues* is Morales's most successful novel to date, given its experimental but still lucid prose style merged with his ongoing historicism.

8. In a 1998 interview at his home, Morales told me of his interest in European postmodern theorists, including Lyotard and Derrida, and of the influence of the "Historians Debate," at the center of which was Daniel Goldhagen's now-notorious *Hitler's Willing Executioners.* Goldhagen's book introduced Morales to the concept of "eliminationist ideologies" and the influence of that critical concept and Holocaust studies in general is evident in both *The Rag Doll Plagues* and the more recent *Waiting to Happen* (2001).

9. Erlinda Gonzales-Berry, in "*Caras viejas y vino nuevo:* Journey Through a Disintegrating Barrio," begins by contrasting Morales's narrative voice against other Chicano writers. Where others, such as Tomás Rivera, amplify the protagonist's experience to speak to a broader Chicano or even universal community, in Morales's work, "the vision the reader receives of that reality is screened through the psyche of one character. . . . It is not the vision of a participant narrator who tells the reader 'here is what I have observed of Chicano reality,' but rather, it is the vision of a narrator who tells us 'here is what [the protagonist] thinks and feels about what he sees,' and what he sees is often transformed according to what he thinks and feels" (289).

10. Primarily, the Spanish word *revuelta* means "over turned," or is synonymous with "mixed"—as in *huevos revueltas* or scrambled eggs. Using this translation would point up Gregory's mixed-race lineage, or *mestizaje* (linking this novel with critiques of colonialism such as Arturo Islas's *The Rain God*), as well as his recurring confusion as to who he is in relation to would-be dichotomized racial groups (making Gregory the wry companion to Richard Rodriguez!). I've chosen to highlight the secondary definition in my translation, "revolution," because "revolution" links the protagonist to the novel's macrohistorical concerns: Each chapter anticipates revolution, and the novel represents a recirculating (rather than dialectical) history. My thanks to the anonymous PMLA consultant who reminded me of the multivalence of "revueltas"—Morales always rewards a multilayered reading.

11. Papa Damian is a transitional figure whose history is not accounted for here, but who appears in Morales's earlier novel, *The Brick People.* In that historical novel, Damian is a Mexican migrant who brings his family north to Los Angeles at the beginning of the twentieth century.

12. Felman is commenting on Albert Camus' *The Plague,* itself a dense allegory of World War II and the Holocaust. Felman is adamant about the uniqueness of the Holocaust. Nonetheless, the problems the Holocaust presents to historians—namely the absence of the witness, and the inadequacy of mimetic narratives—are not themselves unique to that event. With *The Rag Doll Plagues,* we have more than just a citation of the Holocaust, but an invocation of the historical problematic of witnessing and testimony which Camus and Felman describe. If historiography, fiction, and theory all testify to the difficulty of representing the Holocaust, this too must be the challenge for representations of historical traumas of other kinds as well.

13. The legend of Malinche, the concubine-informant of the conqueror Cortés, has long inscribed Mexico's racially mixed culture with a current of shame and self-loathing, according to Octavio Paz and others. In *La Malinche in Mexican Literature: From History to Myth,* Cypress identifies a body of recent Mexican and Chicana writing valorizing the heroic, noble, or pragmatic efficacy of Malinche's role in Mexican history.

14. See Limón's *Mexican Ballads, Chicano Poems,* Gates's *The Signifying Monkey,* or Nguyen's *Race and Resistance* for examples of self-conscious, self-reflexive ethnic critical theories.

15. The quote comes from Dee Cervantes's poem, "Visions of Mexico While at a Writing Symposium in Port Townsend, Washington," in *Emplumada.*

16. See Klepfisz's essay, "*Yom Hashoah, Yom Yerushalayim:* A Meditation," and Cole's *Selling the Holocaust: From Auschwitz to Schindler: How History is Bought, Packaged, and Sold* for two such examples of critiques of Holocaust memory and Zionist interpolations of the Holocaust.

3. "SHE HAS CLAIM"

1. Indeed, as a Marxist movement, Chicano political activism begins with an emphasis on education, including cultural literacy and literary fluency. I expand on this point in my concluding chapter, and more fully in "Writing Ethnicity/Ethnic Writing: The Critical Conception of Chicano Culture."

2. Though I came up with this term originally, I later found Vickroy's citation of Naomi Morgenstern's use of the phrase with regard to *Beloved.* Morgenstern uses the term somewhat differently, calling the novel itself an example of wish-fulfillment for its revision of Margaret Garner's story.

3. I quote Peterson's own term on page 4 of her introduction, because of an ambiguity that runs throughout her book. The book's subtitle is "Contemporary Women Writers and the Crisis of Historical Memory," giving no clue that this is a work of ethnic literary criticism, though all her writers are ethnic American women. Elsewhere in the book, she identifies her writers as "ethnic" and then ambiguously as "women of color." Peterson includes the Polish-born Jewish American writer Irene Klepfisz under this heading, troubling the idea of "color."

4. Caruth adds, "Through the notion of trauma, I will argue, we can under-

stand that a rethinking of reference is aimed not at eliminating history but as resituating it in our understanding, that is, as precisely permitting *history* to arise where *immediate understanding* may not" (*Unclaimed Experience* 11).

5. Walter Benn Michaels complains that readers of *Beloved* perpetuate racist ideologies of the past when they conflate history with what he considers the novel's "mythology," though he does not pause to consider that amnesia produces its own sort of mythology ("You" 188). A more substantive and helpful conflation of the ethics and politics of reading *Beloved* will help us locate our responses to the novel in its true historical moment, the present.

6. See Savitt's article, "Slave Life Insurance in Virginia and North Carolina" for a discussion of how the business of insuring slaves produced problems of category and definition for slave owners and courts.

7. According to documents produced by the California Department of Insurance under the directive of former governor Gray Davis, New York Life Insurance Company's ancestor company, Nautilus, would have been the likely holder of a policy on slaves owned in Kentucky. In response to slave-reparation lawsuits, New York Life has stated on their Web site: "New York Life abhors the practice of slavery, historically and currently, and we profoundly regret that our predecessor company, Nautilus Insurance Company, was associated in any way with it, for even a brief period of time. The fact that slavery was legal in certain parts of the United States at the time doesn't make it any less repugnant. Any lawsuit about events 150 years ago faces huge legal hurdles, and we fully expect to prevail in court. We believe it is far more appropriate to judge a company by its values and actions today." The rhetoric of the statement establishes the present as the negation of the past, and the "move on" attitude is at least ironic in an insurance company.

8. See William Goodell's important and oft-cited *The American Slave Code in Theory and Practice,* published in 1853. Goodell quotes laws establishing the categorical denial of a chattel's right to property, ownership of children, and the right to the term "human." He concludes, "The practice [of slavery] cannot be better than the code itself" (3).

9. Baker is perhaps too celebratory in his analysis of emergent black subjectivity. Saidiya Hartman has examined the economics of manumission and Reconstruction and concludes that for blacks during Reconstruction, "extant and emergent forms of domination intensified and exacerbated the responsibilities and the afflictions of the newly emancipated" (117), primarily because "liberty, property, and whiteness were inextricably enmeshed" (119). Morrison's descriptions of Paul D's experiences with Reconstruction support Hartman's Marxist analysis. I am suggesting that in such an economic and social environment, ex-slaves such as Sethe and Paul D mediate their experiences through the rhetoric of property and economics in order to strategically assess the dangerous and shifting currents of racism.

10. Despite the categorical prohibition of slaves from owning property, it is quite clear that they did own property, albeit meager, and with the obvious con-

sent of their owners, according to Dylan Penningroth. Garden patches, animals, tools, and domestic implements were more or less owned in an extralegal sense. See Huston for a macrohistory of property rights and the Civil War.

11. *General Mining Law of 1872,* 42nd Cong., Sess. 2, May 10, 1872.

12. In order to establish at least local procedures for recognizing claims, and to preempt or prosecute fatal acts of "claim jumping," groups of miners formed "claim clubs," organized around local municipal districts.

13. This is the original German (*Complete Works*), translated by Strachey as "where id was, there ego shall be." I draw on Lupton and Reinhard's analysis of Lacanian readings of trauma for thinking about the "I" emerging out of the "It," though concretizing the "It" as material property is my own suggestion.

14. One interesting confluence: LisaGay Hamilton, who plays the younger version of Sethe at Sweet home in the film of *Beloved* recently produced a version of Eve Ensler's *The Vagina Monologues,* which included Kimberle Crenshaw's reading of her "Black Vaginas"—a monologue suggesting the rational of compensating black women for producing so much productive "property" during slavery.

15. There is substantial evidence that characters do indeed reflect on their social location as property. Consider Baby Sugg's internal meditation on being bought by her son (146); Sixo's lesson learned after stealing the pig (190); Paul D's instruction in his precise monetary value after being caught running away (226); and Sethe's realization that she and her children are her owners' property—an insight that prompts her flight (196–97).

16. Mohanty's analysis of *Beloved* appears at the end of *Literary Theory and the Claims of History,* in which he theorizes an epistemology of reality after postmodernism offering an alternative to reading trauma only or purely from the point of view of psychoanalysis. Mohanty's theory and its companion articulation by Paula Moya in *Learning From Experience* seem to rely on a problematically tautological presumption that people can evaluate their social experience without that evaluation being somehow part of the experience. Representation—the act of narrative imagination or autobiography—is also an experience of the self writing the self, so it is not clear on what ground of objectivity the post-positivist realist auto-evaluator of experience stands. Unlike Mohanty, I am not arguing that Sethe has "objective knowledge" of her experience, nor do we readers, though we are compelled by the novel to reflect on and reorient our own experiences. For a rich forum on Mohanty's argument see essays by Alcoff, Levine, Buell, Saldívar, and Wood in *New Literary History* 32.4 (2001), and Amanda Anderson's review article in *Diacritics*.

17. Moving between psychical and materialist analyses is not an either/or choice. Claudia Tate's *Psychoanalysis and Black Novels* (1998) makes a persuasive case for a nuanced reading of the black psyche as part of the larger project of exploring social protest literature. The impulse to psychoanalyze is part of the same project of elucidating and advancing the claims of social protest in literature and criticism.

18. Rey Chow's creative and compelling analysis of the "protestant ethnic" sug-

gests the trap of materialist-conceived ethnic identification: Chow concludes by summing up: "Admittedly, ethnicity continues . . . to function in a utopian, Marxist/Lukácsian paradigm of protest and struggle, which is grounded in moral universalisms such as democracy, freedom of speech, and human rights. At the same time, this familiar paradigm seems readily to be transforming into something else, something akin to a systematic capitalist ethos of objectification and reification, whereby what is proclaimed to be human must also increasingly take on the significance of a commodity, a commodified spectacle" (48). Turning the human into a commodity—the worst kind of cultural violence. Are protests by and on behalf of the oppressed ethnic subject fated to duplicate the logic of oppression-by-comodification, as Chow surmises? Brogan suggests the reader enters the "scene" of the novel, identifying with characters, or standing at the grave, but this is at least potentially narcissistic, a "seen," or act of looking at one's own self and projecting one's own self into the scene. The question I am trying to answer here is, can we imagine a form of criticism that acknowledges the claims that *Beloved* makes on our present without succumbing to the paralysis of transference, the arrogation of identification, or the assumption of a vocational relation to the text, where criticism requires the traumatized text to support its own critical claims?

19. Countless legal, cultural, and philosophical texts, not to mention Web sites, are devoted to the subject of slave reparations, not to mention Web sites. Boris Bittker's *The Case for Black Reparations* (1973, 2003) lays out the legal and moral case for reparations clearly and comprehensively. Lecky and Wright's *The Black Manifesto* (1969) is a collection of essays on the topic, including the original "Black Manifesto" that gave life to the modern reparations movement. J. Angelo Corlett's *Race, Racism, and Reparations* (2003) suggests how Native American and African American claims for reparation compare. Janna Thompson's *Taking Responsibility for the Past* is one of many works of political philosophy which discusses reparations. Thompson's work is noteworthy for me because she helpfully moves from the most basic terms and concepts to the complexities involved in a political philosophy of reparation. David Delaney's *Race, Place, and Law, 1836–1948* (1998) is not about reparations per se, but sets slavery, emancipation, and Jim Crow in a legal history, thereby laying the grounds for individual and class-action claims by descendants of slaves against the government. Randall Robinson's *The Debt* (2001) is not a scholarly work, but a well-reasoned case for reparations as redress for our current political moment.

20. Ultimately, Sethe has to embrace herself—her "best thing." Ella and the other women, and Paul D can only do so much in this regard. In this way, Ella and Paul D hail Sethe in a way similar to how Baby Suggs hails a community of ex-slaves through her preaching in the clearing, urging them to love themselves. It is debatable as to whether or not Sethe finally claims herself as Paul D suggests she should.

21. Wendy Brown disagrees: "Even as we seek to redress the pain and humiliation consequent to historical deprivation of freedom in a putatively 'free' politi-

cal order, might we thus sustain the psychic residues of these histories as the animus of political institutions constitutive of our future?" (29). Such a question only has teeth in the realm of theory. Where people really live—schools, jobs, polluted communities—psychic residues would be a fine trade for getting rid of the often physically toxic residues of oppression.

22. The South African "Promotion of National Unity and Reconciliation Act, 1995," which established the historic Truth and Reconciliation Commission, "provides a historic bridge between the past of a deeply divided society characterized by strife, conflict, untold suffering and injustice, and a future founded on the recognition of human rights, democracy and peaceful co-existence for all South Africans, irrespective of colour, race, class, belief or sex."

23. "A better understanding of reconciliation . . . is that reconciliation is achieved when the harm done by injustice to relations of respect and trust that ought to exist between individuals or nations has been repaired or compensated for by the perpetrator in such a way that this harm is no longer regarded as standing in the way of establishing or re-establishing these relations" (Thompson 50). See Dwyer's realist discussion of why reconciliation is a first-tier moral response to injury and historical trauma.

24. Michigan congressman John Conyers has sponsored House Bill H.R. 40 as the beginning stage of just this sort of national narrative construction. The bill aims "to acknowledge the fundamental injustice, cruelty, brutality, and inhumanity of slavery in the United States and the 13 American colonies between 1619 and 1865 and to establish a commission to examine the institution of slavery, subsequently de jure and de facto racial and economic discrimination against African-Americans, and the impact of these forces on living African-Americans, to make recommendations to the Congress on appropriate remedies, and for other purposes."

4. BORDERS, DIASPORA, AND EXILE

1. "How proud she had become of her Jewish heritage!" writes Eve Merriam in *Emma Lazarus: Woman with a Torch* (1956). More recently, Bette Roth Young has described Lazarus's simultaneous love and condescension toward Jewish immigrants in America (*Emma Lazarus in Her World: Life and Letters* [1995]). Lazarus was a descendent of one of the earliest Sephardic families to settle in prerevolutionary America, and lived as an aristocrat and an intellectual, with almost no Jewish friends. Yet she was not allowed to forget her Jewish identity as her Christian friends, fascinated or ambivalent toward her Jewishness, kept bringing it up. In Young's account, Lazarus is at first a reluctant, dabbling defender of Jews, then later, in her thirties, a tireless if patronizing muse for Jewish concerns in the United States.

2. See Sharfman, Tobias, and Rochlin for numbers on Jewish migration to the West in the nineteenth century. In most regions, Jews comprised no more than 2 percent of the population of settlement, though it should be noted that the Jewish population increased substantially, sometimes tenfold, in larger cities in the West between 1880 and 1900.

3. The term *galut* is the theological referent of the contemporary term *diaspora,* indicating a metaphysical exile from the biblical Holy Land, and exile from God's immediate presence. The *galut* can only be brought to an end by the coming of the Messiah. An obviously problematic concept for Judaism given contemporary history, *galut* is studied by Arnold Eisen at length in *Galut: Modern Jewish Reflection on Homelessness and Homecoming* (1986).

4. The Philadelphia Conference of Reform Rabbis (1869) adopted a set of principles, the second of which declared: "We look upon the destruction of the second Jewish commonwealth not as a punishment for the sinfulness of Israel, but as a result of the divine purpose revealed to Abraham, which, as has become ever clearer in the course of the world's history, consists in the dispersion of the Jews to all parts of the earth, for the realization of their high priestly mission, to lead the nations to the true knowledge and worship of God" (Isaacs and Olitzky 55). I would argue that such an article of faith could only be declared by Jews in the United States, prior to the second wave of (Russian) immigration in the late 1800s.

5. The charge that Zionism is racism, though false and insidious in my opinion, has been influential on current Jewish theories of diaspora, including Jonathan Boyarin and Daniel Boyarin's proposal for a diasporic model of Judaism, which I look at later in this chapter. Edward Said's debate with them and others on the question of Zionism and racism is reprinted in *"Race," Writing, and Difference,* Ed. Henry Louis , Jr. (1986).

6. The ironic tone is half-hearted here: this is just the path I followed, living my junior year of college in Jerusalem, attending the Hebrew University. Indeed I received a Jewish finishing, but I wasn't finished. Prior to my year in Israel I had read almost no Jewish literature, knew no Hebrew, nor much cared about issues of diaspora or Zionism. I went to Israel because I wanted to get away for a year, and I knew my parents would happily underwrite the effort. Interest in Jewish literature and culture came to me unawares.

7. An Israeli friend of mine has been urging me for years to move to Israel, and his latest appeal is the exceptional quality of life in major cities like Tel-Aviv. "It's just like living in West LA, or parts of Manhattan," he tells me, which, of course, sends all the wrong signals. I suspect (because I am prey to such sentiments myself) that the more bourgeois American Jews become, the more they will long for the romantic portrait of an underdeveloped "frontier" homeland, the Israel marketed to American Jews in the early 1950s, and then again in the 1970s.

8. This raises the interesting question of whether or not Lazarus is participating in the whitening of Jews by troping them as frontier pioneers, or whether her poem is subversive of this mentality. Certainly from the mid-nineteenth century forward Jews hegemonically participated in the construction of America's colonized others as savage and inferior, as Matthew Fry Jacobson has shown. On the other hand, Lazarus's title persists: these Jews, depicted as Semitic, are not at home as budding Americans but Jews in exile.

9. The washerwoman's nationality is not explicitly named, but in the course of

the story she refers to the "Contras" as a possible factor in her son's disappearance. The representative of the military police suggests to her that her son might have been rounded up because he had Contra connections. The term *Contra* is specific to the Nicaraguan civil war—the term *guerrilla* is used elsewhere in Central America—which leads me to my reading. Sonia Saldívar-Hull ("Feminism on the Border: From Gender Politics to Geopolitics") reads the washerwoman as Salvadoran, but without offering any evidence. Her reading, instead, seems intended to conform to the broader thesis that "The Cariboo Cafe" is determinedly anti-U.S., thus the boy's disappearance must likewise occur at the hands of a pro-U.S. government (El Salvador) rather than an anti-U.S. government (Nicaragua). Saldívar-Hull's reading is limited by her own political claims—she strangely links the liminal café owner to the dominant power structure, even though he, like the immigrants in the story, is under police surveillance and coercion—and it suggests to me the need for a broader set of reading strategies that would account for the ambivalence of subject identifications along the axes of race and nationality.

10. In *Barrio Boy*, Ernesto Galarza's important autobiography narrating his immigration from Mexico to Northern California, the narrator is mesmerized when, as a young boy, he encounters a flush toilet in the United States for the first time.

11. See J. D. Saldívar's *The Dialectics of Our America*.

5. OUTING ETHNICITY, "UNDOING" NATIONALISM

1. According to Balderrama and Rodríguez, "by 1930 more than 10 percent of Mexico's entire population was residing in the United States" (7).

2. See Cypress for a historical discussion of *La Malinche* and an analysis of her figuration in Mexican and Chicano literature.

3. Besides research cited above, see Cantú' (2002) and Murray and Dynes (1995).

4. It should be stated at this point that Miguel Grande's self-censure is, among other things, a further inscription of a kind of homophobic code, and though I claim he has "insight," his is not the kind of vision that dismantles social constructions, but rather the kind of (Lacanian) horror that occurs when an individual recognizes he is on the wrong side of those codes. Miguel Grande's conceit of the exposure of the anus, or here the self-exposure, has been theorized as a mode of discipline and punishment by Eve Kosofsky Sedgwick in a remarkable essay linking bare bottoms and spanking to homophobic discipline. In "A Poem is Being Written" she argues that the bared bottom, a synecdoche for the anus, simultaneously represents the desire for and prohibition against male anal penetration (especially, Sedgwick notes, in the absence within cultural discourse of an epistemology of the female anus. Anal sexuality, Sedgwick shows, is so far construed as male and homosexual).

5. Interestingly, at the same time that American minorities are looking to open their ethnicity to include gay culture and issues, gays are increasingly turning to-

ward ethnicity as a model for gay group identification. Alan Sinfield has proffered the "diaspora/ethnicity" model for gay and lesbian group identification, especially as an effective stance against legislative discrimination. Sinfield points out at the beginning of his essay that the ethnicity model for gays and lesbians has been around at least since the 1970s. Sinfield favors, on the one hand, a "strategic essentialism" to unify an otherwise highly diverse group of people. He is skeptical, on the other hand, of bids for citizenship and the nation's rights, which would only replicate nationalisms exclusionary chauvinisms, limiting who is in and who is out of the "ethnic" group—and thus limiting who benefits from the group's claims to rights. In *A Nation by Rights: National Cultures, Sexual Identity Politics, and the Discourse of Rights* (1998), Carl Stychin extensively critiques Sinfield's version of the ethnicity model, picking up on Sinfield's own objections to the reinscription of nationalist hegemony. Lawrence Schimel has explicitly compared Jewish marginality in America with gay marginality. Schimel, who is Jewish and gay, observes the similar stances each identity would have him assume in relation to the dominant culture. Most American Jews are born into assimilated families, while all homosexuals are born "heterosexual-by-default," assimilated a priori into the straight-geist (164). Also, Schimel suggests that gay communities in San Francisco, New York City, West Hollywood, and so on, are "our semi-mythical mini-Zions. . . . These are our cultural homelands, and our visits feel like a return home, even if we've never set foot there before" (167). Finally, Schimel compares the way narratives of peril galvanize Jewish affiliation in America (not to mention support for Israel) to how AIDS forces "queers [to] put aside their difference to fight our common enemy" (170). Schimel's essay is speculative and fairly uncritical; he is playing with ideas rather than arguing an ideology. For a more scholarly and critically rigorous comparison of queer and Jewish subjectivity, see Eve Sedgwick's *Epistemology of the Closet*.

6. Eric Clark succinctly explains, "Tolerance is thus a false hope because it engenders a false sense of democratic sociality and belonging. . . . To move beyond this limiting vision of social and political self-governance demands an ethically attuned judgment that holds accountable a public sphere promising with one hand and retracting with the other" (172). I think Moraga and Kushner—especially in *Angels in America*—both illustrate the limits of tolerance and provoke this sort of ethical accounting.

7. See Rodriguez, *Brown*, especially chapter 5, "Hispanic."

8. Saldívar's remarks come in a response to Satya Mohanty's *Literary Theory and the Claims of History*, a book I cite in chapter 3. Mohanty, a professor at Cornell, is the mentor to Moya and others who point to his work as the basis for their theories of "post-positivist" objectivity in the realm of cultural critique.

9. See Butler's *Gender Trouble*, especially the first chapter, and *Bodies That Matter*.

10. A supremely ironic instance of my point appears in an article in the *Los Angeles Times*: "After hearing graphic stories of suffering directly from persecuted

young people who fled to the United States, President Bush intervened personally to sharply increase the number of refugees admitted to the country—undoing the severe limits placed on such admissions for security reasons after the Sept. 11 attacks" (Hamburger and Wallsten A1). At first glance this would seem to bear out Moraga's point: testimony of personal experience has its own kind of progressive efficacy. However, according to the *Times,* these refugees are sponsored by the various Christian religious groups operating under the umbrella of the Bush administration's Office of Faith-Based Initiatives. The stories of refugees that appeal to religious leaders are pipelined to a like-minded president, who finds in their stories confirmation of his own vision of America. Meanwhile, political persecution and the internal exile of left-wing dissenters, not to mention those "enemy noncombatants" who have been disappeared, persists.

11. Much has been written about that play, including an article in *PMLA* by Jonathan Freedman, arguing that the play ultimately effaces Jewish ethnic identity as the compromise for its assertion of an ethics of gay inclusion in the nation. On the other hand, Freedman notes that Alisa Solomon has argued just the opposite in *Re-dressing the Canon: Essays on Theater and Gender.* Rather than argue what kind of play *Angels* is, I want to look at the larger cultural question Kushner is contributing, too, and think about more generally the yoking together of ethnic and gay identity. For his part Kushner says that the character Louis is "the closest character to myself I've ever written" (220), and that the play is "to a certain extent about being Jewish" (Norman J. Cohen, "Wrestling with Angels," in Vorlicky).

12. The preceding quotation is taken from a 1996 *Village Voice* article by Bob. My background on Klezkamp, the Klezmatics, and the New York Yiddish revival scene relies heavily on local New York reportage, including *Village Voice* and *New York Times* articles from the early 1990s to the present.

13. "Man in a Hat" on the Klezmatics' *Jews with Horns* (1994).

14. For example, see the essays published in *Commentary* in 1969: In the January issue, Earl Raab wrote on "The Black Revolution and the Jewish Divide," and in March, Milton Himmelfarb wrote a piece asking, "Is American Jewry in Crisis?" April's edition featured Nathan Glazer's essay, "Blacks, Jews and Intellectuals," a companion piece to Raab's, and in September Theodore Draper wrote a long historical piece on "The Fantasy of Black Nationalism." Robert Alter, the Dean of American Jewish Studies, wrote attacked the new academic multiculturalism in "What Jewish Studies Can Do" (Oct. 1974).

15. See, for example, Irene Klepfisz's essay collection, *Dreams of an Insomniac,* Laura Levitt's critical and theoretical *Jews and Feminism,* especially chapters 2–5.

16. Though I go against the grain of so many of my subjects here, I am deeply suspicious of the long-term viability of a secular Jewish culture, though I am touched by it nonetheless. Whatever is persistent in Jewish secular culture, including social activism, linguistic and cultural difference, and Jewish philosophy, originates from religion and persists in the diaspora often because of religious difference. I am not positing a stout binary of "religion versus culture," for I do believe

religion, especially Jewish religion, is culture. On the contrary, it seems that those who would claim the status of "secular Jews" and reject religion are themselves locating themselves in a binary that finally collapses.

17. My colleague Scott Klein suggests that the flute sounds Celtic, and he observes that in this song the Klezmatics are accompanied by the Canadian blues group Moxy Fruvous, thereby embodying the diversity described in the lyrics.

18. Quotations by Shreiber come from a chapter titled "'Jewish Trouble' and the Trouble with Poetry," which is part of a book forthcoming from Stanford UP.

19. See Berlant, especially chapter 4.

20. This is Bhabha's point: the normative "pluralism of the national sign, where difference returns as the same, is contested by the signifier's 'loss of identity' that inscribes the narrative of the people in the ambivalent, 'double' writing of the performative and the pedagogical" (154).

CONCLUSION

1. Bhabha has been criticized for articulating a theoretically baroque but socially useless conception of postcolonial identity, and I aim neither to extend this critique nor defend his theory, at least not directly. For example, see E. San Juan Jr.'s critique of Bhabha in *Beyond Postcolonial Theory*.

2. Many critical studies published during the 1980s through mid-1990s were more or less committed either to affirming the validity of racial and ethnic difference as a category for the study of literature or to deconstructing racial thinking and thereby moving beyond a suspect discourse of identity. See Omi and Winant, Takaki, or McKenna as examples of the former, and Sollors, Benn Michaels, and Gilroy as examples of the later. Most scholars of ethnic American literature who have published studies in the last ten years are flexible and canny enough to draw on the theoretical suppositions of materialist criticism and poststructuralist theory without becoming bogged down in the swampy waters of ideology. See Knadler, Karem, and Browder, and Powell, for example.

3. See Omi and Winant, Gutierrez-Jones, and Kaplan and Pease, for example.

4. See Alarcón, R. Saldívar, *Chicano Nation*.

5. See, for example, Boyarin and Boyarin, eds., *Jews and Other Differences: The New Jewish Cultural Studies*.

6. As Henry Louis Gates reminds us, in the West, "writing [is] . . . the visible sign of reason itself" ("Writing 'Race'" 9).

7. Two new Jewish projects actively critique mainstream American Jewish culture, and suggest the look of a new generation's post-Jewish Jewishness. The first is the bimonthly magazine *Heeb*. Billing itself as "The New Jew Review," *Heeb* gathers up whatever is sacred and sentimentalized in Jewish and American culture and submits it to loving satire. The other project is the agit-prop collective known as "Jewish Women Watching." JWW conducts media awareness campaigns and organizes provocative public protests of the mainstream Jewish establishment.

8. For a critique of Lyotard see Boyarin and Boyarin, "Diaspora," above; for a

critique of Deleuze and Guattari see Chana Kronfeld's "Beyond Deleuze and Guattari: Hebrew and Yiddish Modernism and the Age of Privileged Difference."

9. The quote appears on an unnumbered page, inside the cover of Daniel Boyarin's *Unheroic Conduct.*

10. Saldívar expands on his approach to identity in response to Mohanty's theory of post-positivist Realism, in "Multicultural Politics."

11. Further imbricating Jewish and Chicano methodology, Limón cites Harold Bloom's "Anxiety of Influence" thesis as his critical paradigm.

12. I have developed this argument at greater length in an article in *Post Identity* ("Writing Ethnicity/Ethnic Writing").

13. See McKenna and Palumbo-Liu, for example.

BIBLIOGRAPHY

Alarcón, Norma. "Anzaldúa's *Frontera:* Inscribing Gynetics." *Displacement, Diaspora, and Geographies of Identity.* Ed. Smadar Lavie and Ted Swedenburg. Durham: Duke UP, 1996.

Alcoff, Linda Martín. "Objectivity and Its Politics." *New Literary History* 32.4 (Autumn 2001): 835–48.

Almaguer, Tomás. "Chicano Men: A Cartography of Homosexual Identity and Behavior." *The Lesbian and Gay Studies Reader.* Eds. Henry Abelove, Michele Aina Barlae, and David M. Halperin. New York: Routledge, 1993.

Alonso, Ana María, and María Teresa Koreck. "Silences: 'Hispanics,' AIDS, and Sexual Practices." *The Lesbian and Gay Studies Reader.* Eds. Henry Abelove, Michele Aina Barlae, and David M. Halperin. New York: Routledge, 1993.

Anaya, Rudolpho A., and Francisco Lomeli, eds. *Aztlán: Essays on the Chicano Homeland.* Albuquerque: Academia/El Norte, 1989.

Anderson, Amanda. "Realism, Universalism, and the Science of the Human." *Diacritics* 29.2 (1999): 3–17.

Anderson, Benedict. *Imagined Communities.* New York: Verso, 1983.

Anzaldúa, Gloria. *Borderlands/La Frontera: The New Mestiza.* San Francisco: Aunt Lute Books, 1987.

Avelar, Idelber. *The Untimely Present: Postdictatorial Latin American Fiction and the Task of Mourning.* Durham: Duke UP, 1999.

Baker, Houston A., Jr. *Blues, Ideology, and Afro-American Literatures.* Chicago: U of Chicago P, 1984.

Bakhtin, M. M. *The Dialogic Imagination: Four Essays.* Austin: U of Texas P, 1981.

Balderrama, Francisco E., and Raymond Rodríguez. *Decade of Betrayal: Mexican Repatriation in the 1930s.* Albuquerque: U of New Mexico P, 1995.

Barrera, Mario. *Beyond Aztlán: Ethnic Autonomy in Comparative Perspective.* New York: Praeger, 1988.

Bellow, Saul. *Mr. Sammler's Planet.* New York: Viking, 1970.

Benhabib, Seyla. "The Liberal Imagination and the Four Dogmas of Multiculturalism." *Yale Journal of Criticism* 12.2 (1999): 401–13.

Benjamin, Walter. *Illuminations: Essays and Reflections.* New York: Schocken, 1969.

Berger, James. "Ghosts of Liberalism: Morrison's *Beloved* and the Moynihan Report. *PMLA* 111.3 (May 1996): 408–20.

Berlant, Lauren. *The Queen of America Goes to Washington City: Essays on Sex and Citizenship.* Durham: Duke UP, 1997.

Bhabha, Homi. *The Location of Culture.* New York: Routledge, 1994.

Biale, David. "The Melting Pot and Beyond: Jews and the Politics of American Identity." *Insider/Outsider: American Jews and Multiculturalism.* Los Angeles: U of California P, 1998.

Bittker, Boris I. *The Case for Black Reparations.* Boston: Beacon Press, 2003.

Bouson, J. Brooks. *Quiet as It's Kept: Shame, Trauma, and Race in the Novels of Toni Morrison.* New York: SUNY P, 2000.

Boyarin, Daniel. *Intertextuality and the Reading of Midrash.* Bloomington: Indiana UP, 1990.

———. Invention of the Jewish Man. Berkeley: UC Press, 1997.

———. *Unheroic Conduct: The Rise of Heterosexuality and the Invention of the Jewish Man.* Berkeley: U of California P, 1997.

Boyarin, Daniel, and Jonathan Boyarin. "Diaspora: Generation and the Ground of Jewish Identity." *Critical Inquiry* 9 (Summer 1993): 693–725.

———, eds. *Jews and Other Differences: The New Jewish Cultural Studies.* Minneapolis: U of Minnesota P, 1997.

Boyarin, Jonathan. "An Exchange on Edward Said and Difference: III Response." *Critical Inquiry* 15 (Spring 1989): 634–46.

———. *Storm from Paradise: The Politics of Jewish Memory.* Minneapolis: U of Minnesota P, 1992.

———. *Thinking in Jewish.* Chicago: U of Chicago P, 1996.

Brodkin, Karen. *How the Jews Became White Folks and What That Says about Race in America.* Newark: Rutgers UP, 1998.

Brogan, Kathleen. *Cultural Haunting: Ghosts and Ethnicity in Recent American Literature.* Charlottesville: UP of Virginia, 1998.

Brown, Wendy. *States of Injury: Power and Freedom in Late Modernity.* Princeton: Princeton UP, 1995.

Bruce-Nova, Juan. *Retrospace: Collected Essays on Chicano Literature, Theory, and History.* Houston: Arté Público, 1990.

Buell, Lawrence. "Ethics as Objectivity: A Necessary Oxymoron?" *New Literary History* 32.4 (Autumn 2001): 855–57.

Butler, Judith. *Bodies That Matter: On the Discursive Limits of "Sex."* New York: Routledge, 1993.

———. *Gender Trouble: Feminism and the Subversion of Identity.* New York: Routledge, 1990.

———. "Giving an Account of Oneself." *Diacritics: A Review of Contemporary Criticism* 31.4 (Winter): 22–40.

Calderón, Héctor, and José David Saldívar, eds. *Criticism in the Borderlands: Studies in Chicano Literature, Culture, and Ideology.* Durham: Duke UP, 1994.

Camus, Albert. *The Plague.* New York: Vintage, 1972.

Cantor, Norman F. "The End of Zionism: The Renewal of Diaspora Judaism." *Commonweal* 120.20 (1993): 11–13.

Cantú, Lionel. "De Ambiente: Queer Tourism and the Shifting Boundaries of Mexican Male Sexualities." *GLQ: A Journal of Lesbian and Gay Studies* 8.1/2 (2002): 139–66.

Caruth, Cathy. "Traumatic Awakenings." *Performance and Performativity.* Eds. Andrew Parker and Eve Kosofsky Sedgwick. New York: Routledge, 1995. 89–108.

———. *Unclaimed Experience: Trauma, Narrative, and History.* Baltimore: Johns Hopkins UP, 1996.

Castillo, Ana. *So Far from God.* New York: Plume, 1994.

Cervantes, Lorna Dee. *Emplumada.* Pittsburgh: U of Pittsburgh P, 1993.

Chabram, Angie. "Conceptualizing Chicano Critical Discourse." *Criticism in the Borderlands: Studies in Chicano Literature, Culture, and Ideology.* Eds. Héctor Calderón and José David Saldívar. Durham: Duke UP, 1994. 127–48.

Cheng, Anne Anlin. *The Melancholy of Race.* New York: Oxford UP, 2000.

Cheng, Vincent. "Ethnicity" (forum). *PMLA* (May 1998). 449–50.

Chow, Rey. *The Protestant Ethnic and the Spirit of Capitalism.* New York: Columbia UP, 2002.

———. *Writing Diaspora: Tactics of Intervention in Contemporary Cultural Studies.* Bloomington: Indiana UP, 1993.

Chuh, Kandice. *Imagine Otherwise: On Asian Americanist Critique.* Durham: Duke UP, 2003.

Cole, Tim. *Selling the Holocaust: From Auschwitz to Schindler: How History Is Bought, Packaged, and Sold.* New York: Routledge, 1999.

Corlett, J. Angelo. *Race, Racism, and Reparations.* Ithaca: Cornell UP, 2003.

Cypress, Sandra Messinger. *La Malinche in Mexican Literature: From History to Myth.* Austin: U of Texas P, 1991.

Delaney, David. *Race, Place, and the Law, 1836–1948.* Austin: U of Texas P, 1998.

Deleuze, Gilles, and Félix Guattari. *Kafka: Toward a Minor Literature.* Minneapolis: U of Minnesota P, 1986.

Derrida, Jacques. *Acts of Literature.* Ed. Derrick Attridge. New York: Routledge, 1992.

———. *Archive Fever: A Freudian Impression.* Trans. Eric Prenowitz. Chicago: U of Chicago P, 1996.

———. *Specters of Marx: The State of the Debt, the Work of Mourning, and the New International.* Trans. Peggy Kamuf. New York: Routledge, 1994.

Draper, Theodore. "The Fantasy of Black Nationalism." *Commentary* 47.9 (1969): 27–54.

D'Souza, Dinesh. *The End of Racism: Principles for a Multiracial Society.* New York: Free Press, 1995.

————. *What's So Great about America.* Lanham: Regnery Publishing, 2002.

Duran, Roberto, Judith Ortiz Cofer, and Gustavo Pérez Firmat. *Triple Crown: Chicano, Puerto Rican, and Cuban-American Poetry.* Tempe: Bilingual Press, 1987.

Dussere, Erik. "Accounting for Slavery: Economic Narratives in Morrison and Faulkner." *Modern Fiction Studies* 47 (2001): 329–55.

Dwyer, Susan. "Reconciliation for Realists." *Dilemmas of Reconciliation: Cases and Concepts.* Eds. Carol A. L. Prager and Trudy Govier. Ontario: Wilfrid Laurier UP, 2003. 91–110.

Eagleton, Terry. *Criticism and Ideology: A Study in Marxist Literary Theory.* London: NLB, 1976.

Eisen, Arnold M. *The Chosen People in America: A Study in Jewish Religious Ideology.* Bloomington: Indiana UP, 1983.

————. *Galut: Modern Jewish Reflection on Homelessness and Homecoming.* Bloomington: Indiana UP, 1986.

Felman, Shoshana, and Dori Laub, M.D. *Testimony: Crises of Witnessing in Literature, Psychoanalysis, and History.* New York: Routledge, 1992.

Ferraro, Thomas. *Ethnic Passages: Literary Immigrants in the Twentieth Century*

Flanzbaum, Hilene, Ed. *The Americanization of the Holocaust.* Baltimore: Johns Hopkins UP, 1999.

Franco, Dean. "Being Black, Being Jewish, and Knowing the Difference: Philip Roth's *The Human Stain;* or, It Depends on What the Meaning of 'Clinton' Is." *Studies in American Jewish Literature* 23 (2004): 88–103.

————. "Ethnic Writing/Writing Ethnicity: The Critical Conceptualization of Chicano Identity." *Post Identity* 2.1 (1999): 104–22.

Freedman, Jonathan. "Angels, Monsters, and Jews: Intersections of Queer and Jewish Identity in Kushner's *Angels in America.*" *PMLA* (Jan. 1998): 90–102.

Freud, Sigmund. *The Complete Introductory Lectures on Psychoanalysis.* Trans. and ed. James Strachey. New York: Norton, 1966.

————. *The Interpretation of Dreams.* Ed. James Strachey. New York: Avon Books, 1983.

————. "Mourning and Melancholia." *The Standard Edition of the Complete Psychological Works of Sigmund Freud.* Vol. 14. Trans. James Strachey. London: The Hogarth Press and the Institute of Psycho-Analysis, 1973.

Friedlander, Saul, ed. *Probing the Limits of Representation: Nazism and the "Final Solution."* Cambridge: Harvard UP, 1992.

Fukuyama, Francis. *The End of History and the Last Man.* New York: Avon Books, 1987.

Galarza, Ernesto. *Barrio Boy: The Story of a Boy's Acculturation.* Notre Dame: Notre Dame UP, 1980.

Galchinsky, Michael. "Scattered Seeds: A Dialogue of Diasporas." *Insider/Outsider: American Jews and Multiculturalism.* Eds. David Biale, Michael Galchinsky, and Susannah Heschel. Los Angeles: U of California P, 1998.

Galloway, Patricia. "Choctaw Factionalism and Civil War, 1746–1750." *The Choc-*

taw Before Removal. Ed. Carolyn Keller Reeves. Jackson: U of Mississippi P, 1985.

Gardaphe, Fred. *Italian Signs, American Streets,*

Gates, Henry Louis, Jr., ed. *"Race," Writing, and Difference.* Chicago: U of Chicago P, 1985.

———. *The Signifying Monkey: A Theory of Afro-American Literary Criticism.* New York: Oxford UP, 1988.

Gilman, Sander. *Creating Beauty to Cure the Soul: Race and Psychology in the Shaping of Aesthetic Surgery.* Durham: Duke UP, 1998.

———. *Franz Kafka, The Jewish Patient.* New York: Routledge, 1995.

———. *Jewish Self-Hatred: Anti-Semitism and the Hidden Language of the Jews.* Baltimore: Johns Hopkins UP, 1986.

———. "Response." (forum). *PMLA* (May 1998). 450.

Gilroy, Paul. *Against Race: Imagining a Political Culture Beyond the Color Line.* Cambridge: Harvard UP, 2000.

———. *The Black Atlantic: Modernity and Double Consciousness.* Cambridge: Harvard UP, 1993.

———. *Postcolonial Melancholia.* New York: Columbia UP, 2004.

Glazer, Nathan. "Blacks, Jews, and the Intellectuals." *Commentary* 47.4 (1969): 33–39.

———. *Ethnic Dilemmas: 1964–1982.* Cambridge: Harvard UP, 1983.

Glazer, Nathan, and Daniel Patrick Moynihan. *Beyond the Melting Pot: The Negroes, Puerto Ricans, Jews, Italians, and Irish of New York City.* 2nd ed. Cambridge: MIT P, 1971.

Goldhagen, Daniel. *Hitler's Willing Executioners.* New York: Knopf, 1996.

Gomez-Pena, Guillermo.

Gonzales-Berry, Erlinda. *"Caras viejas y vino nuevo:* Journey through a Disintegrating Barrio." *Contemporary Chicano Fiction: A Critical Survey.* Ed. Vernon E. Lattin. Binghamton: Bilingual Press/Editorial Bilingüe, 1986.

González Echevarría, Roberto. *Myth and Archive: A Theory of Latin American Narrative.* New York: Cambridge UP, 1990.

Goodell, William. *The American Slave Code in Theory and Practice: Its Distinctive Features Shown by Its Statutes, Judicial Decisions, and Illustrative Facts.* London: Clark, Beeton, and Co, 1853.

Gordon, Avery. *Ghostly Matters: Haunting and the Sociological Imagination.* Minneapolis: U of Minnesota P, 1997.

Gordon, Avery, and Christopher Newfield, eds. *Mapping Multiculturalism.* Minneapolis: U of Minnesota P, 1996.

Graver, Lawrence. *An Obsession with Anne Frank.* Los Angeles: U of California P, 1995.

Grosz, Elizabeth. *Volatile Bodies: Toward a Corporeal Feminism.* Bloomington: Indiana UP,

Gurpegui, José Antonio, ed. *Alejandro Morales: Fiction Past, Present, Future Perfect.* Tempe: Bilingual Press, 1996.

Gutiérrez-Jones, Carl. *Critical Race Narratives: A Study of Race, Rhetoric, and Injury.* New York: NYU P, 2001.

———. *Rethinking the Borderlands: Between Chicano Culture and Legal Discourse.* Berkeley: U of California P, 1995.

Hamburger, Tom, and Peter Wallsten. "Refugees' Tale Heard by Powerful Audience of One." *Los Angeles Times* Feb. 14, 2005: A1.

Hans, James S. *The Golden Mean.* New York: SUNY P, 1994.

Harpham, Geoffrey Galt. *Getting It Right: Language, Literature, and Ethics.* Chicago: U of Chicago P, 1992.

Harris, Middleton, comp. *The Black Book.* Ed. Toni Morrison. New York: Random House, 1974.

Harris, Trudier. "Escaping Slavery but Not Its Images." *Toni Morrison: Critical Perspectives Past and Present.* Eds. Henry Louis Gates Jr. and K. A. Appiah. New York: Amistad, 1993. 330–41.

Hartman, Geoffrey H., ed. *Holocaust Remembrance: The Shapes of Memory.* Cambridge: Blackwell, 1994.

Hartman, Saidiya V. *Scenes of Subjection: Terror, Slavery, and Self-Making in Nineteenth-Century America.* New York: Oxford UP, 1997.

Heschel, Susannah. "Jewish Studies as Counterhistory." *Insider/Outsider: American Jews and Multiculturalism.* Eds. David Biale, Michael Galchinsky, and Susannah Heschel. Los Angeles: U of California P, 1998. 101–15.

Himmelfarb, Milton. "Is American Jewry in Crisis?" *Commentary* 47.3 (1969): 33–44.

Hollinger, David. *Postethnic America: Beyond Multiculturalism.* New York: Basic Books, 1995.

Howe, LeAnne. *Shell Shaker.* San Francisco: Aunt Lute Books, 2001.

———. "The Story of America: A Tribalography." *Clearing a Path: Theorizing Native American Studies.* Ed. Nancy Shoemaker. New York: Routledge, 2002.

Hungerford, Amy. *The Holocaust of Texts: Genocide, Literature, and Personification.* Chicago: U of Chicago P, 2003.

Huston, James L. *Calculating the Value of the Union: Slavery, Property Rights, and the Economic Origins of the Civil War.* Chapel Hill: UNC P, 2003.

Isaacs, Ronald H., and Kerry M. Olitzky, eds. *Critical Documents of Jewish History: A Sourcebook.* Northvale: Jason Aronson, 1995.

Islas, Arturo. *The Rain God: A Desert Tale.* New York: Avon Books, 1984.

Jacobs, Wilbur R. *On Turner's Trail: 100 Years of Writing Western History.* Lawrence: Kansas UP, 1994.

Jacobson, Matthew Frye. *Whiteness of a Different Color: European Immigrants and the Alchemy of Race.* Cambridge: Harvard UP, 1998.

Jesser, Nancy. "Violence, Home, and Community in Toni Morrison's *Beloved.*" *African American Review* 33 (1999): 325–45.

Jiménez, Francisco, ed. *The Identification and Analysis of Chicano Literature.* New York: Bilingual Press/Editorial Bilingüe, 1979.

Kaplan, Amy, and Donald E. Pease, eds. *Cultures of United States Imperialism.* Durham: Duke UP, 1993.

Karem, Jeff. *The Romance of Authenticity: The Cultural Politics of Regional and Ethnic Literatures.* Charlottesville: U of Virginia P, 2004.

Keefe, Susan E., and Amado M. Padilla. *Chicano Ethnicity.* Albuquerque: University of New Mexico Press, 1987.

Keenan, Thomas. *Fables of Responsibility: Aberrations and Predicaments in Ethics and Politics.* Stanford: Stanford UP, 1997.

Kingston, Maxine Hong. *The Woman Warrior: Memoirs of a Girlhood among Ghosts.* New York: Vintage, 1989.

Klepfisz, Irena. *Dreams of an Insomniac: Jewish Feminist Essays, Speeches, and Diatribes.* Portland: Eighth Mountain Press, 1990.

———. "*Yom Hashoa, Yom Yerushalayim:* A Meditation." *Jewish Women's Call for Peace: A Handbook for Jewish Women on the Israeli/Palestinian Conflict.* Ithaca: Firebrand Books, 1990.

Kramer, Michael P. "Race, Literary History, and the 'Jewish' Question." *Prooftexts* 21.3 (2001): 287–321.

Kronfeld, Chana. "Beyond Deleuze and Guattari: Hebrew and Yiddish Modernism in the age of Privileged Difference." *Jews and Other Differences: The New Jewish Cultural Studies.* Ed. Jonathan Boyarin and Daniel Boyarin. Minneapolis: U of Minnesota P, 1997.

Krumholz, Linda. "The Ghosts of Slavery: Historical Recovery in Toni Morrison's *Beloved.*" *African American Review* 26 (1992): 395–408.

Kushner, Tony. *Angels in America, a Gay Fantasia on National Themes. Part One: Millennium Approaches.* New York: Theater Communications Group, 1992.

———. *Angels in America, a Gay Fantasia on National Themes. Part Two: Perestroika.* New York: Theater Communications Group, 1992.

Lacan, Jacques. *Ecrits, a Selection.* New York: Norton, 1977.

LaCapra, Dominick. *History and Memory after Auschwitz.* Ithaca: Cornell UP, 1998.

———. *Representing the Holocaust: History, Theory, Trauma.* Ithaca: Cornell UP, 1994.

———. *Writing History, Writing Trauma.* Baltimore: Johns Hopkins UP, 2001.

———. *Writing and Rewriting the Holocaust: Narrative and the Consequences of Interpretation.* Bloomington: Indiana UP, 1990.

Langer, Lawrence L. *Admitting the Holocaust: Collected Essays.* New York: Oxford UP, 1995.

———. *Holocaust Testimonies: The Ruins of Memory.* New Haven: Yale UP, 1991.

Lanzman, Claude. *Shoah: An Oral History of the Holocaust. The Complete Text of the Film by Claude Lanzman.* New York: Pantheon, 1985.

Lattin, Vernon E., ed. *Contemporary Chicano Fiction: A Critical Survey.* Binghamton: Bilingual Press/Editorial Bilingüe, 1986.

Lavie, Smadar, and Ted Swedenburg, eds. *Displacement, Diaspora, and Geographies of Identity.* Durham: Duke UP, 1996.

Leal, Luís. *A Decade of Chicano Literature (1970–1979): Critical Essays and a Bibliography.* Santa Barbara: Editorial La Causa, 1982.

Lecky, Robert S., and H. Elliot Wright, eds. *Black Manifesto: Religion, Racism, and Reparations.* New York: Sheed and Ward, 1969.

Lee, Robert. *Multicultural American Literature,*

Levinas, Emmanuel. *The Levinas Reader.* Ed Sean Hand. Cambridge: Blackwell Publishers, 1989.

———. *Outside the Subject.* Trans. Michael B. Smith. Stanford: Stanford UP, 1994.

Levine, George. "Saving Disinterest: Aesthetics, Contingency, and Mixed Conditions." *New Literary History* 32.4 (Autumn 2001): 907–31.

Levitt, Laura. *Jews and Feminism: The Ambivalent Search for Home.* New York: Routledge, 1997.

Limerick, Patricia Nelson. *The Legacy of Conquest: The Unbroken Past of the American West.* New York: Norton, 1987.

Limerick, Patricia Nelson, Clyde A. Milner II, and Charles E. Rankin, eds. *Trails: Toward a New Western History.* Lawrence: Kansas UP, 1991.

Limón, José E. *American Encounters: Greater Mexico, the United States, and the Erotics of Culture.* Boston: Beacon Press, 1998.

———. *Dancing with the Devil: Society and Cultural Poetics in Mexican-American South Texas.* Madison: U of Wisconsin P, 1994.

———. *Mexican Ballads, Chicano Poems: History and Influence in Mexican-American Social Poetry.* Berkeley: U of California P, 1992.

———. *Mexican Ballads, Chicano Epic: History, Social Dramas, and Poetic Persuasion.* Stanford: Stanford UP, 1986.

Loomis, Carol. "Out of the Holocaust." *Fortune* 13 April 1998: 64–84.

Lowe, Lisa. *Immigrant Acts: On Asian American Cultural Politics.* Durham: Duke UP, 1996.

Lupton, Julia Reinhard, and Kenneth Reinhard. *After Oedipus: Shakespeare in Psychoanalysis.* Ithaca: Cornell UP, 1993.

Lyotard, Jean-François. *Heidegger and "the jews."* Trans. Andrea Michel and Mark Roberts. Minneapolis: U of Minnesota Press, 1990.

MacCannell, Juliet. *The Regime of the Brother: After the Patriarchy.* New York: Routledge, 1991.

Maitino, John R., and David Peck, eds. *Teaching Ethnic American Literature.* Albuquerque: U of New Mexico P, 1996.

Malamud, Bernard. *The Magic Barrel.* New York: Farrar, Strauss, and Giroux, 2003.

———. "The Last Mohican." *The Magic Barrel.* New York: Farrar, Straus, and Giroux, 2003. 155–82.

Margolis, Max L., and Alexander Marx. *A History of the Jewish People.* New York: Temple Books, 1969.

McKee, Jesse O., and Jon A. Schlenker. *The Choctaws: Cultural Evolution of a Native American Tribe*. Jackson: UP of Mississippi, 1980.

McKenna, Teresa. *Migrant Song: Politics and Process in Contemporary Chicano Literature*. Austin: U of Texas P, 1997.

———. "On Chicano Poetry and the Political Age: *Corridos* as Social Drama." *Criticism in the Borderlands*. Ed. Héctor Calderón and José David Saldívar. Durham: Duke UP, 1994. 188–202.

Melnick, Ralph. *The Stolen Legacy of Anne Frank: Meyer Levin, Lillian Hellman, and the Staging of the Diary*. New Haven: Yale UP, 1997.

Merriam, Eve. *Emma Lazarus: Woman with a Torch*. New York: Citadel Press, 1956.

Meyer, Michael A. *Response to Modernity: A History of the Reform Movement in Judaism* New York: Oxford UP, 1988.

Michaels, Walter Benn. *Our America: Nativism, Modernism, and Pluralism*. Durham: Duke UP, 1995.

———. *The Shape of the Signifier: 1967 to the End of History*. Princeton: Princeton UP, 2004.

———. "'You Who Was Never There': Slavery and the New Historicism—Deconstruction and the Holocaust." *The Americanization of the Holocaust*. Ed. Hilene Flanzbaum. Baltimore: Johns Hopkins UP, 1999. 181–97.

Mohanty, Satya P. *Literary Theory and the Claims of History: Postmodernism, Objectivity, Multicultural Politics*. Ithaca: Cornell UP, 1997.

Moraga, Cherríe. *The Last Generation: Prose and Poetry*. Boston: South End Press, 1993.

———. *Loving in the War Years: lo que nunca paso por sus labios*. Boston: South End Press, 1983.

Morales, Alejandro. *Barrio on the Edge/Caras Viejas y Vino Nuevo*. Tempe: Bilingual Press, 1998.

———. *The Brick People*. Houston: Arte Público, 1992.

———. *Caras viejas y vino nuevo*. Mexico City: Joaquin Moritz, 1975.

———. *Death of an Anglo*. Tempe: Bilingual Press, 1988.

———. *The Rag Doll Plagues*. Houston: Arte Público, 1992.

———. *Reto en el Paraíso*. Tempe Ariz: Bilingual Review Press, 1997.

———. *La verdad sin voz*. Mexico City: Joaquin Moritz, 1979.

———. *Waiting to Happen*. San José: Chusma House Publications, 2001

Morris, Bob. "Yiddles with Fiddles." *Village Voice* Jan. 23, 1996: 31–34.

Morrison, Toni. *Beloved*. New York: Plume, 1988.

———. *Song of Solomon*. New York: Plume, 1987.

Moya, Paula. *Learning from Experience: Minority Identities, Multicultural Struggles*. Berkeley: U of California P, 2002.

Murray, Stephen O., and Wayne R. Dynes. "Hispanic Homosexuals: A Spanish Lexicon." *Latin American Male Homosexualities*. Ed. Stephen O. Murray. Albuquerque: U of New Mexico P, 1995.

Neusner, Jacob. *Stranger at Home: "The Holocaust," Zionism, and American Judaism*. Chicago: U of Chicago P, 1981.

Newman, Amy. "The Idea of Judaism in Feminism and Afrocentrism." *Insider/ Outsider: American Jews and Multiculturalism.* Ed. David Biale, Michael Galchinsky, and Susannah Heschel. Los Angeles: U of California P, 1998. 150–84.

Newton, Adam Zachary. *Facing Black and Jew: Literature as Public Space in Twentieth-Century America.* New York: Cambridge University Press, 1999.

———. *Narrative Ethics.* Cambridge: Harvard UP, 1995.

Nguyen, Viet. *Race and Resistance: Literature and Politics in Asian America.* New York: Oxford UP, 2002.

Novak, Michael. *The Rise of the Unmeltable Ethnics: Politics and Culture in American Life.* New Brunswick: Transaction, 1995.

Novick, Peter. *The Holocaust in American Life.* New York: Mariner Books, 2000.

Omi, Michael, and Howard Winant. *Racial Formation in the United States: From the 1960s to the 1980s.* New York: Routledge, 1986.

Osherow, Jacqueline. *Conversations with Survivors: Poems.* Athens: U of Georgia P, 1994.

Ozick, Cynthia. *The Cannibal Galaxy.* New York: Knopf, 1983.

———. *The Messiah of Stockholm.* New York: Vintage Books, 1987.

———. *The Shawl.* New York: Vintage Books, 1980.

———. "Who Owns Anne Frank?" *New Yorker* 16 Oct. 1997: 76–87.

Padilla, Genaro. "Imprisoned Narrative? Or Lies, Secrets, and Silence in New Mexico Women's Autobiography." *Criticism in the Borderlands.* Ed. Héctor Calderón and José David Saldívar. Durham: Duke UP, 1994.

Palumbo-Liu, David, ed. *The Ethnic Canon: Histories, Institutions, and Interventions.* Minneapolis: U of Minnesota P, 1995.

Paredes, Américo. *The Hammon and the Beans and Other Stories.* Houston: Arte Público, 1994.

———. *With His Pistol in His Hand: A Border Ballad and Its Hero.* Austin: U of Texas P, 1994.

Parkinson-Zamora, Lois. *The Usable Past: The Imagination of History in Recent Fiction of the Americas.* Cambridge: Cambridge UP, 1997.

Patraka, Vivian M. "Situating History and Difference: The Performance of the Term *Holocaust* in Public Discourse." *Jews and Other Differences: The New Jewish Cultural Studies.* Ed. Jonathan Boyarin and Daniel Boyarin. Minneapolis: U of Minnesota Press, 1997. 54–78.

Penningroth, Dylan C. *The Claims of Kinfolk: African American Property and Community in the Nineteenth-Century South.* Chapel Hill: UNC P, 2003.

Peterson, Nancy J. *Against Amnesia: Contemporary Women Writers and the Crises of Historical Memory.* Philadelphia: U of Pennsylvania P, 2001.

———. *Toni Morrison: Critical and Theoretical Approaches.* Baltimore: John Hopkins UP, 1997.

Powell, Timothy. *Ruthless Democracy: A Multicultural Interpretation of the American Renaissance.* Princeton: Princeton UP, 2000.

Raab, Earl. "The Black Revolution and the Jewish Question." *Commentary* 47.1 (1969): 23–34.

Rapaport, Herman. "Archive Trauma." *Diacritics* 28.4 (1998) 68–81.

Reeves, Carolyn Keller, e. *The Choctaw Before Removal.* Jackson: U of Mississippi P, 1985.

Reising, Russell. *The Unusable Past: Theory and the Study of American Literature.* New York: Methuen, 1986.

Robinson, Randall. *The Debt: What America Owes to Blacks.* New York: Plume, 2001.

Rochlin, Harriet. *Pioneer Jews: A New Life in the Far West.* New York: Mariner, 2000.

Rodriguez, Richard. *Brown: The Last Discovery of America.* New York: Viking, 2002.

Rogin, Michael Paul. *"Ronald Reagan," the Movie: And Other Episodes in Demonology.* Berkeley: U of California P, 1987.

Roskie, David. *The Jewish Search for a Usable Past.* Bloomington: Indiana UP, 1999.

Rosales, Jesús. *La narrativa de Alejandro Morales: encuentro, historio, y compromiso social.* New York: Peter Lang, 1999.

Roth, Philip. *Operation Shylock: A Confession.* New York: Simon & and Schuster, 1993.

———. *The Ghost Writer.* New York: Vintage International, 1995.

Rothberg, Michael. *Traumatic Realism: The Demands of Holocaust Representation.* Minneapolis: U of Minnesota P, 2000.

Rouse, Roger. "Mexican Migration and the Social Space of Postmodernism." *Diaspora* 2 (1991): 8–23.

Ryan, Joseph. *White Ethnics: Their Life in Working Class America.* Englewood: Prentice-Hall, 1973.

Said, Edward. "Ideology of Difference." *"Race," Writing and Difference.* Ed. Henry Louis Gates Jr. Chicago: U of Chicago P, 1988.

Saldívar, José David. *Border Matters: Remapping American Cultural Studies.* Los Angeles: U of California P, 1997.

———. *The Dialectics of Our America: Genealogy, Cultural Critique, and Literary History.* Durham: Duke UP, 1991.

Saldívar, Ramón. *Chicano Narrative: The Dialectics of Difference.* Madison: U of Wisconsin P, 1990.

———. "Multicultural Politics, Aesthetics, and the Realist Theory of Identity: A Response to Satya Mohanty." *New Literary History* 32.4 (Autumn 2001): 849–54.

Saldívar-Hull, Sonia. "Feminism on the Border: From Gender Politics to Geopolitics." *Criticism in the Borderlands: Studies in Chicano Literature, Culture, and Ideology.* Ed. Hector Calderón and Jose David Saldívar. Durham: Duke UP, 1994.

Sale, Maggie. "Call and Response as Critical Method: African-American Oral Traditions and *Beloved.*" *African American Review* 26 (1992): 41–50.

San Juan, E., Jr. *Beyond Postcolonial Theory.* New York: St. Martin's, 1998.

Sanchez, George J. *Becoming Mexican American: Ethnicity, Culture and Identity in Chicano Los Angeles, 1900–1945.* New York: Oxford UP, 1993.

Santner, Eric. *Stranded Objects: Mourning, Memory, and Film in Postwar Germany.* Ithaca: Cornell UP, 1990.

Savitt, Todd L. "Slave Life Insurance in Virginia and North Carolina." *Journal of Southern History* 43 (1977): 583–600.

Schimel, Lawrence. "Diaspora, Sweet Diaspora." *Pomosexuals: Challenging Assumptions about Gender and Sexuality.* Ed. Carol Queen and Lawrence Schimel. San Francisco: Cleis Press, 1997.

Scholem, Gershom. *From Berlin to Jerusalem: Memories of My Youth.* New York: Schocken, 1988.

Sedgwick, Eve Kosofsky. *The Epistemology of the Closet.* Berkeley: U of California P, 1990.

———. *Tendencies.* Durham: Duke UP, 1993.

Sedinger, Tracy. "Nation and Identification: Psychoanalysis, Race, and Sexual Difference." *Cultural Critique* 50 (2002): 40–73.

Sharfman, Harold. *Jews on the Frontier.* Washington, D.C.: Regnery, 1977.

Shreiber, Maeera. *Singing in a Strange Land: Toward a Jewish American Poetics.* Stanford: Stanford UP, forthcoming.

Silko, Leslie Marmon. *Ceremony.* New York: Penguin, 1977.

Sinefeld, Alan. "Diaspora and Hybridity: Queer Identities and the Ethnicity Model." *Textual Practice* 10.2 (1996): 271–93.

Sklare, Marshall, and Joseph Greenblum. *Jewish Identity on the Suburban Frontier: A Study of Group Society in an Open Society.* New York: Basic Books, 1967.

Sollors, Werner. *Beyond Ethnicity: Consent and Descent in American Culture.* New York: Oxford UP, 1986.

———, ed. *The Invention of Ethnicity.* New York: Oxford UP, 1989.

Solomon, Alisa. *Re-dressing the Canon: Essays on Theater and Gender.* New York: Routledge, 1997.

Sommers, Joseph, and Tomás Ybarra-Fausto, eds. *Modern Chicano Writers: A Collection of Critical Essays.* Englewood Cliffs: Prentice-Hall, 1979.

Spillers, Hortense. *Black, White, and in Color: Essays on American Literature and Culture.* Chicago: U of Chicago P, 2003.

Stychin, Carl F. *A Nation by Rights: National Cultures, Sexual Identity Politics, and the Discourse of Rights.* Philadelphia: Temple UP, 1998.

Svigals, Alicia. "Why We Do This Anyway: Klezmer as Jewish Youth Subculture." *Judaism* (Winter 1998): 43–49.

Takaki, Ronald. *From Different Shores: Perspectives on Race and Ethnicity in America.* New York: Oxford UP, 1994.

Tate, Claudia. *Psychoanalysis and Black Novels: Desire and the Protocols of Race.* New York: Oxford UP, 1998.

Thompson, Janna. *Taking Responsibility for the Past: Reparation and Historical Justice.* Malden: Polity Press, 2002.

Tobias, Henry J. *A History of the Jews in New Mexico.* Albuquerque: U of New Mexico P, 1992.

U.S. Congress. *General Mining Law of 1872.* 42nd Cong., 2nd sess., chap. CLII, 1872.

Valdez, Luis, and Stan Steiner, eds. *Aztlán: An Anthology of Mexican American Literature.* New York: Knopf, 1972.

Villa, Raúl Homero. *Barrio-Logos: Space and Place in Urban Chicano Literature and Culture.* Austin: U of Texas P, 2000.

Viramontes, Helena María. *The Moths and Other Stories.* Houston: Arte Público, 1995.

Vorlicky, Robert, ed. *Tony Kushner in Conversation.* Ann Arbor: U of Michigan P, 1998.

Wardi, Anissa Janine. *Death and the Arc of Mourning in African American Literature.* Gainesville: U of Florida P, 2003.

Weissman, Gary. "Lawerence Langer and 'The Holocaust Experience.'" *Response* 68 (Fall 1997/Winter 1998): 78–101.

Wells, Samuel J. "Federal Indian Policy: From Accommodation to Removal." *The Choctaw Before Removal.* Ed. Carolyn Keller Reeves. Jackson: U of Mississippi P, 1985.

West, Cornel. *Race Matters.* New York: Vintage Books, 1994.

White, Richard. "Frederick Jackson Turner and Buffalo Bill." *The Frontier in American Culture: An Exhibition at the Newberry Library, August 26, 1994–January 7, 1995.* Los Angeles: UC Press, 1994. 7–66.

Wiegman, Robyn. *American Anatomies: Theorizing Race and Gender.* Durham: Duke UP, 1995.

Wirth-Nesher, Hana, ed. *What Is Jewish Literature?* Philadelphia: Jewish Publication Society, 1994.

Wood, Allen. "The Objectivity of Value." *New Literary History* 32.4 (Autumn 2001): 859–81.

Yezierska, Anzia. *Hungry Hearts and Other Stories.* New York: Persea.

Young, Bette Roth. *Emma Lazarus in Her World: Life and Letters.* Philadelphia: Jewish Publication Society, 1995.

Young, James. *The Texture of Memory: Holocaust Memorials and Meanings.* New Haven: Yale UP, 1993.

———. *Writing and Rewriting the Holocaust: Narrative and the Consequences of Interpretation.* Bloomington: Indiana UP, 1988.

Young, Robert. *White Mythologies: Writing History and the West.* New York: Routledge, 1991.

Yudkin, Leon, ed. *Hebrew Literature in the Wake of the Holocaust.* Rutherford: Farleigh Dickinson Press, 1993.

INDEX

Adorno, Theodor, 174
African American literature, 73–74
Afro-centrism, 166
Against Race (Gilroy), 8
Almaguer, Tomás, 129
Alonso, Ana María, 129, 131
American Anatomies (Wiegman), 5
anal exposure, 195n4
Anaya, Rudolpho, 60
Anderson, Benedict, 7, 31
Angels in America (Kushner), 144, 151, 196n6, 197n11
Anzaldúa, Gloria, 70, 112, 124, 126, 134
archive, 58–59; culture, 69; and history, 65; Holocaust, 97, 187n5; libraries, 66; in *The Rag Doll Plagues*, 64
Avelar, Adelbar, 57
Aztlán, 102, 112, 138, 140

Beloved (Morrison), 75; claim in, 80–85; community response in, 78; critical reception, 76–80; and ethics, 94; haunting in, 79; and Moynihan report of 1965, 83; and reconciliation, 95; reparation, 93; wish fulfillment, 74. *See also* Southern Claims Commission
Berger, James, 83
Berlin, Irving, 109, 110
Beyond Ethnicity (Sollors), 18
Bhabha, Homi, 7; criticism of, 198n1;

"DissemiNation," 18; on the future, 152; and identity, 155, 168, 174; and memory, 35; and Toni Morrison, 52; and multiculturalism, 31, 198n20; the uncanny, 36
Biale, David, 169, 170
Bittker, Boris, *The Case for Black Reparations,* 90
Black Atlantic, The (Gilroy), 8
Black Book, The (Morrison), 90
Bloom, Harold, 163
border, the, 112, 114, 117–19, 121–23
Borderlands/La Frontera (Anzaldúa), 113, 124
Bouson, J. Brooks, 187n2
Boyarin, Daniel, 147; *Unheroic Conduct,* 171, 175; midrash, 172–74, 178–81
Boyarin, Jonathan, "critical post-Judaism," 157, 167, 170
Boyarin, Jonathan and Daniel, 107–8, 141, 158, 160–61
Brodkin, Karen, 185n8
Brogan, Kathleen, *Cultural Haunting,* 78–79, 89, 93, 187n2
Brook, Van Wyck, 187n4
Brown (Rodriguez), 183n9, 196n7
Bruce-Nova, *Retrospace,* 60
Butler, Judith: and postmodernism, 143; and trauma theory, 11

Cahan, Abraham, 74
"Cariboo Cafe, The" (Viramontes), 114–21
Carnalismo, 138
Caruth, Cathy: "Traumatic Awakenings," 51; *Unclaimed Experience,* 77, 189n4
Castillo, Ana, 60
Cervantes, Lorna Dee, 70, 189n15
Chabram, Angie, 162
Cheng, Anne Anlin, 187n2
Cheng, Vincent, and ethnic literature, 13
Chicano literature: compared with other ethnic literatures, 19, 23; and mainstream literature, 23
Choctaws: civil war of, 1–2; history of, 183nn1–2; *Nanih Wayia,* 1; Redshoes, 1
Chow, Rey, 191n18
Chuh, Kandice, 170
Cisneros, Sandra, 60
Cixous, Hélène, 163
Cole, Timothy, 184n3, 185n7
Commentary, 146
corrido, 176–78, 181
critical post-Judaism, 158
Criticism in the Borderlands (Saldívar and Calderón), 162–63
Cultural Haunting (Brogan), 78–79, 80

deconstruction: and gender, 143; and identity, 170; and Jewish studies, 158–59, 163–64; and multiculturalism, 17
Deleuze, Gilles, and Félix Guattari, 110, 167
de Man, Paul, 162
Denver, and gold mining, 86
Derrida, Jacques: archives of, 87n5; and *différance,* 159; *Specters of Marx,* 1; and Yale, 162, 163
diaspora, 8–10; 104–11
différance, 159
drag, 150
D'Souza, Dinesh, 185n4
Dussere, Erik, 82
Dwyer, Susan, 95

Eagleton, Terry, 176
Englander, Nathan, 55
ethics, 6, 155
Ethnic Canon, The (Palumbo-Liu), 13
ethnicity: and ethnic studies, 5; definition, 13, 14, 16, 18–20, 22; and marginalization, 22; as a process, 178; and race, 103. *See also* post-ethnicity
ethnic literature: and geography, 8; historical developments of, 14; and history, 8; and multicultural literature, 3
exile, 101, 104

Felman, Shoshanna, and Dori Laub, 184n2
feminism, 166
Ferraro, Thomas, 184n12
Fortune Magazine: and anti-Semitism, 33; and the Holocaust, 33
Foucault, Michel, 187n5
Frank, Anne: Amy Bellete (Roth character) and, 34; and assimilation, 41, 45; Broadway production of diaries of, 42, 44, 186n14. *See also under* Ozick, Cynthia
Freud, Sigmund, and dreams, 50
Friedlander, Saul, 184n2
frontier thesis (Turner), 184n4
Fugitive Slave Act, 85

Galarza, Ernesto, 60
galut, 102, 194n3; Arnold Eisen on, 185n7, 185n9. *See also* exile
Gardaphe, Fred, 184n12
gay ethnicity, 195n5
Geiger, Abraham, 165
General Mining Law of 1872, 85, 191n11
geography: and culture, 8; and literature, 25
Gilman, Sander, 13, 186n13
Gilroy, Paul: *Against Race,* 8; *The Black Atlantic,* 8; diaspora, 8–10; *Postcolonial Melancholia,* 9
Glazer, Nathan, 146

Gold, Michael, 74
Goldhagen, Daniel, *Hitler's Willing Executioners,* 188n8
Gomez-Peña, Guillermo, 113
Gonzales-Berry, Erlinda, 188n9
Gonzalez, Corky, 138
Gordon, Avery, 79–80, 93
Grant, Ulysses, 104
Grosz, Elizabeth, 121
Guattari, Félix, and Gilles Deleuze, 110, 167
Gutierrez-Jones, Carl, 88–89

Hans, James, 95
Harby, Isaac, 104
Harpham, Geoffrey, *Getting It Right,* 155
Harraway, Donna, 141
Hartman, Geoffrey, 162, 184n2
Hartman, Saidiya, 190n9
Hasidim, 168
Hebrew Congregation of Newport Rhode Island, 104
Heeb (magazine), 187n1, 198n7
Heschel, Susannah, 164–66
Himmelbarb, Martin, 146
history: American, 33; and culture, 8, 54; and identity, 30; the Holocaust and, 30; and memory, 35, narrative, 55; and trauma, 32. *See also* Holocaust
Hobbes, Thomas, 178
Hollinger, David, and post-ethnicity, 19, 169
Holocaust: Americanization of, 32–35; archives, 47; compared to other traumatic histories, 55, 71–72; and cultural memory, 30; identification, 30; testimony, 48, 184n2
Holocaust of Texts (Hungerford), 39, 184n2
Homestead Act, 85
House Bill H.R. 40, 193n24
Howe, LeAnne, *Shell Shaker,* 1
Hungerford, Amy, *The Holocaust of Texts,* 39, 184n2

identity, 154
Insider/Outsider (Biale, Galchinsky, and Heschel, eds.), 164–67
Islas, Arturo, 60, 126, 135, 140

Jacobsen, Matthew, 20, 21
Jewish literature: compared to Chicano literature, 23; Jewish studies, 165–66, 168, 170; and mainstream literature, 23
Jews: and African Americans, 197n14; in the West, 193n2
Jews with Horns (the Klezmatics), 145

Keenan, Thomas, 80
Kerr, Walter, 44
Klepfisz, Irene, 42, 189n16, 197n15
Klezmatics, the, 144–51
Koreck, María Teresa, 129, 131
Krumholz, Linda, 78
Kushner, Tony, 102, 126, 127, 134, 135, 143–52, 171

Lacan, Jacques, and dreams, 51
LaCapra, Dominick: and Cathy Caruth, 77; cultural mourning, 57, 92, 184n2, 187n2; wish fulfillment, 43
Langer, Lawerence, *Holocaust Testimonies,* 48, 184n2, 185n7
Last Generation, The (Moraga), 136–43, 159–60
Laub, Dori, and Shoshanna Felman, 184n2
Lazarus, Emma: "In Exile," 99, 111; "The New Colossus," 148, 193n1, 194n8
Leal, Luis, 163
Levinas, Emmanuel, 7, 163
Levitt, Laura, 197n15
life insurance, and slavery, 190nn6–7
Limerick, Patricia Nelson, 85, 100
Limón, José, 117; on Américo Paredes, 173–77
Livingston, Jennie, 150
London, Frank (the Klezmatics), 145
Longfellow, Henry Wadsworth, 100

Loving in the War Years (Moraga), 136–43
Lowe, Lisa, and multiculturalism, 20, 185n5
Lyotard, Jean-François, 167

Malinche, La, 189n13, 195n2
Manifest Destiny, 100
McKenna, Teresa, 176
mestizaje, 128, 129, 167
Meyer, Michael, 104
Michaels, Walter Benn: on *Beloved,* 190n5; and identity, 169, 184n2; and reparations, 91
midrash, 171–73
Miller, J. Hillis, 162
Mobius strip, 121
Mohanty, Satya, 87–88, 169; *Literary Theory and the Claims of History,* 191n16, 196n8
Moraga, Cherríe: and identity, 157; and Jewish studies, 166–67, 170, 179; *The Last Generation,* 159–61; and nationalism, 126, 127, 134, 135–43, 150
Morales, Alejandro, 56; biography of, 187n6; critical reception, 60, 187n7; novels of, 59–60; *The Rag Doll Plagues,* 60–69, 172
Morrison, Toni: and reparation, 73, 91. See also *Beloved*
mourning, 52, 89; cultural, 57; and literature, 39; and melancholy, 56. *See also* working-through
Moya, Paula, 139–43, 169, 191n16
Moynihan report (1965), 75, 83
multiculturalism: criticism of, 17, 20; definitions, 5, 183nn9–10; historical, 7, 171

nationalism, 1, 136–40
negative dialectic, 174
Neusner, Jacob: on the diaspora, 105, 114; and Jewish studies, 166
Newman, Amy, 166
new realism, 139

Newton, Adam Zachary, and narrative ethics, 80, 94
Novick, Peter, 185n7, 186n11

Office of Faith-Based Initiatives, 197n10
Omi, Michael, and Howard Winant, *Racial Formation in the United States,* 17
Osherow, Jacqueline, 32
Ozick, Cynthia: on Anne Frank, 45; *The Messiah of Stockholm,* 46–54, 172

Padilla, Genaro, 175
Palumbo-Liu, David, *The Ethnic Canon,* 13
Paredes, Américo: "The Mexico-Texan," 176, 178; *With His Pistol in His Hand,* 173–75, 176
Paris Is Burning (Livingston), 150
Parkinson-Zamora, Lois, 187n4
Penningroth, Dylan, *The Claims of Kinfolk,* 85
Peterson, Nancy, 76, 187n2, 189n3
Philadelphia Conference of Reform Rabbis, 194n4
pluralism, 127
Podhoretz, Norman, 146
Possessed (The Klezmatics), 144–45
Postcolonial Melancholia (Gilroy), 9
post-ethnicity, 19
Powell, Timothy, 7
"protestant ethnic," the (Chow), 191n19

Queer Aztlán, 140, 141, 144, 150
Queer Nation, 150

race, 19, 21
racial privacy initiative (California Ballot Proposition 54), 153
Rain God (Islas), 127–34, 152
Rapaport, Herman, 187n5
Reagan, Ronald, 184n4
reconciliation, 95, 193nn22–23
Reising, Russell, 187n4

reparations, 89; and Boris Bittker, 90–91; criticism of, 91; debate, 192n19, 192n21; and ethics, 90; and memory, 91. *See also* reconciliation

ressentiment, 95

Rivera, Tomás, 60

Robinson, Randall, 92

Rodriguez, Richard, 137, 183n9

Rogin, Michael Paul, 185n4

Rosenbaum, Thane, 55

Roskies, David: on the diaspora, 29; *Jewish Search for a Usable Past*, 71, 187n4; "Library of Jewish Catastrophe," 71–72

Roth, Philip: *The Ghost Writer*, 29–44, 172; *Operation Shylock*, 108–10

Rothberg, Michael, 184n2

Rouse, Roger, 113–14

Saldívar, José David, 113, 167, 170, 174

Saldívar, Ramón, 142, 173–74, 179

Sale, Maggie, 78

Santer, Eric, 187n3

School House Rock, 185n4

Shell Shaker (Howe), 1–4

Shreiber, Maeera, 148

Silko, Leslie Marmon, *Ceremony*, 72

Sklamberg, Lauren (the Klezmatics), 145

slave code, 190n8

Smith, Barbara Herrnstein, 143

Sollors, Werner, 18, 169

Solomon, Alissa, 144

South African Truth and Reconciliation Commission, 193n22

Southern Claims Commission, 85

Spiegelman, Art, *Maus*, 55

Spillers, Hortense, 83

Svigals, Alicia, 146

Swain, Carol, 142

Tate, Claudia, 187n2, 191n17

Thinking in Jewish (Boyarin), 158, 168

trauma theory, 10–12; and literature, 24

"Undoing World, An" (the Klezmatics), 147–52

Unheroic Conduct (Boyarin), 147, 171

United States Holocaust Museum and Memorial, 35

usable past, the, 71, 187n3

Viramontes, Helena María, "The Cariboo Cafe," 103, 114

Wardi, Anissa Janine, 78

Wiegman, Robyn, *American Anatomies*, 5

Winant, Howard, and Michael Omi, *Racial Formation in the United States*, 17

Wirth-Nesher, Hana, 184n1

Wise, Isaac Mayer, 104

wish fulfillment: in literature, 74, 189n2

With His Pistol in His Hand (Paredes), 174

wo Es war, sol Ich werden, 86, 191n13

Woman Warrior, The (Kingston), 183n7

working-through, 50, 56, 58, 89

Wrestling with Zion (Kushner and Solomon), 144

Yezierska, Anzia, 74

yiddishkeit, 144, 145, 147

Young, James, 29, 184n2

Young, Robert, *White Mythologies*, 163

Zionism, 105–7, 141; and racism, 194n5